Interactive Computer Animation

Interactive Computer Animation

Edited by

Nadia Magnenat Thalmann
MIRALab, University of Geneva

and

Daniel Thalmann
Computer Graphics Lab, EPFL

Prentice Hall
London   New York   Toronto   Sydney   Tokyo   Singapore
Madrid   Mexico City   Munich

First published 1996 by
Prentice Hall Europe
Campus 400, Maylands Avenue
Hemel Hempstead
Hertfordshire, HP2 7EZ
A division of
Simon & Schuster International Group

© Prentice Hall Europe 1996

All rights reserved. No part of this publication may be reproduced,
stored in a retrieval system, or transmitted, in any form, or by any
means, electronic, mechanical, photocopying, recording or otherwise,
without prior permission, in writing, from the publisher.

Typeset in 10/12 pt Times
by MHL Typesetting Ltd, Coventry

Printed and bound in Great Britain by
T.J. Press (Padstow) Ltd

Library of Congress Cataloging-in-Publication Data

Interactive computer animation / edited by Nadia Magnenat Thalmann and
    Daniel Thalmann.
        p.   cm.
    Includes bibliographical references and index.
    ISBN 0-13-518309-X (hdb : alk. paper)
    1. Computer animation.   2. Interactive computer systems.
    I. Magnenat-Thalmann, Nadia, 1946–   II. Thalmann, Daniel.
    TR897.7.158   1996
    006.6—dc20   96-634
                                                                CIP

British Library Cataloguing in Publication Data

A catalogue record for this book is available from
the British Library

ISBN 0-13-518309-X

1   2   3   4   5   00   99   98   97   96

Contents

CHAPTER 1

Computer Animation in Future Technologies

Nadia Magnenat Thalmann
MIRALab, University of Geneva

Daniel Thalmann
Computer Graphics Lab, Swiss Federal Institute of Technology

Abstract
In this introductory chapter, we try to situate the role of Computer Animation in the new technologies: digital television, virtual reality, multimedia, cooperative work. We also overview the main techniques which will be further discussed throughout this book by international experts.

1.1 The high-tech role of computer animation

The term "Computer Animation" suggests that computers bring something new to the traditional way of animating. Traditional animation is defined as a technique in which the illusion of movement is created by photographing a series of individual drawings on successive frames of film. Is this definition, due to John Halas (Halas and Manwell 1968), still true for Computer Animation? The definition is essentially correct if we change the definition of the words photographing, drawings, and successive frames. A definition of computer animation could be: a technique in which the illusion of movement is created by displaying on a screen, or recording on a recording device a series of individual states of a dynamic scene. We use the term "recording" also for photographing and we consider both a cine-camera and a videorecorder as a recording device.

There are two ways of considering computer animation and its evolution. The first approach corresponds to an extension of traditional animation methods by the use of the computer. The second approach corresponds to simulation methods based on laws of physics, especially laws of mechanics. For example, traditional methods allow us to create three-dimensional characters with exaggerated movements while simulation methods are

1

used to try to model a human behavior accurately. For example, consider the bouncing ball example as described by Lasseter (1987). The motion is improved by introducing squash and stretch. When an object is squashed flat and stretches out drastically, it gives the sense that the object is made out of a soft, pliable material. This is a well known trick used by many traditional animators. It does not produce a realistic simulation, but it gives an impression to the viewer. A bouncing ball motion may be also completely simulated by computer using laws of mechanics such as Newton's laws and quantum conservation. Deformations may be calculated by using complex methods like finite element theory (Gourret et al. 1989). No approach is better than the other; it is like comparing a painting and a photograph. Both are representations of a particular world. If we consider character animation, it is easier to create emotions using a keyframe approach than using mechanical laws. Emotional aspects could very well be simulated using a more formal approach, they would require emotion models to be incorporated in a physics-based animation system. This means that there is a third way of producing animation using social and behavioral laws on top of physics-based laws.

Computer animation has been considered for many years as a new medium for advertisement and special effects in films. More recently, the fast development of powerful superworkstations has led to new areas like multimedia, interactive games, and Virtual Reality (VR). For these new areas, interactive and real-time animation has become a key issue. Traditional television means that the viewer may only decide which program he/she wants to watch. With the new developments of digital and interactive television and multimedia products, the viewer will be more and more able to interact with programs and this will lead to individual programs for each viewer. Real-time animation and autonomous virtual actors are important in the multimedia industry where an interactive use of the functionality means an immediate asset. Each film and TV producer will be interested in developing new features and programs where the public will be involved interactively. The authors, editors, and publishers of interactive TV programs, CD-I's, and CD-ROM's increasingly exploiting interactivity need real-time animation capabilities.

Historically, we can observe the following evolution: computer animation has started with very simple methods coming from traditional animation and geometry like keyframes. Then, inverse kinematics and dynamics have been imported from robotics leading to complex simulation techniques. At the same time, time-consuming methods for rendering have also been created. Since a few years ago, computer animation has tended to be more and more based on physics and dynamic simulation methods, especially in the areas of deformations and collision detection and response. With the advent of VR-devices and superworkstations, brute force methods like rotoscopy-like methods have tended to come back. In the future, real-time complex animation systems will be developed taking advantage of VR-devices and simulation methods. A typical situation will be the real actor with motion captured by sensors (e.g. Flock of Birds) and autonomous actors completely driven by the computer using real-time behavioral simulation with complex physics-based interaction with the environment. Moreover, these complex scenes could be shared between long-distance partners all over the world. This is one aspect of research we are now putting together in the Virtual Life Network (VLnet) (Pandzic et al. 1995).

1.2   A guide to advanced computer animation techniques

Computer animation means the creation of motion through a computer. There are several ways to do it: performance animation, keyframing, inverse kinematics, dynamics, task-level animation, behavioral animation. Moreover specific techniques like cloth animation, hair animation, and facial animation offer a big challenge.

Performance animation consists of recording the motion by a specific device for each frame and using this information to generate the image by computer. For example, a human walking motion may be recorded and then applied to a computer-generated 3-D character. This approach will provide a very good motion, because it comes directly from reality. However, it has severe limitations since for any new motion, it is necessary to record the reality again. Roberto Maiocchi (Chapter 2) discusses in detail this type of technique.

A popular alternative to performance animation is the well-known technique of keyframing. A brief introduction to the topic is presented in Section 1.3. More details may be found in Magnenat Thalmann and Thalmann (1990).

The use of **inverse kinematics** permits direct specification of end point positions. Joint angles are automatically determined. This is the key problem, because independent variables in a synthetic actor are joint angles. Unfortunately, the transformation of position from Cartesian to joint coordinates generally does not have a closed-form solution. However, there are a number of special arrangements of the joint axes for which closed-form solutions have been suggested. Inverse kinematics is discussed by Boulic and Mas (Chapter 3) and an alternative called inverse kinetics is proposed.

Kinematics-based systems are generally intuitive and lack dynamic integrity. The animation does not seem to respond to basic physical facts like gravity or inertia. Only modeling of objects that move under the influence of **forces** and **torques** can be realistic. Forces and torques cause linear and angular accelerations. The motion is obtained by the **dynamic equations of motion**. These equations are established using the forces, the torques, the constraints, and the mass properties of objects. Methods based on parameter adjustment are the most popular approach to dynamics-based animation and correspond to **non-constraint methods**. There is an alternative: the **constraint-based methods**: the animator states in terms of constraints the properties the model is supposed to have, without needing to adjust parameters to give it those properties. Hégron et al. (Chapter 4) discuss in detail the methods of dynamic simulation.

The coordination of animated objects is a complex problem that is somewhat similar to the **choreography** problem in dance. There are even more similarities and some differences between the ways in which a choreographer composes a dance and an animator composes a sequence of human animation. State of the art animation systems provide the tools for the

animator to "work-out" the detailed movements on an interactive 3-d workstation in a way very similar to that in which the choreographer develops a dance with live dancers. The animator must specify the position and posture of each figure for each step in time. Some simple interpolation may be possible, but there is only limited support for developing movement sequences for complex articulated figures. Just as with the live dance, a complicated animation of articulated figures can take weeks or months to complete. Calvert and Mah (Chapter 5) explore our understanding of the compositional and choreographic processes and describe how some computer-based tools have been developed to support the process.

The **morphing technique** has recently attracted much attention because of its astonishing effects in producing animation sequences dealing with the metamorphosis of an object into another object over time. While three-dimensional object modeling and deformation is a solution to the morphing problem, the complexity of objects often makes this approach impractical. Image morphing is based on warp generation and transition control methods. The most tedious part of image morphing is to establish the correspondence of features between images by an animator. It is very interesting to note that this problem is very similar to the problem of correspondence in keyframe animation as briefly explained in Section 1.3. Lee and Shin (Chapter 6) give an excellent overview of morphing techniques; more details may be found in Wolberg (1990).

In order to solve the major problems in both modeling and animation of natural shapes and movement, there are different ways other than the use of sophisticated physical models to simulate real world action and interaction. We have already discussed the performance animation approach. Another way is to take classic film characters, or video of current-day personalities, and produce computer models and animations of them by **automatic analysis of the video or film footage**. Pentland et al. (Chapter 7) survey progress toward producing such automatic modeling and animation systems.

The face is a small part of a human, but it plays an essential role in communication. People look at faces for clues to emotions or even to read lips. It is a particular challenge to imitate these few details. An ultimate objective therefore is to model human facial anatomy exactly, including its movements to satisfy both structural and functional aspects of simulation. However, this involves solving many problems concurrently. The human face is a very irregular structure, which varies from person to person. The problem is further compounded with its interior details such as muscles, bones, and tissues, and the motion which involves complex interactions and deformations of different facial features. **Facial animation** of synthetic actors is not an easy task, it corresponds to the task of an impersonator. Not only should the actors be realistic in static images, but their motion should be as natural as possible, when a series of images is displayed under the form of a film. Kalra (Chapter 8) gives a complete introduction to the latest techniques in this area.

In order to generate realistic virtual actors, it is essential to create for them clothes and hair. **Cloth animation** is a very interesting problem as it involves all the problems of collision detection, collision response, and deformations. Magnenat Thalmann (Chapter 9) discusses in detail cloth simulation as well as **hair modeling** for the creation of realistic virtual actors.

A **task-level animation system** must schedule the execution of motor programs to control characters, and the motor programs themselves must generate the necessary pose vectors. To do this, a knowledge base of objects and figures in the environment is necessary, containing information about their position, physical attributes, and functionality. With task-level control, the animator need only specify the broad outlines of a particular movement and the animation system fills in the details. Task-level motor control is a problem under study by roboticists. **Planning**, described by Badler et al. (Chapter 10), is a key issue in task-level animation.

For many Virtual Reality applications and telecooperative work, virtual worlds should be also inhabited by virtual people. These people could be actors controlled by the VR participant or completely autonomous agents. In this latter case, there is a need for a way of providing autonomy or artificial smartness to these virtual humans. By autonomy we mean that the actor does not require the continual intervention of a viewer. Smart actors should react to their environment and take decisions based on perception systems, memory, and reasoning. Badler et al. (Chapter 10) also discuss some of these aspects and Thalmann et al. (Chapter 11) present the concepts of complex **virtual sensors** like virtual vision, audition, and tactility for fully **autonomous virtual actors**.

1.3   A brief survey of traditional computer animation methods

For many years, most authors (Hanrahan and Sturman 1985; Parke 1982; Magnenat Thalmann and Thalmann 1985; Steketee and Badler 1985; Zeltzer 1985) distinguished between three types of computer animation methods: image-based keyframe animation, parametric keyframe animation, and procedural animation.

1.3.1   Image-based keyframe animation

Keyframe animation consists of the automatic generation of intermediate frames, called in-betweens, based on a set of keyframes supplied by the animator. In image-based keyframe animation, the in-betweens are obtained by interpolating the keyframe images themselves. This is an old technique, introduced by Burtnyk and Wein (1971). Figure 1.1 shows the principles to create in-between frames by linear interpolation between corresponding vertices. When corresponding images do not have the same number of vertices, it is necessary to add extra vertices. A linear interpolation algorithm produces undesirable effects such as lack of smoothness in motion, discontinuities in the speed of motion and distortions in rotations. Alternate methods have been proposed by Baecker (1969), Burtnyk and Wein (1976), and Reeves (1981). The method may be extended to three-dimensional objects. The

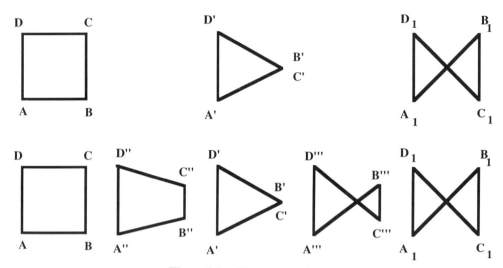

Figure 1.1.   *Linear interpolation.*

principle is the same when objects are modeled in wire-frame. However, the technique is much more complex when objects are facet-based, because a correspondence between facets and between vertices must be found. Vertices and facets must be added in order to have the same numbers for both objects. A complete algorithm has been introduced by Hong et al. (1988).

1.3.2   Parametric keyframe animation

Parametric keyframe animation is based on the following principle: an entity (object, camera, light) is characterized by parameters. The animator creates keyframes by specifying the appropriate set of parameter values at a given time (see Fig. 1.2 for an example), parameters are then interpolated and images are finally individually constructed from the interpolated parameters. Linear interpolation causes first-derivative discontinuities, causing discontinuities in speed and consequently jerky animation. The use of high-level interpolation such as cubic interpolation or spline interpolation is generally necessary. A good method is the Kochanek–Bartels spline interpolation (Kochanek and Bartels 1984) because it allows the curve to be controlled at each given point by three parameters: tension, continuity, and bias. A time value should be added to each control point to control the motion. The method is valid for interpolation between scalar values like angles and vector values like positions.

To explain the method, consider a list of points P_i and the parameter t along the spline to be determined. The point V is obtained from each value of t from only the two nearest given

Figure 1.2. *Key position for a synthetic actress.*

points along the curve (one behind P_i, one in front of P_{i+1}). But, the tangent vectors D_i and D_{i+1} at these two points are also necessary. This means that we have:

$$V = THC^T \qquad (1.1)$$

where T is the matrix $[t^3\ t^2\ t^1]$, H is the Hermit matrix, and C is the matrix $[P_i, P_{i+1}, D_i, D_{i+1}]$. Kochanek and Bartels start from the cardinal spline:

$$D_i = 0.5(P_{i+1} - P_{i-1}) = 0.5[(P_{i+1} - P_i) + (P_i - P_{i-1})] \qquad (1.2)$$

This equation shows that the tangent vector is the average of the source chord $P_i - P_{i-1}$ and the destination chord $P_{i+1} - P_i$. Similarly, the source derivative (tangent vector) DS_i and the destination derivative (tangent vector) DD_i may be considered at any point P_i.

Using these derivatives, Kochanek and Bartels propose the use of three parameters to control the splines — **tension**, **continuity**, and **bias**.

The tension parameter t controls how sharply the curve bends at a point P_i; the parameter c controls the continuity of the spline at a point P_i and the direction of the path as it passes through a point P_i is controlled by the bias parameter b.

Equations combining the three parameters may be obtained:

$$DS_i = 0.5[(1-t)(1+c)(1-b)\,(P_{i+1}-P_i) + (1-t)(1-c)(1+b)(P_i-P_{i-1})] \quad (1.3)$$

$$DD_i = 0.5[(1-t)(1-c)(1-b)\,(P_{i+1}-P_i) + (1-t)(1+c)(1+b)(P_i-P_{i-1})] \quad (1.4)$$

A spline is then generated using Eq. (1.1) with DD_i and DS_{i+1} instead of D_i and D_{i+1}.

1.3.3   Procedural animation

In this kind of animation, motion is algorithmically described by a list of transformations (rotations, translations etc.). Each transformation is defined by parameters (e.g. an angle in a rotation). These parameters may change during the animation according to any physical law. These laws may be defined using an analytical form or using a complex process such as the solution of differential equations. Control of these laws may be given by programming as in ASAS (Reynolds 1982) and MIRA (Magnenat Thalmann and Thalmann 1983) or using an interactive director-oriented approach as in the MIRANIM (Magnenat Thalmann et al. 1985) system. As an example of algorithmic animation, consider the case of a clock based on the pendulum law:

$$\alpha = A\sin(\omega t + \phi) \tag{1.5}$$

A typical animation sequence may be produced using a program such as:

```
create CLOCK (...);
for FRAME:=1 to NB_FRAMES
    TIME:=TIME+1/25;
    ANGLE:=A*SIN (OMEGA*TIME+PHI);
    MODIFY (CLOCK, ANGLE);
    draw CLOCK;
    record CLOCK
    erase CLOCK
```

1.4   References

Baecker R. (1969) "Picture-driven Animation", Proc. AFIPS Spring Joint Comp. Conf., Vol. 34, pp. 273–288.
Burtnyk N. and Wein M. (1971) "Computer-generated Key-frame Animation", Journal SMPTE, Vol. 80, pp. 149–153.
Burtnyk N. and Wein M. (1976) "Interactive Skeleton Techniques for Enhancing Motion Dynamics in Key Frame Animation", Comm. ACM, Vol. 19, No. 10, pp. 564–569.
Gourret J.P., Magnenat Thalmann N., Thalmann D. (1989) "Simulation of Object and Human Skin Deformations in a Grasping Task", Proc. SIGGRAPH '89, Computer Graphics, Vol. 23, No. 3, pp. 21–30.

Halas J. and Manwell R. (1968) "The Technique of Film Animation", Hastings House, New York.

Hanrahan P. and Sturman D. (1985) "Interactive Animation of Parametric Models", The Visual Computer, Vol. 1, No. 4, pp. 260–266.

Hong T.M., Laperrière R. and Thalmann D. (1988) "A General Algorithm for 3-D Shape Interpolation in a Facet-Based Representation", Proc. Graphics Interface '88, Edmonton.

Kochanek D. and Bartels R. (1984) "Interpolating Splines with Local Tension, Continuity and Bias Tension", Proc. SIGGRAPH '84, Computer Graphics, Vol. 18, No. 3, pp. 33–41.

Lasseter J. (1987) "Principles of Traditional Animation Applied to 3D Computer Animation", Proc. SIGGRAPH '87, Computer Graphics, Vol. 21, No. 4, pp. 35–44.

Magnenat Thalmann N. and Thalmann D. (1983) "The Use of High Level Graphical Types in the MIRA Animation System", IEEE Computer Graphics and Applications, Vol. 3, No. 9, pp. 9–16.

Magnenat Thalmann N. and Thalmann D. (1990) "Computer Animation: Theory and Practice", Springer, Tokyo (2nd edition).

Magnenat Thalmann N., Thalmann D. and Fortin M. (1985) "MIRANIM: An Extensible Director-Oriented System for the Animation of Realistic Images", IEEE Computer Graphics and Applications, Vol. 5, No. 3, pp. 61–73.

Pardzic I., Capin T., Magnenat Thalmann N. and Thalmann D. (1995) "VLnet: A Networked Multimedia 3D Environment with Virtual Humans", Proc. Multi-Media Modeling MMM '95, World Scientific Publ., Singapore, pp. 21–32.

Parke F.I. (1982) "Parameterized Models for Facial Animation", IEEE Computer Graphics and Applications, Vol. 2, No. 9, pp. 61–68.

Reeves W.T. (1981) "Inbetweening for Computer Animation Utilizing Moving Point Constraints", Proc. SIGGRAPH '81, pp. 263–269.

Reynolds C.W. (1982) "Computer Animation with Scripts and Actors", Proc. SIGGRAPH '82, pp. 289–296.

Steketee S.N. and Badler N.I. (1985) "Parametric Keyframe Interpolation Incorporating Kinetic Adjustment and Phrasing Control", Proc. SIGGRAPH '85, pp. 255–262.

Wolberg G. (1990) "Digital Image Warping", IEEE Computer Society Press, Los Alamitos.

Zeltzer D. (1985) "Towards an Integrated View of 3D Computer Animation", The Visual Computer, Vol. 1, No. 4, pp. 249–259.

CHAPTER 2

3-D Character Animation Using Motion Capture

Roberto Maiocchi
Pacific Data Images

Abstract

The increasing interest of the entertainment industry for the creation of products involving 3-D characters is due to the development of techniques that can raise computer animation to the challenge of rendering lifelike performers. One such technique is performance animation, or motion capture. Motion capture is the measurement and recording of the performance of an actor for immediate or delayed analysis and playback. The use of motion capture for 3-D character animation requires the mapping of these measurements onto the motion of the character. Motion capture can be adopted both for body and for facial animation.

The purpose of this chapter is to give an overview of the state of the art in performance animation. After an historical perspective on motion capture, the chapter presents a critical survey of current classes of performance animation systems and an in-depth analysis of the methodologies developed to animate 3-D characters with performance data.

2.1 Introduction

Three-dimensional computer animation can be described as the specification and display of moving objects. Generally this process is decomposed into object modeling, motion specification, and image rendering. Although all three phases contribute to the making of a computer animated film sequence, it is the second phase that deserves to be considered as the essence of animation, because without it one can only generate still images.

In the early days of computer animation, when the objects to be moved were independent, rigid bodies like flying logos, motion specification was fairly straightforward. As the complexity of the objects and their potential movements has increased, motion control has grown to become a critical issue. The animation of articulated bodies such as humans and animals is particularly challenging. The human body for instance can be represented by a hierarchical structure of rotational joints with over a hundred degrees of freedom and is capable of such complex movements that ongoing research is still trying to measure it, analyse it, and represent it (Winter 1979). The animation of realistic human models with skin and muscles introduces additional problems, and issues such as the control of facial expressions and lip-synchronizing have to be resolved (see Chapter 8).

Regardless of the complexity of the task at hand, the entertainment industry is looking towards the capability to create 3-D character animation with increasing interest. Films, commercials, videos, and especially games and interactive forms have shown the need for convincing computer generated human figures and animals.

Early attempts at using computer-based techniques were disappointing due to the mechanical quality of the movements as well as the simplistic look of the models. The vast majority of character animation up until today has been accomplished by **keyframing** (see Section 1.3). Using this method, the creation of a complex motion can require the specification of a value for each degree of freedom of the articulated body every three of four frames. Techniques such as inverse kinematics (see Chapter 3) and dynamic simulation (see Chapter 4) allow animators to control several degrees of freedom at once, but despite these sophisticated tools, keyframing is a tedious process that does not achieve the realism necessary for say a complex film effect. An alternative method for generating character animation is **procedural animation** (see Section 1.3 and Magnenat Thalmann and Thalmann 1991). With this approach, the values of the degrees of freedom are generated automatically by a physical model. Although providing a powerful way for creating more complex motion, this technique is not a viable solution to the problem.

The attempt to overcome the limitations related to keyframing and procedural animation has led to an increasing interest in **performance animation**, or **motion capture**. Motion capture is the measurement and recording of the direct actions of an actor for immediate or delayed analysis and playback. The information captured can be as simple as the value given by an input device such as a joystick or as complex as the deformations of the face of a mime. Motion capture for computer animation involves the mapping of such measurements onto the motion of the digital character. The mapping can be direct, such as human arm motion controlling a character's arm motion, or indirect, such as mouse movement controlling a character's eyes and head direction.

There are a number of techniques for capturing motion consisting of a combination of hardware devices and software tools of various capabilities. For instance, one technique requires the parameters controlling the motion of the character to be connected to simple input devices such as the mouse, the joystick, and the keyboard. Thanks to the image generation speed of today's workstations, the effect of the direct manipulation of multiple control parameters can be immediately seen, allowing the equivalent of puppeteering. If

more sophisticated input devices such as potentiometers are used, the character can be directly acted. Performance animation systems based on this technique are called **mechanical systems**. Another live-action technique consists of attaching some sort of indicator to key points on a person's body. By tracking the positions of the indicators, one can get the locations for the corresponding key points in an animated model. For example, if we attach small sensors at the joints of a person and we record the position of these sensors from several different directions, we can reconstruct the 3-D position of each key point at each time. **Optical motion capture systems** are designed according to this principle. Yet another popular performance animation technique adopts **magnetic systems**. This technique requires the actor to wear a set of sensors that are capable of measuring their spatial relationship to a centrally located magnetic transmitter; the position and orientation of each sensor is then used to drive the animated character.

There are several uses of motion capture for animation productions: to replicate the movement of a particular actor; to do a lot of animation quickly; to give directors the ability to direct a 3-D character in the same way they direct an actor; for use as a rotoscoping device for 3-D cartoons; to easily recreate a character that keeps appearing in a TV series; and to capture all the nuances of a realistic motion. But there are also various reasons why performance animation is not as widely adopted as it could be: all the existing motion capture systems present limitations such as the encumbrance of the sensors and the area in which the performer can move. Transforming the raw data into a more usable shape and turning it into a file that can be exported into a commercial software package has, up until now, required the involvement of expert software programmers; the technology does not yet exist to capture a performance with sufficient accuracy and display the resulting imagery in a timely enough manner with sufficient resolution for a director to effectively evaluate the performer's actions.

Besides going beyond the current technical capabilities, the main challenge of performance animation is to establish its unique ground of applications. Too often motion capture has been considered as a mere replacement of current production methods. Up until today, performance animation has been used for the creation of special visual effects in the realm of established art forms like film and video; in the near future, it will also allow the creation of 3-D interactive art installations and performances, the immersion in virtual realities, and the development of sophisticated 3-D interactive contents.

In the meantime, the new medium has to be understood in terms of previous forms or related artistic expression before it can be freely utilized and properly appreciated. For instance, if we consider performance animation from the point of view of traditional animation, it is obviously unreasonable to consider motion capture as a replacement, let alone an improvement, over keyframing. The real power of motion capture is for characters that can be acted, while it is less appropriate for cartoon characters. In the context of traditional animation, motion capture can be used as a sophisticated rotoscoping device for 3-D cartoon animation as film was used for 2-D animation. Vice versa, the twelve principles of character animation established by the Disney masters have been effectively applied to keyframed computer animation (Lasseter 1987), and clearly apply to performance animation as well. Similarly, art forms such as puppeteering, acting, and dance are looked to for reference and lessons for creating performance animation strong enough to stand on its own; in turn, as performance animation grows, such art forms might benefit from its achievements.

The purpose of this chapter is to give an overview of the state of the art in performance animation in both the academic and production environments. The chapter is organized as follows. In Section 2.2, the history of the main research and productions projects that have employed motion capture is outlined. Section 2.3 presents a critical survey of current input systems by comparing the characteristics of three classes of systems: mechanical systems, magnetic systems, and optical systems. Capturing motion data is only one step of the performance animation process. Motion data is raw material that must be further edited and manipulated in a 3-D animation system where skin and other elements of the character to be animated are added. A discussion of how this task is achieved in relation to both body and facial animation is given in Section 2.4. In the concluding remarks of Section 2.5, we finally argue about the future developments of performance animation that will streamline the production process and add to its general functionalities.

2.2 A brief history of motion capture

The use of motion capture for computer character animation is relatively new, having begun in the late 1970s, and only now beginning to become widespread. In fact, the idea of copying human motion for animated characters is not new. Traditional animation has extensively used **rotoscoping**. For rotoscoping, a film is made in which people or animals act out the parts of the character in the animation, then animators draw over the film, enhancing the backgrounds and replacing the actors with their animation equivalents. This technique, which provides exceptionally realistic motion, was first introduced at the Disney studios in the 1930s and successfully used for several characters ever since (Thomas and Johnston 1991).

The advantage of using rotoscoping for traditional animation depends on how the live action is conceived, shot, and used. Disney animators found out that whenever they just copied directly the recorded action, the results looked very strange because even though the moves appeared real enough, the figure lost the illusion of life. Not until they realized that photographs must be redrawn in animatable shapes, were animators able to transfer live action to cartoon animation. This task required making the cartoon figure go through the same movements as the live actor, with the same timing and the same staging, but because animatable shapes called for a difference in proportions, the figure and its model could not do things in exactly the same way. Essentially the actor's movements had to be reinterpreted in the world of design, shapes, and forms.

In the late 1970s, when it became feasible to animate characters by computer, animators adopted traditional techniques for their 3-D animations including rotoscoping. For instance, at NYIT Rebecca Allen used a half-silvered mirror to superimpose videotapes of a real

dancer onto a computer screen to pose a computer generated dancer for a piece called ''The Catherine Wheel''. The computer used these poses as keys for generating a smooth animation; the complexity of the dancer's motion required the setting of keys every few frames.

Rotoscoping can be thought of as a primitive form or precursor to motion capture, where the motion is basically captured by hand. More automatic methods for tracking motion have been developed for studying **biomechanics of human movement**. The aim of this discipline is the description, analysis, and assessment of human movement, and is built on the basic body of knowledge of several disciplines including physics, chemistry, mathematics, physiology, and anatomy. In biomechanics, movements are described and analysed using parameters that can be categorized as kinematics, kinetics, anthropometry, muscle mechanics, and electromyography (Winter 1979). For the purposes of animation, we are interested in methods for the acquisition of kinematics variables, which provide a description of movement independent of the forces causing it. Such variables include linear and angular displacements, velocities, and accelerations. The displacement data are taken from any anatomical landmark: center of gravity of body segments, centers of rotations of joints, extremes of limb segments, or key anatomical prominences.

To gather information about the actual patterns of movement described by kinematics variables, several systems have been developed and refined since the beginning of this century. In 1885 Marey, a French psychologist, built a photographic gun to record displacements in human gaits and chronophotographic equipment to get the stick diagram of a runner (Dagognet 1992). At about the same time in California, Muybridge sequentially triggered a sequence of cameras to record the patterns of moving people and animals (Muybridge 1955; Muybridge 1957). Progress has been rapid during this century, and motion capture systems developed for biomechanics adopt today a wide spectrum of techniques ranging from prosthetic devices to optical systems. In fact, computer animation first approached motion capture using direct measurement techniques developed in the field of biomechanics, and still today most of the optical systems employed for performance animation come from that field.

In Table 2.1 and Table 2.2 we report the main **research projects** and **commercial productions** that have relied on performance animation to give life to their digital characters.

The projects are classified according to the type of character (human, non-human, animal), the type of animation shown by the character (body and facial), and the type of motion capture method adopted (mechanical, magnetic, optical). For each research project we indicate the name of the institution where it was developed, the year in which the results of the research were published, and the corresponding bibliographical reference. For each production project, the name of the character, the computer graphics facility that produced the animation, the motion capture system used, and the year in which it was produced are given. In the rest of this section, we review some of the most significant projects appearing in the tables.

Table 2.1 *Performance animation projects in the research environment.*

Character	Animation	Methodology	Project	Research Institution	Reference
Human-like	Face	Optical		Sony Corporation, Japan	Oka et al. 1987
				University of Toronto, Canada	Terzopoulos and Waters 1991
				Apple Computer, USA	Williams 1990
			The Audition	Apple Computer, USA	Patterson et al. 1991
				University of Tokyo, Japan	Saji et al. 1992
				MIT, USA	Pentland et al. 1994
	Body	Mechanical		SFU, Canada	Calvert et al. 1982
		Optical	Graphical Marionette	MIT, USA	Ginsberg and Maxwell 1983
			Pinocchio	Politecnico di Milano, Italy	Maiocchi and Pernici 1990

The initial interest in acquiring motion data for the synthesis of human movement was raised at Simon Fraser University in Canada at the beginning of the 1980s by a group of researchers of the Kinesiology and Computer Science departments of that school. Their animation system used the motion capture apparatus together with Labanotation and kinematics specifications to drive computer animated figures for choreographic studies and clinical assessment of movement abnormalities (Calvert et al. 1982). The apparatus used analog inputs derived from electrogoniometers. To track knee flexion, for instance, they strapped a sensor to each leg, positioning a potentiometer alongside each knee so as to bend in concert with the knee. The analog output was then converted to digital form and fed to the computer animation system.

The first animation system that adopted an automated optical technique for motion capture was also developed in the academic environment at MIT in 1983 for a project called ''Graphical Marionette''. Two cameras with special photo detectors tracked the positions of LEDs wired on a body suit in correspondence to anatomical landmarks. The system used this

Table 2.2   *Performance animation projects in the entertainment environment.*

Character	Animation	Methodology	Project	Production Company	System	Year
Human-like	Face	Mechanical	Mike	DeGraf/Wahrman	proprietary	1988
			Mario	SimGraphics	VActors	1992
			Poupidoo	Medialab	proprietary	1992
			Chipie and Clyde	Medialab	proprietary	1993
			Tazor	Medialab	proprietary	1994
			Moxy	Colossal Pictures	Alive!	1994
		Optical	Monkeys	MetroLight Studios	Elite	1994
			Ratz	SimGraphics	VActors	1994
	Body	Mechanical	Toys	Pacific Data Images	proprietary	1988
		Magnetic	Mr. Scratch	Mr. Film	Flock of Birds	1992
			Poupidoo	Medialab	proprietary	1992
			Chipie and Clyde	Medialab	proprietary	1993
			Tazor	Medialab	proprietary	1994
			Weldon Pond	Windlight Studios	Flock of Birds	1994
			Moxy	Colossal Pictures	Alive!	1994
			Jackie Lenny	Pacific Data Images	Flock of Birds	1994
		Optical	Dozo	Kleiser/Walczack	Expert Vision	1989
			Walk and Run	SuperFluo	Elite	1989
			Ciao Italia 90	SuperFluo	Elite	1990
			Lawnmower Man	Homer & Associates	Elite	1992
			Steam	Homer-Colossal Pictures	Elite	1992
			Sister Pain	Homer & Associates	Elite	1993
			Luxor	Kleiser/Walczack	Expert Vision	1993
			Blockheads	Colossal Pictures	Expert Vision	1993
			Space Boy	Blue Sky Productions	Elite	1993
			Duel	Acclaim	proprietary	1993
			Copa 94	GloboGraph	Elite	1994
			Alien	Acclaim	proprietary	1994
Non-human	Face	Mechanical	Waldo C Graphic	Pacific Data Images	proprietary	1988
			Mat	Videosystem	proprietary	1991
		Optical	Party Hardy	Homer & Associates	Elite	1992
	Body	Magnetic	Shell Oil	R/Greenberg & Associates	Flock of Birds	1994
		Optical	Party Hardy	Homer & Associates	Elite	1992
		Mechanical	Yoozer Friendly	Interactive Personalities	Alive!	1992
Animal	Body	Optical	Olympic Deer	Rez.n8 Productions	Elite	1993

information to drive a stick figure for immediate feedback, and stored the sequence of points for later rendering of a more detailed character (Ginsberg and Maxwell 1983).

Since that time, methods similar to the one employed for Graphical Marionette have become quite popular for computer character animation in productions. In 1989, Kleiser/ Walczack created ''Dozo'', a singer who danced in front of a microphone in a computer animated music video. For that piece, Kleiser/Walczack used an optical system called Expert Vision produced by Motion Analysis to capture a dancer's motion with 3-D data. They then converted this data into line segments onto which the animators draped a body with flexible skin. Dozo succeeded in bringing the attention of the computer animation community to the capabilities offered by performance animation, and in 1992 several music videos and film effects were produced with this technology. The fire and ice scene for Peter Gabriel's music video ''Steam'' (see Figure 2.1 below and the plate section between pages 152 and 153) and several other scenes of the video were created by Homer & Associates using motion captured from the singer himself and from a group of professional dancers. For

Figure 2.1. *The fire and ice scene from Peter Gabriel's music video ''Steam''. Courtesy Homer & Associates*

the video, co-produced with Colossal Pictures, SuperFluo's Elite optical performance animation system was employed to track the motion. The same system had also been previously used by Homer for the burning priest scene in *The Lawnmower Man*, the first feature film with motion capture (Sorensen 1992). 1992 was also the year of *Toys*. In this film, one scene shows a congress of Pentagon generals as seen by an X-ray surveillance camera, which reveals the conferees as greenish skeletons (Figure 2.2). For *Toys*, an actor was fitted with a plastic upper-body armature that went from his waist to his neck; the actor also wore data gloves to record finger movement at the same time. These devices measured different angles based on specific movements, which were displayed on the computer monitor in the form of skeletal images. As the skeletons had to interact, their movements had to be orchestrated by recording one skeleton's motion, and then play back those movements while recording the second skeleton, and so on. The animation for *Toys* was created at Pacific Data Images (PDI) (Cotta Vaz 1993).

Skeletons have always been a very popular and effective way of representing human characters in computer animation. Recently PDI used Ascension's Flock of Birds combined with proprietary software to create ''The Late Jackie Lenny'' (Figure 2.3), a skeleton comedian for Limboland on cable channel Comedy Central. Flock of Birds is a magnetic system that allows capture and display of the motion in real time. For this reason, the

Figure 2.2.   *The fighting skeletons' scene in* Toys. *Courtesy PDI.*

Figure 2.3. *The Late Jackie Lenny. Courtesy PDI.*

director of the show was able to watch a low resolution version of the character move as the performer moved and thus really control the final animation (the performer was in fact the director himself).

PDI has actually been committed to performance animation for several years, experimenting with different technologies. The company gained its initial exposure to motion capture producing a character called "Waldo C. Graphic" for the television series "The Jim Henson Hour" (a **waldo** is the generic name for a control device that mimics the thing it is controlling). "The Jim Henson Hour" was a weekly television series which initially aired on NBC in the fall of 1988, with a Muppet-Show-meets-MTV variety format. PDI designed a system which allowed a puppeteer to perform the character's motion using an eight degrees of freedom waldo built by the Henson puppet workshop. The waldo was fitted with the same components as a dial box and the motion was fed to the computer using the dial box driver. A low resolution version of Waldo was generated in real time allowing the performer to see the motion. This image was also composited over the image of the other Muppet characters so that all the puppeteers could see Waldo in relation to the other puppets during the performance. The series lasted only six weeks, but Waldo made a comeback in

Muppet Vision 3-D, a stereoscopic 75mm 3-D film/attraction showing in Disney World in Florida (Walters 1989).

Puppeteering was also the method used in the same year by DeGraf/Wahrman to create "Mike, the Talking Head" for Silicon Graphics to show off the real-time capabilities of their at the time new 4D machines. Mike was driven by a specially built device that allowed a single puppeteer to control many parameters of the character's face including mouth, eyes, expression, and head position. The set-up allowed shaded images to be moved interactively thanks to SGI's new workstations and to DeGraf/Wahrman's software ability to smoothly control the interpolation between facial expressions that changed whenever someone moved an input device (Robertson 1988).

Among the successful productions based on the use of digital puppeteering there is also Videosystem's "Mat the Ghost", a friendly green ghost that interacted with live actors and puppets on a daily children's show called "Canaille Peluche" on French television, and more recently Colossal Pictures' "Moxy", a dog serving as the real-time digital host of the Cartoon Network in the USA. Videosystem, now become Medialab, has actually continued to develop its performance system to the point where it is a reliable production tool for large

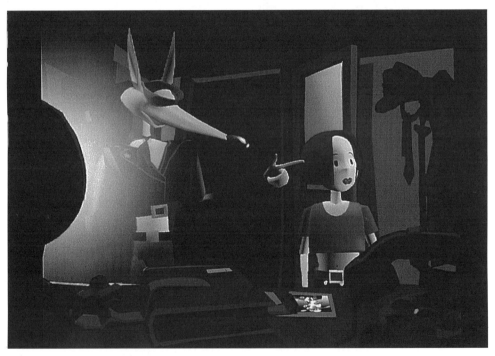

Figure 2.4. *Chipie and Clyde. Courtesy Medialab.*

volumes of animation in a short time. Medialab's performance animation set-up is based on the use of the magnetic system developed by Polhemus for the tracking of gross body motion and of a mechanical system for digital puppeteering for facial animation. The most interesting characters created by Medialab include ''Poupidoo'', ''Chipie and Clyde'' (Figure 2.4), and ''Tazor''.

A different example of 3-D character animated with a mechanical system is ''Mario'' from Nintendo's Super Mario Brothers designed by SimGraphics. Mario, a disembodied head, was controlled by an actor wearing a face waldo. Using mechanical sensors attached to the chin, lips, cheeks, and eyebrows, and electromagnetic sensors on the supporting helmet structure, the most important motions of the face could be tracked and mapped in real time on to Mario. In this case the mechanical system allowed the character to be acted rather than puppeted.

Among the various projects that have successfully adopted motion capture, two are particularly noteworthy for the technical and production challenges involved. Both projects relied on the services provided by SuperFluo with the Elite optical system. In ''Party Hardy'', a spot promoting the Pennsylvania Lottery produced by Homer & Associates in 1992, a crowd of humanoid lottery tickets cavort and gossip at a costume party while they wait for the surprise guest of honor (Figure 2.5).

Figure 2.5. *The lottery tickets in ''Party Hardy''. Courtesy Homer & Associates.*

Each ticket has a different movement, voice, and facial expression that matches his or her costume. To animate the rubbery lottery tickets, an actor held up in front of himself large pieces of foam dotted with reflectors and acted each character's part. In three days, motion was captured that might have taken months to create with keyframes due to the number of characters. Each character's face was also animated using motion capture data: reflectors were attached to the actor's face so as to record facial expressions and lip-sync movements as he acted each character's part. The captured motion was then mapped to predefined target expressions as for instance a smile or a frown, and the animation between the targets was achieved by custom interpolation software.

If "Party Hardy" was particularly challenging for the unusual use of motion capture and for the number of characters to be animated, the promotional piece created by Rez.n8 Productions for the **1994 Winter Olympic Games** held in Norway's Lillehammer Valley is unique for the actual actor whose motion was captured: a real **deer**. In the 30-second piece aired by CBS, the deer wanders through a computer generated forest and is startled by a golden light shining in the night sky (Figure 2.6).

The light is actually the Olympic flame being carried by a torch bearer off in the distance. The deer follows the vision to the edge of Lillehammer, where the trademark Olympic rings

Figure 2.6.   *The Olympic Deer. Courtesy Rez.n8 Productions.*

come into view. To ascribe a sense of naturalness and fluidity to the computer generated deer, the motion of a live deer hired from an agency called Animal Actors was captured. The challenge was to condition the deer to wear the reflective markers that were placed all over its body during the motion capture session and to perform the movements outlined in the storyboard. The computerized model of the deer was digitized from a clay sculpture of the animal matching the exact proportions of the live deer so that the captured motion of the key joints would line up with the respective joints of the animated model.

Another interesting project where the animation of the 3-D character was based on the use of motion capture is "Weldon Pond", a half-hour CBS Television situation comedy pilot that starred a computer animated spokesanimal. The main challenge faced in this project was the integration of the character with the live action: in the show Weldon, an animated sheep whose gross body motion was created by Windlight Studios with Flock of Birds, interacts with his human counterparts in real world settings, including an office (see Figure 2.7 below and the plate section between pages 152 and 153) and a golf course. Despite the promising results achieved in the pilot, the show was never broadcast.

Figure 2.7. *Weldon Pond, a Windlight Studios production for CBS. Courtesy CBS Inc.*

Finally, we would like to mention Acclaim's "Duel" and "Aliens", two amazing demo sequences for video games done entirely with an optical proprietary motion capture system able to track over 100 points simultaneously in real time. The two pieces are outstanding for the realism shown by the characters involved; particularly impressive is the complex interaction between the human character and the humanoid in "Duel" during a long fight scene.

Looking at Table 2.2, we can see that performance animation is a relatively new technique that has been adopted in projects of a small scale. In the past few years various motion capture systems have been released and several software vendors have integrated the possibility of loading data generated with such systems automatically. In fact, the technology does not yet exist to capture the performance with sufficient accuracy and display the resulting images in a timely enough manner to evaluate effectively the performance. However it is easy to see that there is much that motion capture can offer today, and this is confirmed by the increasing interest in performance animation in the computer graphics community (Chase 1994; Kaufman 1994; Robertson 1992; Robertson 1994; SIGGRAPH 93; SIGGRAPH 94). As the technology develops, there is no doubt that motion capture will become one of the basic tools of the animator's craft.

2.3   Techniques for capturing motion data

In this section we present a critical survey of current motion capture systems by comparing the characteristics of three approaches: mechanical systems, magnetic systems, and optical systems. We can distinguish three main phases in the use of any performance animation system (Figure 2.8):

1. **System set-up**. This phase consists of the preparation of the performance animation system for the actual motion capture session. The performance animation system has first to be calibrated for the proper interpretation of the input data. The process of calibration consists of the specification of the area where the performance takes place. Mechanical systems allow data acquisition without limitations on the space, but the range of values of each input device must be mapped to values allowed for the motion parameter it controls. For magnetic systems, the capture area depends on the position of the central transmitter; for optical systems, the capture area varies with the position of the cameras and their focal lenses. In any case, the capture area must be located in an environment that avoids any potential interference that causes erroneous reading of the motion data such as metal sources, environmental lighting, and magnetic and electrical fields.

2. **Performance planning**. The success of a motion capture session requires a careful planning of the performance. The motion sensors have to be placed on the actor's body in correspondence to particular landmarks. The number of sensors necessary to capture

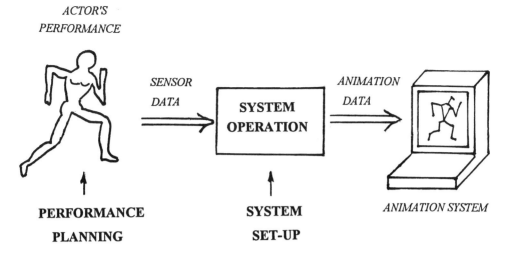

ACTOR'S
PERFORMANCE

SENSOR
DATA

**SYSTEM
OPERATION**

ANIMATION
DATA

PERFORMANCE

PLANNING

SYSTEM

SET-UP

ANIMATION SYSTEM

Figure 2.8.   *The performance animation process.*

gross body motion and facial animation depends on the information given by the sensors. For instance, the sensors used for magnetic systems return the values of their position and orientation, while optical systems track just the position of the reflectors placed on the actor's body, thus requiring an additional number of markers to capture the same information. Sensors also vary in size from system to system, and many require cabling for their operation; both these factors have an impact on the encumbrance, i.e., the limitations in the range of movements of the performer.

3. **System operation**. In this phase the sensor data are recorded and manipulated for the creation of animation data. One of the properties of a motion capture system affecting the actual recording of the data is the sampling rate at which the system operates, i.e., how many readings per second it is able to record. Mechanical systems allow direct animation of the character from the readings of the input devices. Optical systems work at a very high frequency, while magnetic systems require accurate design of the transmission of motion data from the sensors to the computer for the collection of sufficient animation information. The data collected needs proper filtering to reduce any noise that can affect its value without eliminating the nuances that characterize the movements. Such a process affects the actual quality of the data that is fed into the animation system for display. While the motion data is captured in real time for any class of performance animation systems, its availability for animating a 3-D character may require a non real-time process. This is typically the case with optical systems, because the conversion from multiple two-dimensional views of the reflector's positions into 3-D information is achieved through a software process called triangulation.

In the following presentation of the various techniques for capturing motion data, the main advantages and disadvantages related to system set-up, performance planning, and system operation for each class of performance animation system are reviewed in some detail. The primary aspects characterizing the three aforementioned approaches are summarized in Table 2.3. The columns labeled *capture area, calibration*, and *environment limitation* are related to the system set-up; *body, face, encumbrance*, and *sensor number* to performance planning; *sampling rate, data quality*, and *real-time display* to system operation. An additional column labeled cost indicates the relative current cost of each system.

2.3.1   Mechanical systems

In this class we include systems that collect motion data for performance animation from the mechanical characteristics of a wide spectrum of input devices varying from joysticks, mice, dial boxes, and keyboards to more sophisticated devices like potentiometers and face waldos. The way in which the captured data is mapped onto the action of the character varies with the device, the desired effect, and the trade-offs between ease of use, cost, flexibility, and capability.

At one end of the spectrum we have very cheap and general devices that can be used for many purposes. However, such devices are somewhat removed from the direct action they are controlling and thus require an adjustment on the part of the performer. The use of the devices of this class is most appropriate for inexpensive layered motion, that is, not for live performances. Character animation with these devices is similar to **puppeteering**. At the other end of the spectrum there are input devices capable of measuring and mapping movements onto the 3-D character more directly and transparently, but that also are more expensive and cannot be used for any other purposes than for what they were originally designed. This type of device is particularly useful for live performances where many motion parameters must be captured at once, and fine control is less important than direct response. Character animation with these devices is similar to **acting**.

Digital puppetry

Digital puppetry allows the animation of a 3-D character through the use of any number of real-time input devices: the mouse, joysticks, data gloves, the keyboard, dial boxes, or any other desirable device, including magnetic sensors. The information provided by the manipulation of such devices is used to control the variation of parameters over time for every animating feature of the character. For example, the puppeteer can synchronize a character's lips to a soundtrack by moving them with the input coming from a mouse and at the same time modify facial expressions with a dial box. If all parameters are connected to real-time control devices, the characters can be performed live. In Figure 2.9, we show how the motion of Poupidoo is controlled at Medialab: one puppeteer wears a set of magnetic

Table 2.3   *Comparative view of classes of performance animation systems*

	Body	Face	Capture Area	Encumbrance	Calibration	Sensor Number	Real-Time Display	Environment Limitation	Sampling Rate	Data Quality	Cost
Mechanical Systems	yes	yes	no limit	armature limits the range of motion	set min-max correspondence between device and model	no limit	both body and facial animation	no limit	direct measurement from device	low	low
Magnetic Systems	yes	no	up to 9 cubic feet (0.25 m^3)	wires limit the range of motion	specify positional and rotational offset for each sensor	related to sampling rate	only body animation	far from magnetic and electrical fields and metal sources	30–50 Hz for body motion	medium	medium
Optical Systems	yes	yes	varies with cameras; up to 12 cubic feet (0.34 m^3)	none	specify camera's position with respect to sampling area	over 100 reflectors	only facial animation	requires control on lighting conditions	up to 200 Hz	high	high

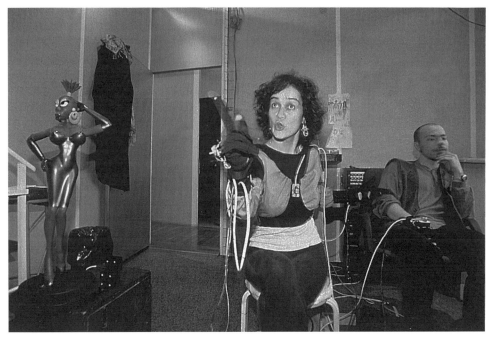

Figure 2.9.   *Puppeteer Tamar Barush gives life to Poupidoo at Medialab. Courtesy Canal +.*

sensors for capturing gross body motion, while another puppeteer controls the facial expressions of the same character with a data glove.

On the other hand, sometimes the results of one type of manipulation are saved and then, while that animation plays back, a second layer of motion can be added. For instance, eye movement can be recorded after the character's facial expressions have been established. Additional layers can be created until the entire animation is accomplished: in this case the character does not obviously perform in real time.

As a production tool, digital puppetry is a relatively inexpensive approach to performance animation that has proven itself successful for both real-time and layered animation. Digital puppetry is particularly appropriate when the characters to be animated are simple and their range of movement limited, or when special cartoon effects are to be added to the basic motion. The great number of degrees of freedom that need to be controlled for complex human motion does not make digital puppetry a viable solution for realistic looking animation.

Performance acting
The typical devices adopted by mechanical systems in this category to collect full body motion data are electrical potentiometers that can be attached to the actor to measure joint

angles. A potentiometer has two arms: one arm must be attached to one limb segment, the other to the adjacent limb segment, and the axis of the potentiometer must be aligned to the joint axis. When a constant voltage is applied across its terminals, a wiper arm inside the device moves to pick off a fraction of the total voltage which depends on the joint angle.

The main advantages of this approach are the low cost and the immediate availability of output signals for recording and conversion into a computer. On the other hand, there are serious restrictions limiting the use of this technique that have caused the progressive discarding of these types of device for character animation. The main drawback is that if a large number of potentiometers is needed, movement can be encumbered by straps and cables, especially if we consider that more complex potentiometers than the one described above are required for joints that do not move as hinge joints. Also, the proper placement of the potentiometers on the performer's body can be difficult and it usually requires the design and construction of ad-hoc support. Additional problems related to this approach include noise in the electronics and excessive length of time to fit and align the devices for calibration of the system before the actual performance.

For facial animation that can be acted, one of the most successful implementations of a face waldo uses mechanical sensors attached to the chin, lips, cheeks, and eyebrows, and electromagnetic sensors on a supporting helmet structure. This type of system is able to track the most important motions of the face and map them in real time onto a character. The encumbrance of the helmet supporting the mechanical sensors and the limited number of sensors that can be controlled at one time are the main problems of mechanical face waldos: real-time animation is traded-off for data accuracy.

2.3.2   Magnetic systems

Magnetic systems involve the use of a centrally located transmitter and a set of receivers which are strapped onto various parts of the performer's body. Each receiver is capable of measuring its spatial relationship to the transmitter and is connected to an interface that can be synchronized so as to prevent data skew. The data stream from the receivers to a host computer consists of 3-D positions and orientations for each receiver. For gross body motion, as many as eleven sensors are needed: one on the head, one on each upper arm, one on each hand, one in the center of the chest, one on the lower back, one on each ankle, and one on each foot. As the human body has more degrees of freedom than those that can be specified with eleven sensors, the captured data must be applied to an inverse kinematics system that calculates the rest of the necessary information.

The primary advantage of a magnetic system is that it can capture and display the movement of 3-D characters in real time, albeit in low resolution to get a decent slow frame rate. In production environments this allows a director to see immediately whether or not the motion works well for the digital character and to make adjustments in much the same way as directing a live action shoot. On the other hand, the primary disadvantage of a magnetic

system is the tether. Each receiver worn by the performer is connected by a long wire to a decoder that sends data to the host computer, and this restricts the range and complexity of movement. It is generally best to connect all of the sensors' wires together at the center of the back and to attach the bundle securely to a belt. The cables can then be bundled together and run back to the receiving units. Another limitation to the movement consists of the need to build a harness for attaching the sensors to the actor's body. The harness must balance comfort with rigid placement of the sensors: in other words, the harness must hold the sensors tightly against the skin and must not move, but cannot be so tight as to be uncomfortable.

Once the sensors have been placed onto the actor's body, calibration must be carried out in two steps: 1. orient the sensors to a default configuration; 2. measure the joint position offsets from each sensor. The calibration process is quite time consuming and needs to be repeated for every adjustment in the receivers' placement on the actor's body during the performance. Other problems inherent to the use of magnetic systems are: a confined working area for the performer, the need to remove all metal sources from the area to avoid noise in the data, and difficulties in setting up communication lines between the sensor hardware and the host computer that controls the animation of the 3-D character. Such difficulties can actually impact the number of sensors that can be utilized at the same time, providing a sampling rate sufficient for animation.

2.3.3   Optical systems

An optical system's ability to track motion is based on small reflective sensors called markers attached to the actor's body and on a series of two or more cameras focused on the performance space. Each camera is equipped with a light source that is aligned to illuminate its field of view and is connected to a synchronized frame buffer that stores the 2-D camera views. A combination of special hardware and software picks out the markers in each camera view and, by comparing the images, calculates the 3-D position of the markers through time. The sampling rate of these systems does not depend on the number of markers attached to the performer; it generally varies between 50–60 Hz and 100–120 Hz but it can also reach 200 Hz, therefore providing detailed information even for the most rapid movements.

Optical systems have become quite popular over the last few years in the computer animation community despite their cost, which is two or three times that of a magnetic or mechanical system. In fact, it is convenient for a production company to buy an optical system only if the system is going to be used heavily. Alternatively, the production company can hire one of the various service companies owning a system for the supply of motion data; in this case, the cost of the service is usually proportional to the time involved in the capturing of the data and in its following post-processing. The expensive components of an optical system are the cameras, which have to be customized for their particular use, the hardware for the synchronization of the cameras and for the image processing to extract the 2-D markers' positions from the camera views, and the computer on which the software dedicated to the 3-D tracking of the reflectors runs.

The main reasons for the rapid success of optical systems are the freedom of movement that they can offer to the performer since they do not require any cabling (Figure 2.10), the high sampling rate, the larger capture area which varies with the camera lenses, and the high accuracy of the motion data resulting from the process. Like every other current motion capture system, optical systems present various limitations. Typically, the intermediate step to process the 2-D markers' positions to obtain the final 3-D animation information discourages people who need real-time feedback. In fact, few examples of real-time data capture for facial animation have been proposed, although with a limited number of reflectors; the complexity of the 3-D tracking for gross body motion does not currently allow the immediate availability of animation data.

Among the problems affecting the tracking process are occlusion, i.e., the lack of data resulting from hidden markers such as when the performer lies on his or her back, and identification, i.e., the lack of an automatic way of distinguishing the reflectors when they get very close to each other during motion. The problem of occlusion can be minimized by

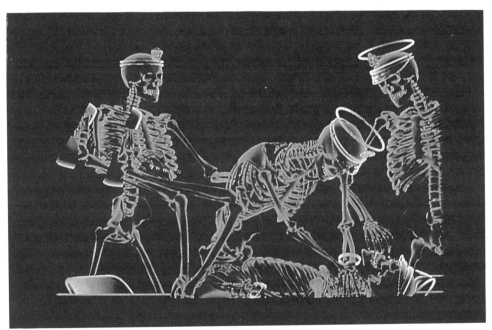

Figure 2.10.   *A scene from Vince Neil's music video "Sister Pain". Courtesy Homer & Associates.*

adding more cameras to increase the chance of always having all markers in view (most of the systems currently available operate with four or six cameras), but this solution has an impact on the cost of the system; an alternative solution is the ability to create by interpolation the data between the extremes of the interval where the marker has disappeared. The problem of identification generally requires the direct intervention of the system operator to specify which marker is which, so that the system can continue its automatic tracking without interruptions. An intelligent tracking software based on an extensive knowledge of human motor behavior could be of great help in minimizing this problem and could actually be a step forward in the implementation of a real-time optical system.

As results from the discussion above, none of the performance animation systems currently available is the ultimate solution to the problem of capturing motion to animate 3-D characters. The most appropriate approach for a particular production depends on several factors such as the required realism and range of motion of the character, the need for real-time visualization of the animation, the type of character, what has to be animated, and of course the production costs.

2.4 Animating with motion capture data

Capturing motion data is only the first step of the performance animation process. Motion data is raw material that must be finessed and further animated in a 3-D animation software where final rendering of the character is carried out, and movements are adjusted and completed. Translating the raw data into a shape that can be exported into a commercial, or for that matter also proprietary, package has not, up until now, been very straightforward due to the lack of a consistent standard file format. In the attempt to make motion capture more accessible, several animation software companies have recently developed drivers capable of reading different data formats. Nevertheless, managing all the captured information can be overwhelming not only for the amount of data itself, but also because it requires knowledge of complex hierarchical structures, inverse kinematics, and biomechanics of movement. In addition, the way that motion data is mapped to the character's actions varies with the input device and with the character's model, and often such mapping can only be achieved by the development of ad-hoc programs; in fact, there is a total lack of software tools specifically tailored to the editing and manipulation of motion capture data. Finally, several layers of motion must generally be added to create more complex animations, to enhance the primary captured motion in some way.

In this section we tackle the main issues related to body and facial animation with motion capture data. For each case we discuss:

a) the main traditional methodologies.
b) how to use motion capture data in relation to such methodologies.

c) how to manipulate the motion capture data both for mapping the input channels to the character's motion and for enhancing the performance.

d) how to add secondary actions that complete the animation.

2.4.1 Body animation

The most natural and popular way of animating 3-D characters is **skeletal animation**. With this approach, animators control the movement of the characters by manipulating the skeletal structure underlying the skin model. Skeletal models are best represented by a hierarchical structure where each node corresponds to one body segment: in this way, when one segment is rotated around its joint, all the segments that are parented to it move along. For example, if we move the right upper leg of a character to reach a certain position, the right lower leg and foot will be repositioned as well. This can create a problem if, say, we would like to be able to move the right upper leg, keeping the foot in its original position. A solution to the problem is to rotate the lower leg and foot back to the desired location at every event or keyframe. An alternative approach uses a popular technique for 3-D character animation called **inverse kinematics**. Inverse kinematics finds, given an arbitrary chain of joints and a position in space, the joint angles such that the distal end of the chain reaches that position in space. If we take the chain corresponding to the right leg, for instance, the hip and knee angles can be computed by the inverse kinematics algorithm once the position of the foot has been defined. More details on inverse kinematics may be found in Chapter 3.

Using skeletal systems, animators can concentrate on animating the character regardless of the geometric model that represents how the character appears. Attaching a skin to the animated skeleton is actually the next step in creating 3-D characters that move. There are two main approaches to 3-D character modeling: one approach uses separate 3-D objects for each limb, like the bones of a skeleton; the other describes the body's skin as a single continuous surface. The former approach is particularly appropriate for characters that do not intend to be realistic, like for example a robot, a skeleton, or an artist's dummy. This type of character design falls short in dealing with individual objects interpenetrating each other at the joints during motion and in not considering deformations of the limbs caused by the bulging of the muscles. Defining the skin as a single continuous surface allows the achievement of a more realistic look of the character not only because it avoids the problem of interpenetration, but also because with this approach it is possible to create the complex range of deformations that occur when the arms and legs bend. In fact the achievement of this goal depends to a large extent on the software tools that control the manipulation of the surface; deformations are generally induced by the hierarchical rotational information about body motion.

Since the most natural way of animating 3-D characters is by controlling the hierarchical structure underlying the skin, motion capture data is best employed to make characters move if it is organized in a hierarchical fashion as well: raw positional data must then be translated

into the appropriate format. For a character modeled by using separate objects for each limb, the data does not have to be hierarchical: the position and orientation of each limb can be given as absolute values in respect to the origin of the world space.

The need to manipulate motion capture data for mapping the input channels to a character whose size is different from the performer and for further enhancement of the performance to obtain special animation effects requires knowledge of the positional information of each sensor. This information can be associated to the end effectors of kinematics chains corresponding to body segments; by manipulating the curves describing the motion of the end effectors, one can modify the captured data. The manipulation must be handled carefully to respect environmental constraints such as floor position and biomechanical constraints such as joint rotation limits. The 3-D character's motion can also be built by combining data from different takes: for example one could substitute the arm motion of a particular take with a more expressive arm motion from another take, while maintaining the motion of the rest of the body. This allows data reusability if proper motion libraries are built.

Enhancement of the primary captured motion can also be achieved by layering motions in an additive fashion. For instance, most performance animation systems do not allow the capture of complex finger actions at the same time as gross body motion movements are recorded; in the case of optical systems, for instance, this is due to the need to use smaller markers for the finger joints and to the potential problems of occlusion. Finger motion can then be performed using performance animation for a separate delayed capture that is later combined with the main motion. Alternatively, a different motion capture device can be used to track finger movements in conjunction with the main system: for instance, data gloves worn by the performer strapped in a harness supporting magnetic sensors can capture hand motion together with body movements.

2.4.2   Facial animation

Facial animation is concerned with techniques for specifying and controlling the positioning and motion of the face into and between facial expressions. In most facial animation systems to date, the visible surfaces of the face are modeled as networks of connected polygons. The goal of the various animation methods is to control the polygon vertex positions over time such that the rendered facial surfaces have the desired shapes in each frame of the animated sequence. The three main traditional approaches to expression control are key expression interpolation, parametrized models, and physical simulation (Parke 1991).

The basic idea underlying **key expression interpolation** is to collect by some means geometric data describing the face in various expression poses and then to change the face from one expression into another by using a control parameter that varies over time. Although this idea has been expanded in several ways, all key pose interpolation schemes have limitations. For example the range of expression control is directly related to the number of expression poses available, and expressions falling outside the bounds of the key pose set are very difficult to control. In addition, since each of the key poses requires an explicit geometric description, covering a wide range of expressions requires the management of a huge quantity of data. **Parametrized models** have been developed in the attempt to overcome the difficulties associated with the key pose interpolation approach. The goal of such models is to allow the creation of any possible face with any possible expression through the specification of the values of an appropriate set of control parameters, which essentially apply deformations to various regions of the face. Examples of control parameters include eyelid opening, eyebrow arch, mouth expression, jaw rotation, and so on.

Most of the parametrized models proposed to date are fairly low level and do not account for the complexity of facial anatomy. More detailed models provide the ability to manipulate facial expressions simulating the characteristics of the underlying bone and muscle structure and of the facial tissues. Such models, usually referred to as **physical models**, appear to be a promising research direction for the achievement of maximum control of facial animation. Nevertheless, sophisticated physical modeling does not directly address the performance problem, i.e., the gestures and expressions of a human actor are not the solution to a dynamic system; outside the scope of computation are the volition of the performer and the meaning the performer intends to express.

Traditional facial animation control techniques have then been extended or redefined to use information from human performances. Facial animation data can be collected from video sources or by tracking the position of reflectors attached to the face of an actor with an optical motion capture system. Alternatively, puppetry provides a means to control facial expressions by mapping the data coming from an input device onto the model of the face. Unlike body animation, current performance driven methodologies for facial animation lack generality and cannot be classified in broader categories; this is due in part to the complexity of the task at hand and also to the little experience gained in using performance data for facial animation. Therefore in the following discussion we outline the methodologies adopted by some of the most successful projects in the entertainment and academic environments without providing any specific classification.

The first ground breaking use of performance animation for facial animation dates back to 1988 when DeGraf/Wahrman created "Mike, the Talking Head". We have already reviewed this project in the presentation of the history of motion capture; here we discuss the methodology used for facial animation. The interactive character was created as follows: first, the basic facial action poses that define the space of the character's expressions were determined, and the basic topology of the character's face generated with a laser scan was deformed to obtain each expression. These facial objects were then used as interpolation units combined using a low level geometry interpolator. The inputs to the interpolator were an expression driver and a phoneme driver, both of which were higher level groupings of the basic facial-action codes. The drives were controlled by various input devices, including a voice recognizer, MIDI interfaces, and various puppet interfaces. The approach adopted for "Mike" is basically a traditional key pose interpolation method controlled by performance data.

Similar methods have been adopted using performance data coming from optical motion capture systems in various projects including "Party Hardy" by Homer & Associates. Here several reflectors were positioned on the actor's face along the eyebrows, the mouth, and the cheeks (Figure 2.11). The positions of the reflectors in time were then used to drive the interpolation between various key poses. Direct deformation of the basic facial model has also been attempted successfully in a few productions. The key to the success of this methodology lies in the proper mapping of the reflectors' positions to the control points governing facial deformations.

Recently, various projects developed in the research environment have employed video based tracking techniques to control facial animation. In Williams (1990), the author proposes a means for acquiring the expressions of real faces and applying them to computer generated faces called "electronic masks". This method can be considered as an attempt to extend the mapping of texture and expression to continuous motion mapping. Facial animation with the electronic mask is accomplished through the following steps. First, motion is captured on video from the actions of a live performer. Control points are then obtained from the video, and this acquired motion is spatially mapped to conform to a

Figure 2.11.   *Director Michael Kory interprets one of the lottery tickets in "Party Hardy". Courtesy Homer & Associates.*

synthetic actor's face. Finally, animation is generated by deforming the texture and geometry of the synthetic face around the control points. A group of researchers at Apple Computer has developed additional work on this approach, focusing on the improvement of tracking techniques, surface modeling methods, and cross-mapping for applying expressions to a face very different from that of the performer. Their improved method was used in the film *The Audition* to animate a talking dog (see Section 8.2.1 and Patterson et al. 1991).

The previously described facial animation technique is not based on an underlying model of bones or skin, but is simply accomplished by local deformations of textures and geometry. Experimentation with the use of video sequences for driving a physically-based model of the face has been conducted by Terzopoulos and Waters. In Terzopoulos and Waters (1991), the authors reported on the development of an automated technique for estimating face muscles contraction parameters from video sequences. Briefly, the proposed method works as follows: through straightforward image processing, digitized image frames are converted into 2-D potential functions whose ravines (extended local minima) correspond to salient facial features such as eyebrows, mouth, and chin. Each of these functions describes the behavior of a dynamic deformable contour in the image plane called "snake". The snakes lock on to the ravines, thereby tracking the non-rigidly moving facial features from frame to frame. The proposed method estimates dynamic muscle parameters for use by a physically-based face model by automatically interpreting the state variables of the snakes in successive image frames. Other experiments are reported by Kalra (see Chapter 8) and Pentland et al. (see Chapter 7).

Little if no work has been proposed to date to enhance or manipulate the captured facial performances for animation purposes. Little experimentation has also been conducted in matching facial animation with body animation. Other relevant facial components such as the eyes, the tongue, and hair must be taken into consideration to create convincing facial animations. The most successful technique developed so far for including these elements into the final animation has been the layered approach.

2.5 Concluding remarks

The entertainment industry is looking towards the capability to create convincing 3-D character animation with increasing interest. Performance animation is indeed one of the most promising techniques for the creation of 3-D characters. Despite the amazing results achieved so far in numerous productions, current technical capabilities have limited the widespread use of motion capture. **Motion tracking systems** have limitations related to the capture area, the actor's encumbrance, the availability of data for real-time display, and the possibility of recording movement of multiple actors at the same time. **Methodologies for the use of motion capture data** to drive the animation of a character have mainly been developed to solve specific production needs, and there is therefore lack of a global perspective in approaching the problem. For instance, little experimentation has been

conducted in order to verify the possibility of integrating different methodologies to offer a broad range of solutions to the animators, and a standard data format needs to be defined so that the performance data can be easily loaded in any animation system. There is a complete lack of **software tools** for editing and manipulating motion capture data to allow animators the ability to operate on the data. During a production, several problems may arise like, for instance, how to scale the data to match the dimensions of the character if they are not exactly like those of the performer, how to join two motions obtaining a smooth transition between them, how to enhance the original performance to create cartoon effects, or how to modify the data for the particular needs of a scene that were not considered at the time of the shoot. Finally, current **motion capture facilities** are unable to satisfy all production needs related to performance animation. An ideal facility should offer the possibility of choosing between various solutions to capture the data and should support the production throughout its development from production design, to data capturing, to final animation.

Besides going beyond the current technical capabilities, the main challenge of performance animation consists of establishing its unique ground of applications. Too often motion capture has been thought of as a mere replacement of traditional production methods. Up until today, performance animation has been used for the creation of special visual effects in the realm of established art forms like film and video; in the near future, it will also allow the creation of 3-D interactive art installations and performances, the immersion in virtual realities, and the development of sophisticated 3-D interactive contents. We believe that performance animation will soon grow to the status of a performance art strong enough to stand on its own.

2.6 Acknowledgments

We would like to thank all the companies that have kindly provided the pictures included in the chapter. We would also like to thank Umberto Lazzari at SuperFluo for his critical contribution in several discussions on performance animation and Ronan Boulic at EPFL for some reference material.

2.7 References

Calvert T.W. et al. (1982) ''Aspects of the Kinematics Simulation of Human Movement'', IEEE CG&A 2, 9, pp. 41–50.
Chase D. (1994) ''The Human Factor: Figuring It Out with Performance Animation'', Millimeter, February 1994, pp. 34–44.
Cotta Vaz M. (1993) ''Toy Wars'', Cinefex 54, May 1993, pp. 54–73.
Dagognet F. (1992) ''Etienne-Jules Marey: A Passion for the Trace'', Zone Books, 1992.
Ginsberg C.M. and Maxwell D. (1983) ''Graphical Marionette'', Proc. ACM SIGGRAPH/SIGART Workshop on Motion, ACM Press, New York, pp. 172–179.

Kaufman D. (1994) "Motion Capture", In Motion, October issue, pp. 21–25.

Lasseter J. (1987) "Principles of Traditional Animation Applied to 3D Computer Animation", Computer Graphics 21, 4, pp. 35–44.

Magnenat Thalmann N. and Thalmann D. (1991) "Complex Models for Visualizing Synthetic Actors", IEEE CG&A, 11, 5, pp. 32–44.

Maiocchi R. and Pernici B. (1990) "Directing an Animated Scene with Autonomous Actors", The Visual Computer 6, 6, pp. 359–371.

Muybridge E. (1955) "The Human Figure in Motion", Dover, New York.

Muybridge E. (1957) "Animals in Motion", Dover, New York.

Oka M. et al. (1987) "Real-Time Manipulation of Texture-Mapped Surfaces", Computer Graphics 21, 4, pp. 181–188.

Parke F. (1991) "Control Parametrization for Facial Animation", in: N. Magnenat Thalmann and D. Thalmann (eds.), Computer Animation '91, Springer International, Tokyo, pp. 3–13.

Patterson E. et al. (1991) "Facial Animation by Spatial Mapping", in: N. Magnenat Thalmann and D. Thalmann (eds.), Computer Animation '91, Springer International, Tokyo, pp. 31–44.

Pentland P. et al. (1994) "Visually Guided Animation", in: Computer Animation '94, IEEE Computer Society Press, Los Alamitos, pp. 112–121.

Robertson B. (1988) "Mike the Talking Head", Computer Graphics World, July issue, pp. 15–17.

Robertson B. (1992) "Moving Pictures", Computer Graphics World, October issue, pp. 38–44.

Robertson B. (1994) "Caught in the Act", Computer Graphics World, September issue, pp. 23–28.

Saji H. et al. (1992) "Extraction of 3D Shapes for the Moving Human Face Using Lighting Switch Photometry", in: N. Magnenat Thalmann and D. Thalmann (eds.), Creating and Animating the Virtual World, Springer International, Tokyo, pp. 69–84.

SIGGRAPH 1993, "Course Notes: Character Motion Systems", ACM SIGGRAPH '93, Anaheim, CA, August.

SIGGRAPH 1994, "Course Notes: Character Animation Systems", ACM SIGGRAPH '94, Orlando, FL, August.

Sorensen P. (1992) "Cyberworld", Cinefex 50, May 1992, pp. 48–71.

Terzopoulos D. and Waters K. (1991) "Physically Based Facial Modeling, Analysis, and Animation", Journal of Visualization and Computer Animation, 1, 2, pp. 73–80.

Thomas F. and Johnston O. (1991) "Disney Animation: The Illusion of Life", Abbeville Press, New York.

Walters G. (1989) "The Story of Waldo C. Graphic. Course Notes: 3D Character Animation by Computer", ACM SIGGRAPH '89, Boston, MA, July issue, pp. 65–79.

Williams L. (1990) "Performance-Driven Facial Animation", Computer Graphics, 24, 4, pp. 235–242.

Winter D. (1979) "Biomechanics of Human Movement", John Wiley & Sons, New York.

CHAPTER 3

Hierarchical Kinematic Behaviors for Complex Articulated Figures

Ronan Boulic

Computer Graphics Laboratory, Swiss Federal Institute of Technology

Ramon Mas

Department of Mathematics and Computer Science, Balearic Islands University

Abstract

The hierarchical control decomposition provided by inverse kinematics is seldom used in the field of Computer Animation. In this chapter we first review the properties and limitations of inverse kinematics compared to other techniques dedicated to the motion control of complex articulated figures. Then, beyond the sole pseudo-inverse solution, we examine the homogeneous solution allowing the partial realization of a secondary task (or *optimization* or *behavior*). Case studies are presented in two distinct application areas of this technique: balance control and motion correction.

3.1 Introduction

In this chapter we explore the high potential of the *homogeneous solution* from inverse kinematic control. Its main interest is to allow partial fulfilment of a secondary task in the so-called *null space* without disturbing the achievement of the main task. We examine here the reasons why this property is of crucial interest for posture and animation design of complex articulated structures. The human articulated structure is considered as a good illustration of the degree of complexity we address here and it is used for most of the examples. We first review the properties and limitations of inverse kinematics compared to other techniques when applied to the control of complex articulated figures. Then, we focus on secondary tasks, especially approaches for posture and animation design. We concentrate on two distinct application areas of this technique: balance control and motion correction.

3.2 Animating complex articulated structures

Our purpose is to control and animate the posture of significantly complex articulated figures while still providing the end-user with the necessary interactivity and specification flexibility. We first recall the order of complexity that we consider here and stress the specific requirements for the interactive manipulation of such entity. This will lead us to compare the inverse kinematics approach with other motion control techniques. We then develop a general expression of inverse kinematics with special emphasis on practical issues such as the calculation of Jacobian and its inversion, the joint limits and the singularity management.

3.2.1 Key characteristics of complex articulated structures

We consider the animation of vertebrate animals including the human being. For our articulated figure a mechanical model of such an entity requires at least thirty *degrees of freedom* (referred to as *dof*) for the limbs alone plus twelve dofs for a crude representation of the relative motion of the pelvis, the abdomen, the thorax, the neck and the head. So, even excluding the mobility of the clavicle and scapula, the simplest 3-D model contains at least forty-two dofs (see Chapter 5) (Badler et al. 1993; Boulic et al. 1995). Then, a supplementary minimal set of forty dofs is necessary if simplified hands are to be considered too. Finally, after adding eight to twelve dofs approximating the clavicle and the scapula joints and some "aggregate vertebrae" for a smoother back bending (Monheit and Badler 1991), the total can easily raise to more than one hundred and twenty dofs depending on the resolution of the vertebrae model. The same evaluation is valid for most of the terrestrial vertebrate animals. The only significant variations are the following: first, the foot and hand models can be either more complex (a primate foot is similar to a hand) or simpler (horses have only one "finger"); second, the spine can hold more (lizard) or less (frog) vertebrae and may include a tail.

From this statement we show in Section 3.2.3 that inverse kinematics, although very simple, is still a pertinent tool for designing postures and animation compared to other control techniques.

The second characteristic of these articulated structures directly results from its high dimension. These structures are extremely redundant, that is to say they have many more dofs than are theoretically necessary to perform goal-oriented tasks in the Cartesian space. This can be illustrated by the infinite number of possible postures to grasp an object. As a result it becomes very difficult to design and determine the "proper" posture to do so. Additional constraints or criteria have to be considered in order to guide the posture control. In such contexts, the hierarchical decomposition of inverse kinematics becomes a powerful feature as developed in Sections 3.2.4 and 3.3.

A fundamental aspect makes the articulated structure we consider here very specific compared to the traditional investigation field of Robotics. Apart from the dimension

mentioned before, we want to stress that all bipedal animals have to face an intrinsic unstable balance problem whereas robots are normally rigidly fixed to their supporting area. Moreover, studies of mobile robots barely focus on such unstable structures. Some notable exception are the control studies of monopods, bipeds and quadrupeds in Hodgins and Raibert (1991) and Raibert and Hodgins (1992). However, they only deal with the control of single support or flying phases, as in a running motion or hopping, due to the difficulty of managing double support phases, as in walking motion or standing.

3.2.2   Animation design criteria

The animation of such a complex structure as the human being has a long history (Calvert 1991; Badler et al. 1993; Magnenat Thalmann and Thalmann 1990). Chapter 5 is especially dedicated to the management of human animation involving multiple entities. We just recall here our requirements on motion control technique for such a complex entity:

Maintain an interactive manipulation rate in order to allow direct user-intervention during motion control or any optimization process. In such a way, the animator can ''shape'' the motion or the posture concurrently with its evaluation.

Retain techniques producing realistic, if not physically-based, output while involving the simplest possible control variables, i.e. joint angles, position and orientation of end effectors, mass distribution and temporal derivatives of these variables.

Provide input variables and operative concepts from which the animator has a very clear and intuitive understanding. Otherwise the high dimension of the system quickly overloads the animator capabilities. Some of these mental representations with low cognitive burden are the posture, position, displacement, mass and center of mass.

3.2.3   A comparison of inverse kinematics with other control techniques

Physically realistic approaches, such as dynamic or optimal control are not yet suited to interactive design of human postures due to the delicate handling of their associated parametric space (torque, muscle activation) or the additional parameters added by the control approach (energy storage, management of the ground reaction force). They are hard to handle for an animator as stated in Raibert and Hodgins (1992). Regarding optimal control, the major limitation comes from the high dimension of the human figure preventing on-line interaction on current workstations (see Chapter 4).

An interesting approach incorporates human strength into the solution of the motion control problem within a dynamic system paradigm (Lee et al. 1990). The belief is that strength is the foundation of a figure's posture (Lee 1993). A complete behavioral model is proposed to control deliberate movements (those not heavily influenced by dynamics). At each time step, it proceeds by selecting various path planning schemes (available torque, reduce moment, pull back, add joint) according to the current state of the system and some proposed external variables (force trajectory, comfort level, desired comfort level, perceived exertion). However, as it is related to biomechanical variables, this approach suffers from the arduous task of establishing the whole human strength model. There is no general model of human strength in the literature and partial results are often based on various simplifying assumptions, one of which is the degree of consideration of adjacent joints' influence on a joint's strength (Lee 1993).

Conversely, pure inverse kinematic control has some limitations. It provides a local solution (see Section 3.2.4) without simple means of knowing whether other solutions exist (Klein and Huang 1983) except by using a global method which optimizes an integral cost criterion (Won et al. 1993). But such a global approach suffers from a lack of interactive capability. The local minima problem is the direct consequence of the local solution of inverse kinematics especially for highly redundant structures. However the optimization of secondary criteria can be used to improve that aspect as already demonstrated in Robotics (Cleary and Tesar 1990) (see Sections 3.2.4 and 3.3) while still being careful about unrealistic demands on mechanism performance induced by their naive use (Maciejewski 1989). In fact the large range of possible secondary tasks greatly helps to ground inverse kinematics into more physically-based solutions.

Finally, a pertinent usage of the secondary task allows full advantage of inverse kinematics' intrinsic qualities to be taken: a low computational cost allowing interactive control, and a great flexibility of specification and manipulation of easy-to-understand control variables. In such a way, we can greatly extend the interactive postural design (Girard and Maciejewski 1985; Boulic et al. 1994b; see also Chapter 5) to posture control with higher realism. Its application to motion still requires negligible dynamics, i.e. a slow speed with minimal frictional and inertial effects, as already mentioned in Badler et al. (1993).

3.2.4 An explicit task hierarchy

Here we review the principle of direct and inverse kinematics and describe its general expression, then we discuss how to define the main task and evaluate the achievement potential of the secondary task. The Jacobian construction and inversion is presented in detail prior to a discussion on two important aspects: joint limits and singularities.

Principle of direct and inverse kinematics

As stated before, inverse kinematics is a technique mostly used to control or constrain strategic parts of the articulated figure, the so-called *end effectors*. Let us recall the technical justification of this technique. An end effector location depends on the current state of the joint parameters. The set of non-linear equations establishing the end effector location as a function of the joint state is called the direct geometric model in Robotics. Inverting it is

possible as long as the dimension of both spaces is the same (Paul 1981). This problem has been solved for standard classes of robotic manipulators (i.e. with up to six dofs). However, as emphasized in Section 3.2.1, we address classes of complex articulated structures which are highly redundant in accomplishing tasks. In such a context the inversion of the geometric model is not possible. For these reasons, an alternate approach, the kinematic model, has become the privileged tool for positioning and animating such structures.

Let us now examine the principle of the direct kinematic model. It is based on the evaluation of instantaneous variations of the end effector(s) position and orientation, for each individual joint parameter, at the current state of the articulated system (direct kinematics). Figure 3.1 shows the resulting linearization of the direct geometric model obtained in this way (1D analogy shown for clarity).

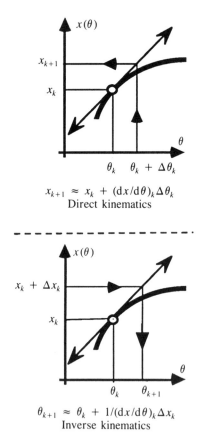

$$x_{k+1} \approx x_k + (\mathrm{d}x/\mathrm{d}\theta)_k \Delta\theta_k$$
Direct kinematics

$$\theta_{k+1} \approx \theta_k + 1/(\mathrm{d}x/\mathrm{d}\theta)_k \Delta x_k$$
Inverse kinematics

Figure 3.1. *Linearization of the direct geometric model.*

The so-called Jacobian of the system is the matrix gathering the first order variations. It is inverted (Whitney 1969; Liégeois 1977) in order to obtain the joint variation realizing a desired variation of the end effector (inverse kinematics).

As shown on Figure 3.1, the linearization is valid only in the neighborhood of the current state of the articulated system and, as such, any desired variation has to comply with the hypothesis of small movements. We now explore in greater detail the mathematical expression of direct and inverse kinematics and then describe the construction of its components.

General expression
The hierarchical decomposition resulting from the redundancy of the articulated system with respect to the task space was first introduced in Liégeois (1977). The first term of the solution is called the *pseudo-inverse solution* while the second term is called the *homogeneous solution*:

$$\Delta\theta = J^+\Delta x + (I - J^+J)\Delta z \tag{3.1}$$

where

$\Delta\theta$	is the unknown vector in the joint variation space, of dimension n.
Δx	describes the so-called *main task* (or *behavior*) as a variation of one or more end effector(s) position and/or orientation in Cartesian space of dimension m.
J	is the Jacobian matrix of the linear transformation representing the first order approximation of the direct geometric model for the *main task* (Figure 3.2).
J^+	is the unique pseudo-inverse of J providing the minimum norm solution, the so-called pseudo-inverse solution, which achieves the *main task* (Figure 3.2).
I	is the identity matrix of the joint variation space ($n \times n$).
$(I-J^+J)$	is a projection operator on the *null space* of the linear transformation **J**.
Δz	describes a *secondary task* (or *behavior*) in the joint variation space. Its projection on the null space constitutes the homogeneous solution which is mapped by J into the null vector of the Cartesian variation space, thus not affecting the realization of the main task (Figure 3.2).

Defining the main task
Inverse kinematics has been successfully applied to the design of complex postures by interactively moving some end effector(s) attached to the articulated structure (Figure 3.3). It is possible to control only the end effector position or only its orientation (Girard and Maciejewski 1985; Zeltzer and Sims 1988; Boulic et al. 1994a; see Chapter 5). Another approach considers the simultaneous position control of multiple end effectors attached at any places on the human tree structure (Badler et al. 1987). The resulting posture is a compromise depending on the relative weights which are also associated with each end effector. This method has been extended further to include combinations of position and

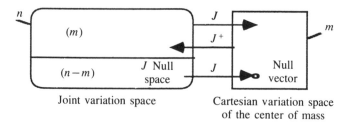

Figure 3.2. *Illustration of the joint variation space partitioning with inverse kinematics.*

a) Pseudo-inverse solution for a reaching task of the right hand (reach the white cube).

b) Homogeneous solution for the right hand (retain the white cube location).

Figure 3.3. *Inverse kinematics on complex articulated figure.*

orientation control under the generic name of goals (Phillips et al. 1990). In fact these goals are constraints analogous to mechanical joints as point on point, point on line, point on plane, as well as plane on plane, ball and socket, etc. (Dombre et al. 1985).

Now, we should explain the local character of the solution provided by this method (Klein and Huang 1983). Figure 3.4 illustrates it in both the posture and Cartesian spaces. Given a goal x_{final} to reach with an end effector, the final posture of the articulated figure (final 1 or final 2) depends on its initial configuration (respectively initial 1 or initial 2). The other postures belonging to the gray sub-space of Figure 3.4 also complete the goal for the end effector. However, they cannot be evaluated directly; they can only be estimated from the dimension of the null space. Again, it is possible to improve this aspect with the choice of a pertinent secondary behavior as introduced in the next section.

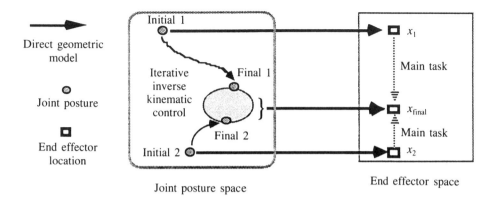

Figure 3.4. *Inverse kinematics provides a local solution depending on the initial posture.*

Evaluating the potential of the secondary task

By definition the secondary task (or behavior) is partially realized by the projection on the null space (Figure 3.2). This way the projected component does not modify the achievement of the main behavior because it is mapped into the null vector of the Cartesian variation space by the linear transformation J. The secondary task usually expresses the minimization of a cost function and it is important to evaluate the potential of this optimization to succeed. First, let us assume that the main task belongs to the image space of $\mathbf{J}$ (i.e. all the target goals defined by the main task can be realized with the articulated structure). Then the null space's dimension is $n-m$.

From this information we can deduce to what extent the secondary behavior may be fulfilled, or rather, may not be fulfilled. To begin with, the joint space's dimension n must be greater than m in order to allow the null space to exist. Then it is easy to imagine the tradeoff between the dimension of the main task m and the remaining dimension to realize the secondary task $n-m$. The high redundancy of the human articulated structure is a very favorable context for the secondary tasks to be realized. Section 3.3 reviews the various approaches proposed for the secondary task and highlights the ones useful for computer animation.

Constructing the Jacobian matrix

We have seen that the Jacobian matrix can hold translation and/or rotational constraints in a very flexible manner according to the controlled dimensions.

We illustrate here how to build it for articulated systems with rotational joints. First we describe the translation Jacobian followed by the Jacobians for the rotation and the general case. Figure 3.5 shows the construction of the translation Jacobian in the 2-D case from the end effectors' velocities due to the rotational joints θ.

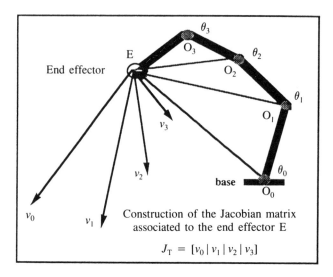

Figure 3.5.   *Building a translation Jacobian.*

For each joint θ_i, the instantaneous velocity v_i on the end effector E due to a unit variation of θ_i is given by:

$$v_i = \omega_i \times O_i E \tag{3.2}$$

where $\times$ is for the cross product of the unit instantaneous rotation vector ω_i of joint θ_i with the lever arm vector O_iE. All the vectors have to be expressed in a common frame. In this 2-D case all the rotational vectors are perpendicular to the plane. However formula (3.2) is still valid in the 3-D case where the rotational vectors are freely oriented. So, finally the translation Jacobian is given by:

$$J_T = [v_0 \vdots v_1 \vdots v_2 \vdots v_3] \tag{3.3}$$

Building the rotational Jacobian is even simpler. The instantaneous rotations on the end effector due to a unit variation of the joints θ_i are simply the instantaneous rotation vectors ω_i themselves. The reason for this comes from the rigid solid hypothesis for the so-called *augmented body* including all the body segments after joint θ_i (on the end effector side of the articulated structure). This hypothesis is intrinsic to the kinematic model and states that the instantaneous rotation is the same for any part of the solid, i.e. at location O_i as at location E. So the rotational Jacobian just gathers the set of ω_i vectors expressed in a common frame:

$$J_R = [\omega_0 \vdots \omega_1 \vdots \omega_2 \vdots \omega_3] \tag{3.4}$$

$$J = \begin{bmatrix} J_\mathrm{T} \\ \hline J_\mathrm{R} \end{bmatrix} \tag{3.5}$$

The complete Jacobian for one end effector integrates the translation and rotational Jacobians just by combining them as a column matrix. As mentioned before, some dimension may be omitted to reflect the behavior of a mechanical joint. In the multiple end effectors' case the associated Jacobian can be built by piling the partial Jacobians representing the goals associated with each end effector.

Inverting the Jacobian matrix
The first iterative algorithm proposed to compute the pseudo-inverse of a rectangular matrix is given in Gréville (1960). Although efficient, this approach cannot be adapted to overcome the singularities. For this reason, an approach based on the Singular Value Decomposition is to be preferred (Press et al. 1992). A specific nonlinear programming approach with variable metric, which avoids the computation of the pseudo-inverse, has been chosen in Phillips et al. (1990).

Handling joint limits
Only the approach described in Phillips et al. (1990) and Badler et al. (1993) explicitly takes into account the joint limits as additional inequality constraints for their nonlinear programming problem. In the classical and more general case of equation (3.1) the joint limits do not explicitly appear. So, when a joint reaches such a limit, various approaches can be followed:

- Eliminating this variable is a bad solution as it remains locked there.
- A simple approach is to evaluate the solution and to truncate the joints values which are beyond their joint limits. However, such a blind truncation of both main and secondary behaviors introduces a bias into the solution which can lead to a local minimum different from the expected main behavior.
- Using the secondary task to avoid the joint limits has been proposed in the literature (Liégeois 1977) but there is no guarantee of permanent avoidance as it is only partially realized on the null space. Moreover such optimization may not be desirable as discussed in Section 3.2.3.
- An alternate method is to remove all variables which are at their limit range from the Jacobian matrix, but only for the computation of the projection operator onto the null space (Boulic and Mas 1994). In this way, the secondary behavior has no component along these dimensions. The joint value truncation alters only the main component of the joint variations for the angles at their limit value. Then the remaining error in the main goal is further reduced in the next iteration, thus exponentially converging to its realization without local minimum.

Furthermore, the secondary behavior should not be evaluated whenever the number of joints reaching their limit value is equal to the dimension of the null space. It is easy to understand that, for each degree of freedom reaching its limit, the dimension of the null space is also decreased until there is no "space" for a secondary task.

Managing singularities

Another limitation of inverse kinematic control appears whenever the configuration becomes singular. This situation is due to an alignment of the segments constituting the articulated figure leading to a loss of mobility of the effector(s) in that direction. The Jacobian has a loss of rank or, even worse, a very small singular value along that Cartesian dimension. Then, inverting the matrix leads to a very large singular value for the pseudo-inverse. Finally, the resulting pseudo-inverse solution has its norm growing accordingly to infinity when a movement is required along the singular Cartesian direction. Such problem appears quite frequently for a human model. For example, it should be mentioned that the usual standing position is nearly singular regarding displacements along the vertical dimension.

An elegant solution to this problem has been proposed in Maciejewski (1990) which limits the norm of the solution provided by inverse kinematics. The computation of the so-called damped least square solution is related to the Singular Value Decomposition (Press et al. 1992) by preventing the singular values of the Jacobian from being zero with a so-called damping factor. Then, the singular values of the inverted damped Jacobian are prevented from reaching the important values inducing the former instabilities of the joint variation solution.

3.2.5   Controlling the center of mass position

The center of mass is one of these fundamental concepts which are intuitive and well mastered by an animator. It is especially useful to evaluate the state of balance of a static posture from the relative position of the center of mass and the support area. If its vertical projection lies in the support area then the posture can be considered well balanced. Otherwise, if we want to design complex balanced postures (e.g. for dance postures), it is necessary to provide a simple means for its position control in order to move it over the support area.

Inverse kinematics has been first used for that purpose by envisioning the center of mass as an end effector attached to the lower torso because its average human location is slightly frontal to the base of the spine (Phillips and Badler 1991). Unlike the true center of mass which local coordinates are changing in the lower torso coordinate system after each posture update, Phillips and Badler's end effector remains fixed until the constraint satisfaction process is solved. Then the center of mass is recomputed and usually it does not coincide with the end effector. Therefore, the constraint satisfaction process is repeated until the center of mass position is close enough to the end effector. In this approach, the only articulated chain influencing the center of mass position is of the dominant leg; i.e. the one bearing most of the body weight (hip, knee, ankle). The authors can achieve balance behaviors for a standing human model (Phillips and Badler 1991; Badler et al. 1993). However it is too complex to generalize this method for any arbitrary articulated figure and even for a human structure with a different support or attach (hanging by the hands, sitting etc.). Furthermore, the influence of the joint variables is not related to the mass distribution in the body but to the geometrical lever arm (Figure 3.5). Such a geometric approach clearly explains the observed distortions between the positions of end effector and the real center of mass.

Several other approaches have also considered the control of the center of mass. The system presented in Girard (1987), dedicated to bipedal walking, is mostly kinematic but also includes some dynamic rules so as to maintain the center of mass within the support polygon. A similar approach has defined kinematic and dynamic rules so as to partially control the balance via the position of the center of mass, and to minimize the effort developed by the muscles (Maiocchi 1991). The approach is applied to optimize various motions such as walking, sitting on a chair and climbing stairs. Despite the fact that the author can successfully manage the balance in the case of sitting (and, especially, getting up from a seat), the control of the center of mass is actuated only with the bending of the torso, which limits its range of application.

Recently, a general approach has been introduced in Boulic and Mas (1994) and Boulic et al. (1994a) which overcomes the theoretical weakness previously mentioned. The key point of this approach is to evaluate the **kinetic** influence of the joints based on the fraction of the total body mass they support, i.e. their *augmented body*. Here, the augmented body concept is used for both the imaginary rigid solid it represents and the equivalent mass it holds. Figure 3.6 shows the center of mass of all the augmented bodies of an arbitrary articulated chain and also outlines the augmented body associated with one joint. It also highlights related variables for the following demonstration of direct kinetics principle.

The basic principle of direct kinetics is to relate instantaneous joint rotations to the corresponding instantaneous translation of the total center of mass. According to the hypothesis of an instantaneous rigid body, the instantaneous velocity $V_{G_{ai}}$ on the center of mass G_{ai} from the augmented body associated with joint θ_i is given by:

$$V_{G_{ai}} = \omega_i \times O_i G_{ai} \qquad (3.6)$$

where the instantaneous rotation ω_i is of unit magnitude and O_i is the center of rotation (Figure 3.6). For direct kinetics we need to evaluate the corresponding velocity V_{G_i} of the center of mass of the whole body. It is given by applying the principle of the conservation of the momentum to the augmented body of mass m_{ai} and velocity $V_{G_{ai}}$ and to the whole body of mass m and velocity V_{G_i}:

$$m V_{G_i} = m_{ai} V_{G_{ai}} \qquad (3.7)$$

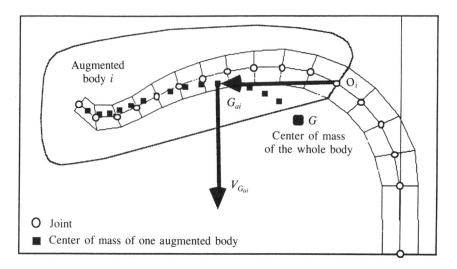

Figure 3.6.   *Total and partial (augmented bodies) centers of mass for a simple articulated chain.*

So

$$V_{G_i} = \left(\frac{m_{ai}}{m}\right) V_{G_{ai}} \tag{3.8}$$

V_{G_i} constitutes one column of the direct kinetic Jacobian matrix J_G (an alternate demonstration of direct kinetics is developed in Boulic and Mas (1994)). Conversely, *inverse kinetics* provides the instantaneous joint rotation realizing a desired instantaneous translation of the total center of mass. The kinetic Jacobian is inverted in exactly the same way as the kinematic Jacobian. Inverse kinetic control is equivalent to expression (3.1).

3.3   Beyond the pseudo-inverse solution

In Computer Animation very few applications of inverse kinematics go beyond the pure inverse kinematic control. We first review how the secondary task has been treated in Robotics and then we present a selection of secondary tasks tailored for Computer Animation.

3.3.1   The robotics viewpoint

Various secondary tasks have been proposed to enhance the control of redundant manipulators. Their purpose is to optimize a cost function while carrying out a task in

Cartesian space. Two great classes of secondary tasks can be found depending on the space of interest: the configuration space (internal criteria) or the Cartesian space (external criteria). The following sections present them in greater detail. The next section highlights the kinetic limitation of the secondary task.

Optimization criteria

The literature is rich with cost functions designed to improve various and sometimes conflicting aspects of the manipulator state, either internal or external. We now briefly explain the chief advantages for the most important of them.

Joint limits avoidance:

It was the first secondary task to be proposed in Liégeois (1977). In order to achieve a joint limit avoidance behavior the cost function to minimize is the squared norm of the difference between the current posture θ and the mid-range posture θ_M. The mid-range posture is the one for which each joint holds the middle value of its range. The gradient vector is simply twice the difference vector:

$$\Delta Z = -2(\theta - \theta_M) \tag{3.9}$$

Singularities avoidance:

Singular configurations of the manipulator are linked to a loss of rank in the Jacobian matrix and their proximity is linked to the vanishing of the Jacobian singular values to zero. So, any measure reflecting the current state of the singular values is a measure of the proximity to a singular configuration. The singular values should be globally maximized in order to balance the potential end effector movements in all the directions of the Cartesian space (including rotation). For these reasons the cost functions aimed at the singularity avoidance are sometimes called dexterity or manipulability. The dexterity index (Klein 1984) is the smallest singular value while the manipulability index (Yoshikawa 1985) is the product of all the singular values. This latter is also equal to:

$$\sqrt{|JJ^T|} \tag{3.10}$$

Another approach minimizes the condition number which is defined as the ratio of the higher singular value to the lower one (Cleary and Tesar 1990). Finally, let us recall that the damped least square method successfully overcomes the inherent instabilities occurring at the singularity neighborhood (Maciejewski 1990) with a modified pseudo-inverse (see Section 3.2.4). However, it does not improve the manipulability which remains very small along some Cartesian dimensions in such context.

Obstacle avoidance:

Obstacle avoidance is the main concern of the secondary tasks expressed in the Cartesian space. In Maciejewski and Klein (1985) the manipulator point closest to the obstacles is

given an instantaneous repulsive velocity. We can call this point a secondary end effector with its specific Jacobian J_s and pseudo-inverse J_{s^+}. The main task clearly has some influence on the secondary effector motion. It is necessary to evaluate it and subtract it from the desired repulsive velocity in order to compensate it in the final solution. Expression (3.11) summarizes the successive transformations realizing that behavior (Maciejewski 1989):

$$\Delta\theta = J^+\Delta x + [J_s(I - J^+J)]^+(\Delta x_s - J_s J^+ \Delta x) \tag{3.11}$$

In Espiau and Boulic (1985) and Boulic (1986) the collision avoidance is based on the simulation of multiple proximeter sensors providing an approximation of the short range distance to the obstacles (from one to twenty centimeters with narrow and wide fields). Their small size allows installing a great number of them (from twelve to thirty-two) on the end effector and the segments of the manipulator. Furthermore, their fast measurement processing guarantees the real-time control. The distance measurements are exploited to synthesize a repulsive kinematic torsor on each segment of the manipulator (translation and rotation velocities). The repulsive torsor associated to the end effector is integrated in the main task thus adapting to changing environments. The other repulsive torsors are mapped onto the joint variation space with the transpose Jacobian associated with each segment. Expression (3.12) recalls the final solution of this approach (k is indexing the segments and k_{max} is the end effector):

$$\Delta\theta = J^+(\Delta x + \Delta x_{k_{\mathrm{max}}}) + (I - J^+J)\left(\sum_{k=k_{\mathrm{min}}}^{k_{\mathrm{max}}-1} J_k^T \Delta x_k\right) \tag{3.12}$$

Other interesting approaches worth mentioning are:

- manipulator workspace investigation (Kumar and Waldron 1981)
- improvement of the dynamic response (Salisbury and Abramowitz 1985)
- minimization of the joint torque (Suh and Hollerbach 1987)
- improvement of the kinetic energy distribution (Cleary and Tesar 1990)
- multiple criteria integration with normalization and prioritization (Cleary and Tesar 1990)
- global optimization for various performance indexes (Won et al. 1993)

Kinetic limitations of the secondary task
Despite the pleasant theoretical partitioning of task provided by inverse kinematics, its solution can be physically inaccurate when applied to real redundant manipulators. Imposing an arbitrary secondary task for their control can induce significant error tracking for the main task and generate unrealistic joint torques (Klein and Chirco 1987).

Manipulators have a mass distribution and therefore a kinetic energy whenever moving. Consequently, the kinetic behavior of the homogeneous solution should be controlled and limited in order to obtain realistic torque requirements. This is especially true when redundancy is solved at the level of acceleration as has been demonstrated in Maciejewski (1989).

3.3.2 The animation viewpoint

Again let us recall that the articulated systems we deal with are, at least kinematically, much more complex than the one simulated in Robotics. This may explain the lukewarm interest of Computer Animation researchers in Robotics secondary tasks. For example, the joint limits avoidance and singularity avoidance are of little interest for the human figure because the natural resting postures mostly adopted by humans while standing are close to some joint limits (knee and elbow extension, hip and shoulder adduction) and nearly singular for vertical displacements of any part of the body.

Specific secondary tasks have to be proposed bringing solutions for such problems as:

- interactive posture manipulation with goal-oriented constraints
- automatic enhancing of posture realism with respect to balance, natural postures etc.
- automatic correction of pre-recorded joint motions with goal-oriented constraint

We review now the significant propositions made in these directions.

Interactive posture manipulation
The hierarchical nature of inverse kinematics solution always guarantees the realization of the main task. For example, it is possible to move and/or orient some end effector interactively, then to decide that it remains fixed (<=> null vector for the main task) and work on adjusting the posture within the null space of the main task. Thus, the posture adjustment does not affect the goal-oriented constraints of the main task.

This can be achieved in two ways:

- specifying a cost function attracting the current posture to an interactively defined posture in the same way we were avoiding the joint limits with an attraction to the mid-range posture (Liégeois 1977). This is used in Girard and Maciejewski (1985) with an additional weighting factor for each joint (also interactively defined).
- using the Cartesian space secondary tasks with attracting velocities instead of repulsive velocities. The user can easily pick any part of the articulated chain as a secondary end effector and interactively attract it to some desired location.

Global balance optimization
The global balance optimization was introduced in Boulic and Mas (1994). It focuses on the minimization of torques due to the gravitation force around the center of support (also called

support torques). These torques tend to rotate the whole body around the center of support under the influence of gravity. The cost function C_S to minimize expresses that all independent support torques T_i should be geared to zero rather than their algebraic sum alone:

$$C_S = \sum_{i=1}^{n} \|T_i\|^2 \tag{3.13}$$

The relation between cost function C_S and the joints has been established in order to express its gradient vector in term of joint variations. Figure 3.7 illustrates the different elements entering this relationship for the augmented body associated with joint I.

First, its support moment comes from the action of the weight p_i and is directly proportional to the distance d_i between G_{ai} and the vertical support line.

Minimizing M_i is equivalent to minimizing d_i.

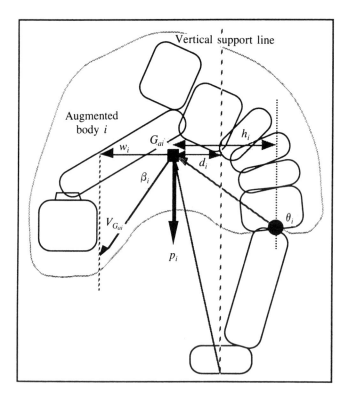

Figure 3.7. *Variables for the balance and rest posture secondary tasks.*

Now, the influence of a joint variation on d_i can be deduced from its influence $V_{G_{ai}}$ on point G_{ai} projected on the axis supporting distance d_i (referred to as W_i).

The resulting term of the gradient vector is proportional to:

$$\Delta Z_{S_i} = -2 \cdot m_{ai} \cdot d_i \cdot \|W_i\| \tag{3.14}$$

The global minimum of this cost function corresponds to the configuration sub-space where the centers of gravity of all the augmented bodies lie on the vertical line of support (see Figure 3.7).

Attraction to a natural rest posture

The approach presented in Boulic and Mas (1994) considers the rest posture as a useful concept for the posture optimization of complex mechanisms presenting an active behavior as animals and human models. They assume it to be the global minimum among standing postures regarding muscular cost according to some biomechanical and physiological studies (Jouffroy et al. 1990; Kuo and Zajac 1993). For this reason, they propose a cost function converging to the rest posture based on kinetic information.

Although an attraction gradient vector like the one of expression (3.9) clearly leads to the rest posture θ_r, it does not convey kinetic information and therefore is not a valid rest performance index. For this reason, a second factor representing such effort scales this cost function. This is the torque exerted by the augmented body weight with respect to the origin O_i of the joint rotation axis. Figure 3.7 illustrates the quantity h_i directly influencing the torque for joint i. Finally, the gradient term retained for the effort minimization is proportional to:

$$\Delta Z_{E_i} = -2 \cdot m_{ai} \cdot h_i \cdot (\theta_i - \theta_{ri}) \tag{3.15}$$

Some gradient terms can be locally null whenever their torque vanishes due to the vertical alignment of the G_{ai} and O_i. By construction, all terms vanish only for the rest posture.

Cascaded control

Kinetic and kinematic control schemes share a common space, i.e. the joint variation space, thus allowing their integration into more sophisticated architecture as developed in Boulic and Mas (1994). Extending expression (3.1) to integrate the center of mass control as a secondary behavior of a classic kinematic control is straightforward and bears some similarity with expression (3.11) from Maciejewski and Klein (1985).

Such a secondary task is equivalent to ensure the algebraic sum of support moment to be null, i.e. to maintain the total center of mass on the vertical line of support. This sub-optimal approach has been identified in Phillips et al. (1990) but not treated kinetically and globally. In discrete form, the cascaded architecture with an additional level of secondary task is:

$$\Delta\theta = J_e^+ \Delta x_e + (I - J_e^+ J_e)(J_G^+ \Delta x_G + (I - J_G^+ J_G)\Delta z_0) \tag{3.16}$$

where J_e is the Jacobian of the kinematic transformation describing the effector control (for example a reach behavior), J_G is the Jacobian of the kinetic transformation describing the center of gravity control (balance behavior). Here the optimization behavior Δz_0 is integrated through a second partitioning level of the joint variation space. It could also directly share the kinematic null space with the kinetic control.

Moreover, the underlying hierarchy of expression (3.16) can be inverted to favor the center of mass control over the reach behavior:

$$\Delta\theta = J_G^+ \Delta x_G + (I - J_G^+ J_G)(J_e^+ \Delta x_e + (I - J_e^+ J_e)\Delta z_0) \tag{3.17}$$

Reference motion deformation

One nice feature provided by inverse kinematics is the goal-oriented motion specification in Cartesian space. Keyframing of the goal parameters is also possible as was demonstrated in Phillips et al. (1991).

However, unlike Robotics where high level specification of complex tasks is better made in the Cartesian space, in Computer Animation the space truly expressing the character of an articulated figure motion is the joint space. It is well known that the motion developed using inverse kinematics is poor in that respect, resembling puppet motion. So it is rarely used to animate characters directly. Rather, it is a valuable tool to define realistic postures for an interpolation tool (Girard and Maciejewski 1985; see Chapter 5). There are several other important motion sources expressed in the joint space:

- simulation of physically-based motions (see Chapter 4)
- functional models based on dynamics and keyframing (Bruderlin and Calvert 1989) or biomechanical studies of specific motion pattern as walking (Boulic et al. 1990)

Furthermore, strong requirements on the motion realism have recently stimulated the development of performance animation systems (see Chapter 2). One challenging task in this domain is to elaborate robust and versatile tools converting raw measurement data into joint trajectories of the performer model. It is easy to understand this interest as motion patterns expressed in joint space can be played back by a reasonable range of virtual human models without noticeable dynamic discrepancies (see Raibert and Hodgins (1992) on scaling and dynamics). The second reason comes from the large set of joint motion manipulating tools allowing refinement of the motion (filtering, editing, layering etc.).

However, even the best of converters cannot exactly translate the motion character accurately and precisely in the joint space because all the articulated models of the human being (or other animal) heavily rely on simplifying assumptions. One example among others is the knee joint which has six degrees of freedom biomechanically, while only two rotations are usually retained in computer animation models (Boulic et al. 1994a). Moreover, the parameters of the performer skeleton are never very accurate due to the difficulty in measuring such characteristics. So, from these statements we already know that the motion reproduced on the performer model can be significantly different from its real counterpart. Finally, the computer animation character itself can be radically different from the performer.

All these problems generally have the cascading effect losing the initial Cartesian constraints achieved by the performer (e.g. the foot may enter the ground etc.). So, in such a context the reusability of a joint space motion is quite poor. There is a need for tools editing highly coordinated motion while retaining the coordination information at the joint level. This analysis has led to the proposal of combining direct and inverse kinematic control schemes (Boulic and Thalmann 1992a). Its purpose is to deform coordinated joint motion by distributing on all joints the motion deformation resulting from Cartesian constraints. The secondary task plays the key role in that approach. So, given an original joint motion to edit, let us now review the concepts guaranteeing that objective:

- Tracking a reference joint motion as secondary task:
  The basic idea is to consider the original joint motion as a reference motion which tracking is enforced through inverse kinematics secondary task. The simplest tracking approach is realized with an attraction to each successive reference posture (Figure 3.8) and the associated gradient vector is similar to expression (3.9). The main task simultaneously ensures the realization of desired Cartesian constraints over some specified end effectors.
- Half-space as a convenient class of Cartesian constraints:
  The user is more interested in local reshaping of the motion both in time and space. For this reason half-space constraints (planar, cylindrical, spherical) are preferred as they divide the Cartesian space into an "allowed zone" and a "forbidden zone".
- The Coach–Trainee Metaphor:
  In order to ensure a continuity requirement on the corrected motion, the most important concept of this approach is to duplicate the part of the articulated structure which requires motion correction (e.g. a leg, an arm, more). The original articulated structure is simply replicating the reference motion, also called the *coach* motion. It serves as a guide for the duplicated articulated structure supporting the corrected motion, also called the *trainee* motion. This *coach–trainee* metaphor is suggested by sport training

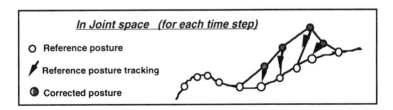

Figure 3.8. *Reference configuration tracking as a secondary task.*

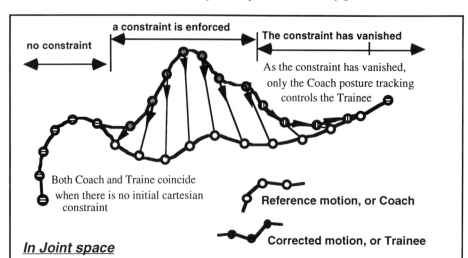

Figure 3.9.   *The coach–trainee metaphor.*

as the adaptation of the coach reference movement into a trainee movement. This movement is the closest possible with respect to a different context of body structure and/or Cartesian constraints (Figure 3.9).

- The transition function:
  Even with the coach–trainee concept, the solution presents a first order discontinuity at the interface of the half-space constraint. For this reason the boundary of the half-space constraints is given a thickness and a smooth switching is performed on the resulting *transition zone* (using a *transition function f*). Then, the formulation of the combined direct and inverse kinematic control scheme is given by the following equation (one dimensional constraint case):

$$\Delta\theta = J^+(f\Delta x + (1-f)J\Delta z) + (I - J^+J)\Delta z \qquad (3.18)$$

with $0 \leq f \leq 1$

  $f = 1$ provides $\Delta\theta = J^+\Delta x + (I - J^+J)\Delta z$ (equation (3.1))
  $f = 0$ provides Δz (secondary task only)

When multiple constraints are defined, each constrained dimension is associated with one transition function and the previous scalar term f in (3.18) becomes a diagonal matrix F containing the transition function. The transition function f has two parameters: first, trainee goal, the relative position of coach with respect to the transition zone; and second, trainee deviation, the relative position of the trainee with respect to its goal. Details can be found in Boulic and Thalmann (1992a).

3.4 Case studies

The following case studies illustrate most of the techniques presented in Section 3.2. Regarding the methods dedicated to automatic posture optimization (from Section 3.2.2 to 3.2.4) let us recall that only the model mass distribution information is required in addition to standard inverse kinematics information. This can be derived as a first approximation from a volume distribution or identified roughly from photographs or X-ray multiple views. Conversely, it is very difficult to find data on more complex quantities such as strengths and general joint modeling as required by other approaches. Whenever possible the simulation results are compared with real postures obtained from images.

3.4.1 Balance control

First some 2-D examples clearly demonstrate the efficacy of the balance control as a secondary task for chain structures (at least fifteen dofs). Then a complex 3-D human model (tree-structure with at least forty dofs) confirms these approaches as a valid alternative to complex physically-based simulations. The 2-D drawing convention reflects the mass distribution of the articulated structure in the following way: a segment S_i is defined between joint i and joint $i+1$. It has a length L_i and a mass m_i. The idea is to have the segment surface proportional to the segment mass. So its width l_i is proportional to (m_i/L_i). The segment width is displayed only at the end effector side of the segment in order to draw a continuous envelop reflecting a continuous mass distribution.

Global balance optimization in joint space (2-D)
A simple fern ''fiddle head'' simulation highlights the interest of minimizing the support moments.
   Although there is no explicit specification to unroll the fern ''fiddle head'', this motion implicitly derives from the support moment minimization (Figure 3.10). Here, the center of gravity is moving upward from the combined opening and closing variations of the augmented bodies in order to align their center of gravity on the vertical line of support. One can also notice the slight swaying along the vertical line of support. The torques display these characteristics (Figure 3.11) while globally decreasing to zero (Boulic and Mas 1994).

Comparison of cascaded control with other approaches
The bird example is of great interest due to some radiographs (see p. 79 in MacLelland (1989)) which have been used to identify the initial rest posture of the bird and to validate the posture predicted with cascaded control. Three of the body segments are rigidly connected in this simulation. Their purpose is to adjust the mass distribution so that the center of mass projection lies just in front of the ''palm'' joint in the rest posture.

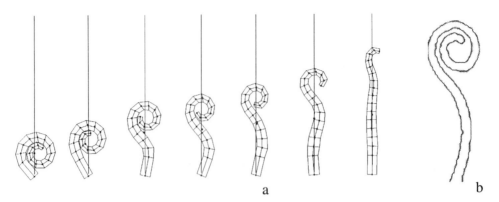

Figure 3.10.   *(a) Unrolling of a fern with a minimization of the support moments. (b) Outline of a real fern "fiddle head", Polypodium aspidium (Blossfeldt, 1929).*

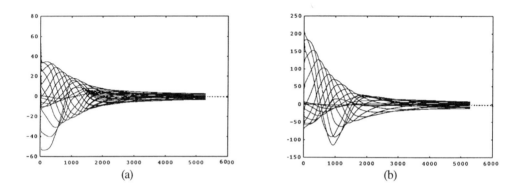

Figure 3.11.   *Evolution of support torques (a) and joint torques (b) for the fern simulation.*

The cascaded control of inverse kinematics with inverse kinetics as a secondary task is used to ensure a reaching and orienting task of the beak as main behavior (for drinking) while maintaining the balance of the subject as secondary behavior.

Figure 3.12 shows the initial (real posture) and final stages (real and simulated). The simulated posture has a thicker neck; this is just to model the mass distribution of the water drunk. As can be seen in Figures 3.13a and 3.13b the cascaded control is clearly superior regarding the balance control. However, the real drinking posture bears some similarities with the one resulting from the attraction to the rest posture (Figure 3.12a) as also suggested in the neurobehavioral morphology literature (Zweers et al. 1994). A complementary simulation would be to integrate the attraction to the rest posture as the secondary task of inverse kinetics, itself being the secondary task of the reach behavior.

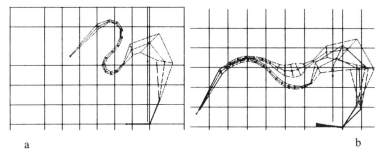

Figure 3.12.   *(a) rest posture (from a radiograph); comparison of final drinking postures (b) real drinking posture (thin neck) and cascaded control (thick neck base).*

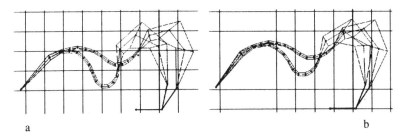

Figure 3.13.   *(a) Cascaded control (black) and inverse kinematics alone (gray) (b) cascaded control (black) and inverse kinematics with attraction to rest.*

Human posture optimization

As can be seen in Figure 3.3, the human posture space is highly redundant for simple reach tasks. We illustrate here how to take advantage of the redundancy to optimize the balance of the human model while carrying complex reach tasks with one or more end effector(s).

The general tree structured human model is rooted at the right foot. The projection of the center of gravity should be in the so-called support polygon made by the foot between the ankle and toe joints. It should always remain in that space to maintain the balance of the whole body.

When the toe joint is locked the so-called vertical line of support passes through the center of support located a few centimeters in front of the ankle joint.

In the present simulations, the cascaded control is used with priority given to reach behaviors (Figures 3.14, 3.15, 3.16).

In the first example, the balance is difficult to achieve because the reach target lies far in front (Figure 3.14) and on the left side of the body while the support is on the right foot (Figure 3.15). In the second example, three end effectors are attracted by one another to simulate the action of lacing a shoe (Figure 3.16).

We suggest readers try themselves.

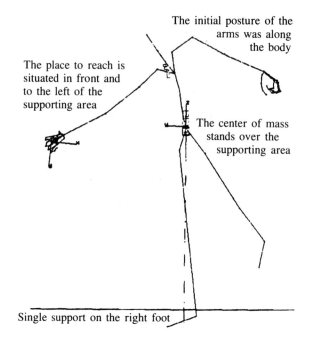

The initial posture of the arms was along the body

The place to reach is situated in front and to the left of the supporting area

The center of mass stands over the supporting area

Single support on the right foot

Figure 3.14.   *Side view.*

Figure 3.15.   *Front view.*

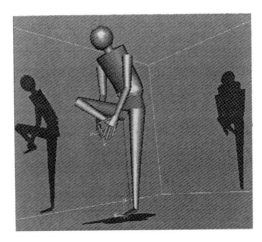

Figure 3.16. *Multiple effector case.*

3.4.2 Walking motion correction

The coach–trainee method for motion correction is illustrated on a walking motion. Unlike other walking motion generators (Girard and Maciejewski 1985; Ko and Badler 1993; Bruderlin and Calvert 1989) the one proposed in Boulic et al. (1990) is established in the joint space. It relies on normalized trajectories coming from multiple biomechanical studies in order to retain the natural dynamics of the motion. As such it is intrinsically associated with a statistical average of the human articulated structure. So it may happen that the walking motion associated to a specific instance of human skeleton faces some Cartesian discrepancies during the support phase (i.e. foot entering the floor). This problem is in fact very common and happens each time one wants to reuse a motion expressed in joint coordinates on a different articulated structure than the one used for performing the motion (or simulating or designing etc.). We recall now two examples from Boulic and Thalmann (1992a) with a single end effector (Figure 3.17) and two end effectors (Figure 3.19).

Figure 3.17a highlights the type of correction which is handled by the method. First the vertical dimension only is corrected resulting in a backward sliding of the foot (Figure 3.17b), then an additional vertical planar half-space is added to prevent the backward sliding without restraining the forward motion (Figure 3.17c).

The correction is distributed on the chain including the hip, knee, ankle and toe flexion–extension joints (Figure 3.18). As can be noticed on these curves, it is preferable to perform small corrections in order to retain the natural dynamics of the initial motion. If larger corrections are required, an incremental methodology is preferred (Boulic and Thalmann 1992b). The curves on the left show the raw sampled data of the coach and the trainee motions; it is important to reduce the number of samples without affecting the shape of

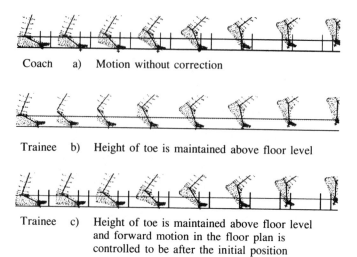

Coach   a)   Motion without correction

Trainee   b)   Height of toe is maintained above floor level

Trainee   c)   Height of toe is maintained above floor level
and forward motion in the floor plan is
controlled to be after the initial position

Figure 3.17.   *Single end effector with one and two constrained dimension(s) (planar half-space).*

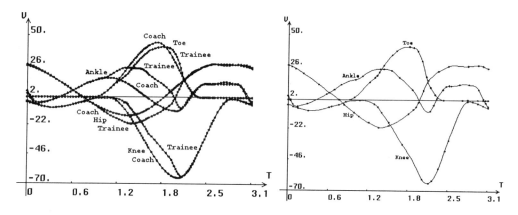

Figure 3.18.   *The correction is distributed on all the joints of the trainee articulated chain.*

curves (Boulic and Thalmann 1992b). Then it becomes easy to edit and adjust them with standard curve design tools; the curves on the right show the slight adjustment of the trainee motion after data reduction (Boulic et al. 1994c).

Figure 3.19 shows an example with two end effectors corrected only along the vertical dimension. First we can see that the motion is unchanged as the end effectors do not violate the forbidden zone (Figure 3.19a), then we can evaluate the motion deformation resulting from an effective correction on both effectors simultaneously (Figure 3.19b).

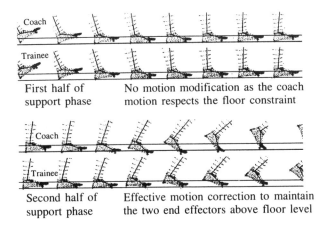

First half of support phase — No motion modification as the coach motion respects the floor constraint

Second half of support phase — Effective motion correction to maintain the two end effectors above floor level

Figure 3.19. *Two end effectors with one constrained dimension (planar half-space).*

3.5 Future directions

Within the present context of complex articulated structures, other secondary tasks have to be proposed in the following directions:

- *Strength optimization*: once normalized data on human strength is available for the whole body, it is important to build a comfort performance index based on the human strength in order to obtain more realistic postures (important concepts are introduced in Lee (1993) in a dynamic context). Associated with the balance control, such a secondary task would greatly enhance ergonomics studies for workplace evaluation.
- *Multiple support inverse kinetics*: humans and animals rely most of the time on multiple support to ensure an equilibrium state. Until now the motion has been rooted on the dominant support, i.e. the one bearing most of the body weight (Badler et al. 1993; Boulic et al. 1994c). It is highly desirable to be able to control the center of mass position by taking into account how the body mass is distributed on the different supporting sites.
- *Enhancing the motion correction*: first order correction of the motion with the coach–trainee approach shows interesting results but the resulting motion still has to be improved with traditional tools. In fact the correction provides useful hints on how the correction should be distributed on the articulated chain and the designer can locally adjust the smoothness of the joint curves. Furthermore, the coach–trainee approach can be applied to the inverse kinetics context where the center of mass would be a special case of end effector and the motion would be corrected whenever the posture becomes out of balance.

3.6 Conclusion

The various examples shown in this chapter clearly demonstrate the interest of inverse kinematics for the posture and motion control of complex articulated structures. The main condition is to associate the pseudo-inverse solution with a homogeneous solution driven by a pertinent secondary task.

Owing to the hierarchical nature of inverse kinematics control we can ensure the realization of the main task while optimizing the secondary task.

Thus we feel that inverse kinematics can be physically grounded while still providing a low cost computational solution for complex articulated structures (forty dofs and more). Moreover, using intuitive concepts and variables allows the designer to overcome the great complexity of the posture design of such articulated structure.

3.7 Acknowledgments

The research was partly supported by the Swiss National Research Foundation and OFES. The authors are grateful to Srikanth Bandi and Serge Rezzonico for improving the style, and to Roberto Maiocchi for fruitful discussions.

3.8 References

Badler N., Manoocherhi K. and Walters G. (1987) "Articulated Figure Positioning by Multiple Constraints", IEEE CGA, 7(6), pp. 28–38.

Badler N., Phillips C. and Webber B. (1993) "Simulating Humans, Computer Graphics Animation and Control", Chapter 4 "Behavioral Control", Oxford University Press, Oxford 1993.

Blossfeldt K. (1929) "Art Forms in Nature: Examples from the Plant World Photographed Direct from Nature", New-York E. Weyhe, ISBN 0-486-24990-5, republished by Dover, NY.

Boulic R. (1986) "Conception Assistee par Ordinateur de Boucle de Commande Referencee Capteurs en Robotique et en Teleoperation", These de Docteur-Ingenieur, IRISA-Universite de Rennes I.

Boulic R. and Mas R. (1994) "Inverse Kinetics for Center of Mass Position Control and Posture Optimization", Technical Report 94/68, Computer Science Department, EPFL, DI-LIG, Switzerland.

Boulic R. and Thalmann D. (1992a) "Combined Direct and Inverse Kinematic Control for Articulated Figure Motion Editing", Computer Graphics Forum, 2(4), pp. 189–202.

Boulic R. and Thalmann D. (1992b) "TRACK, a Kinematic Goal-Oriented Animation System for Coordinated Editing of Joint-Space Based Motions", Third Eurographics Workshop on Animation and Simulation, Cambridge England, September 5 & 6th.

Boulic R., Thalmann D and Magnenat Thalmann N. (1990) "A global human walking model with real time kinematic personification", The Visual Computer, 6(6).

Boulic R., Balmer D., Huang Z. and Thalmann D. (1994a) "A Stereoscopic Restitution Environment for 3D Analysis of Gait", Third Symposium of 3D Analysis of Human Motion, Stockholm, July.

Boulic R., Mas R. and Thalmann D. (1994b) "Inverse Kinetics for Center of Mass Position Control and Posture Optimization", Race Workshop on "Combined real and synthetic image processing for broadcast and video production (Monalisa Project)'', Hamburg, 23–24 November 1994. Y. Parker & S. Wilbur (Eds), Workshop in Computing Series, Springer-Verlag, ISBN 3-540-19947-0.

Boulic R., Huang Z., Magnenat Thalmann N. and Thalmann, D. (1994c) ''Goal Oriented Design and Correction of Articulated Figure Motion with the TRACK System'', Journal of Computer and Graphics, 18 (4), pp. 443–452.

Boulic R., Capin T., Kalra P., Lintermann B., Moccozet L., Molet T., Huang Z., Magnenat Thalmann N., Saar K., Schmitt A., Shen J. and Thalmann D. (1995) ''A System for the Parallel Integrated Motion of Multiple Deformable Human Characters with Collision Detection'', EUROGRAPHICS '95, Maastricht, Computer Graphics Forum, 14(3), pp. 337–348.

Bruderlin A. and Calvert T.W. (1989) ''Goal-Oriented Dynamic Animation of Human Walking'', Computer Graphics, Proc. SIGGRAPH '89, 23(3), pp. 233–242.

Calvert T. (1991) ''Composition of Realistic Animation Sequences for Multiple Human Figures'' in ''Making Them Move: Mechanics, Control, and Animation of Articulated Figures'', Badler, Barsky & Zeltzer, ed., Morgan Kaufmann, San Mateo, California, pp. 35–50.

Cleary K. and Tesar D. (1990) ''Incorporating multiple criteria in the operation of redundant manipulators'', IEEE Conf. RA Vol. 1, pp. 618–624.

Dombre E., Fournier A., Quaro C. and Thevenon J.B. (1985) ''Design of a CAD-CAM system for robotics on a microcomputer'', Proc. of 3rd Int. Symposium on Robotic Research, Gouvieux, France.

Espiau B. and Boulic R. (1985) ''Collision Avoidance for Redundant Robots with Proximity Sensors'', 3rd Int. Symposium on Robotics Research, Gouvieux, France.

Girard M. (1987) ''Interactive Design of 3D Computer-Animated Legged Animal Motion'', IEEE CGA, 7(6).

Girard M. and Maciejewski A.A. (1985) ''Computational Modeling for the Computer Animation of Legged Figures'', Computer Graphics, 19(3), pp. 263–270.

Gréville T.N.E (1960) ''Some application of the pseudo-inverse of a matrix'', SIAM Review, 2(1).

Hodgins J.K. and Raibert M. (1991) ''Adjusting Step Length for Rough Terrain Locomotion'', IEEE Trans. on Robotics and Automation, 7(3), pp. 289–298.

Jouffroy F.K., Niemitz C. and Stack M.H. (1990) ''Nonhuman Primates as a Model to Study the Effect of Gravity on Human and Nonhuman Locomotor Systems'', in ''Gravity, Posture and Locomotion in Primates'', Jouffroy, Stack and Niemitz, eds, ''Il Sedicesimo'', Firenze, Italy.

Klein C.A. (1985) ''Use of redundancy in the design of robotic systems'', Proc. of Second Int. Symposium of Robotic Research, H. Hanafusa and H. Inoue, Eds, MIT Press, Cambridge, MA, pp. 207–214.

Klein C.A. and Chirco A.I. (1987) ''Dynamic Simulation of a Kinematically Redundant Manipulator System'', Journal of Robotic Systems, 4(1), pp. 5–23.

Klein C.A. and Huang C.H. (1983) ''Review of Pseudo-Inverse Control for use with Kinematically Redundant Manipulators'', IEEE Trans. on SMC, 13(3).

Ko H. and Badler N.I. (1993) ''Intermittent Non-Rhythmic Human Stepping and Locomotion'', First Pacific Conference on Computer Graphics and Applications, Seoul.

Kumar A. and Waldron K.S. (1981) ''The Workspaces of a Mechanical Manipulator'', ASME Journal of Mechanical Design, 103(3), pp. 665–672.

Kuo A.D. and Zajac F.E. (1993) ''Human Standing Posture: Multi-Joint Movement Strategies Based on Biomechanical Constraints'', in ''Progress in Brain Research'', Vol 97, Allum, Allum-Mecklemburg, Harris & Probst, eds, Elsevier Science Publishers, Barking.

Lee P.L.Y. (1993) ''Modeling Articulated Figure Motion with Physically- and Physiologically-based Constraints'', PhD Dissertation in Mechanical Engineering and Applied Mechanics, University of Pennsylvania.

Lee P., Wei S., Zhao J. and Badler, N.I. (1990) ''Strength Guided Motion'', Computer Graphics, 24(4), pp. 253–262.

Liégeois A. (1977) ''Automatic Supervisory Control of the Configuration and Behavior of Multibody Mechanisms'', IEEE Trans SMC, 7(12), pp. 868–871.

Maciejewski A.A. (1989) ''Kinetic Limitations on the Use of Redundancy in Robotics Manipulators'', Proc. of IEEE Conf. on Robotics and Automation, pp. 113–118.

Maciejewski A.A. (1990) "Dealing with Ill-Conditioned Equations of Motion for Articulated Figures", IEEE CGA, 10(3), pp. 63–71.

Maciejewski A.A. and Klein C.A. (1985) "Obstacle Avoidance for Kinematically Redundant Manipulators in Dynamically Varying Environment", Int. Journal of Robotic Research, 4(3), pp. 109–117.

MacLelland J. (1989) "Form and Function in Birds", vol. 4, King & MacLelland, Eds, Academic Press, London, p. 79.

Magnenat Thalmann N. and Thalmann D. (1990) "Synthetic Actors in 3D Computer Generated Films", Springer-Verlag, New York.

Maiocchi R. (1991) "A Knowledge Based Approach to the Synthesis of Human Motion", IFIP TC5/WG5.10 "Modeling in Computer Graphics", Tokyo.

Monheit G. and Badler N. (1991) "A Kinematic Model of the Human Spine and Torso", IEEE CGA, 11(2), pp. 29–38.

Paul R. (1981) "Robot Manipulators: Mathematics Programming and Control", MIT Press, Cambridge, MA.

Phillips C.B., Zhao J. and Badler N.I. (1990) "Interactive Real-Time Articulated Figure Manipulation Using Multiple Kinematic Constraints", Computer Graphics, 24 (2), pp. 245–250.

Phillips C.B. and Badler N. (1991) "Interactive Behaviors for Bipedal Articulated Figures", Computer Graphics, 25 (4), pp. 359–362.

Press W.H., Teukolski S.A., Wetterling W.T. and Flannery B.P. (1992) "Numerical Recipes in C", Press Syndicate of the University of Cambridge, second edition.

Raibert M.H. and Hodgins J.K. (1992) "Animation of Dynamic Legged Locomotion", Computer Graphics, 25 (4), pp. 349–358.

Salisbury J. and Abramovitz J. (1985) "Design and Control of a Redundant Mechanism for Small Motion", IEEE Int. Conf. on Robotics and Automation, pp. 323–328.

Suh K.C. and Hollerbach J.M. (1987) "Local versus Global Torque Optimization of Redundant Manipulators", IEEE Int. Conf. on Robotics and Automation, pp. 619–624.

Whitney D.E. (1969) "Resolved Motion Rate Control of Manipulators and Human Prostheses", IEEE Trans. Man-Machine Systems MMS-10, pp. 47–53.

Won J.H., Choi B.W. and Chung M.J. (1993) "A Unified Approach to the Inverse Kinematic Solution for a Redundant Manipulator", Robotica, 11, pp. 159–165.

Yoshikawa T. (1985) "Manipulability of Robotics Mechanism", Int. Journal of Robotic Research, 4(2).

Zeltzer D. and Sims K. (1988) "A Figure Editor and Gait Controller to Task Level Animation", SIGGRAPH 88 Tutorial Notes on Synthetic Actors: The impact of A.I. and Robotics on Animation.

Zweers G., Bout R. and Heidweiller J. (1994) "Motor Organization of the Avian Head–Neck System", Davies M.N.O. and Green P.R. (Eds) "Perception and Motor Control in Birds", Springer-Verlag, Berlin, Heidelberg, pp. 201–221.

CHAPTER 4

Dynamic Simulation and Animation

G. Hégron
Ecole des Mines de Nantes

B. Arnaldi and C. Lecerf
IRISA/INRIA

Abstract

The main goal of computer animation is to synthesize any dynamic behavior of an object like motion and deformation. Motion control models are the heart of any animation system because they determine the friendliness of the user interface, the class of motions and deformations produced and the application fields. Among the different approaches, physical models are taking a preponderant position in computer animation because they display the following advantages: realism, genericity and simplicity. They are also suitable for both animation and simulation. In this chapter the physical models and the formalisms used to build the motion equations of a mechanical system are presented. The application of the Lagrangian formalism to complex articulated rigid objects is developed and the simulation results of a 3-D vehicle based on forward dynamics are compared to real measurements. The motion control of physical objects remains a tedious task for an animator. Two classes of techniques are proposed: on-line control techniques allowing the animator to interact with the animation evolution while it is simulated (Proportional Integral Derivative control, control by constraints) and off-line control techniques where animator interaction is no longer possible (optimal control). These techniques are illustrated with two examples: a hopping one-legged robot and a vehicle.

4.1 Introduction

To animate means to bring to life. Therefore the main goal of computer animation is to synthesize any desired effects evolving through time: motion (position and orientation

changes) and deformation (shape changes). The designer conceives the object's dynamic behavior with its mental representation of causality which is a mixture of natural phenomena, perception and imagination. He imagines how it moves, gets out of shape or reacts when he pushes, presses, pulls or twists it. Motion control models are the heart of any animation system because they determine the friendliness of the user interface, the class of motions and deformations produced, and the application fields. Physical models take a preponderant position in computer animation because they display the following advantages:

- realism: tasks are performed in a realistic fashion due to the application of physical laws such as gravity;
- genericity: for a given physical object, a physical model represents the class of all possible movements;
- simplicity: physical models take advantage of the intrinsic behavior of the objects, their reactions and interactions. The motion specification of complex linked figures becomes easier thanks to the reduction of the number of parameters and to the use of high level motion control techniques.

The scope of this chapter is first to introduce the physical models and the formalisms used to build the motion equations of a mechanical system. The second section presents the structure of articulated rigid objects and the method for handling motion equations and simulation results. The third section is dedicated to motion control problems introducing general control techniques with examples.

4.2   Physical models and formalisms

4.2.1   Physical models

To take into account natural phenomena in a computer animation system, a physical model has to be chosen to represent the objects. The choice of this model is essential and depends on the way the animator wishes to describe the desired result because, in order to control the behavior of an object, he acts on its representation. In a more structured approach, the following classification of physical models can be considered (Luciani et al. 1991):

- The continuous distributed model: this is the model proposed by classical analytical physics which describes object behavior with a set of differential equations. This model is concerned with the physical simulation field and provides accurate though time consuming solutions. The articulated rigid object model falls into this class.
- The continuous localized constants model: this model deals with a structural discretization of the object. For each component, a continuous distributed model is used to express its mechanical behavior. Some analytical equations link the different

components to provide motion equations for the entire mechanical system. The finite elements method lies in this family.

- The discrete localized constants model: this model also contains a structural discretization of the object but implicitly defines a computation algorithm for obtaining the emergent mechanical behavior of the object. A particle system belongs to this class.

4.2.2 Mechanical formalism

Once a physical model for the objects has been chosen, mechanical formalism provides the laws to obtain the equations of motion expressing the dynamic behavior of the object. In analytical mechanics we find the fundamental laws of mechanics, the principle of virtual works with Lagrange's equations, Hamilton's equations and the methods based on Lie's groups. On the basis of assumptions about the nature of mechanical systems and dynamic constraints, all these methods lead to the same set of motion equations. The first two formalisms are presented below because they are the two that are used in the relevant literature.

Fundamental laws
The fundamental principles of mechanics can be expressed as three laws:

- in a Galilean frame, for a system S the motion of the center of gravity is the motion of a point where all the masses are concentrated and on which all the external forces are applied:

$$M_S\gamma = F_E \tag{4.1}$$

where

M_S: mass of S
γ: linear acceleration of the center of gravity
F_E: net external forces

- the law of moment of momentum: the absolute time derivative of the absolute angular momentum with respect to a reference point fixed in inertial space equals the resultant torque with respect to the same reference point:

$$J_S\dot{\omega} = M_\varepsilon \tag{4.2}$$

where

J_S: inertial matrix of S at the center of gravity
ω: center of gravity angular velocity
M_ε: momentum of all applied forces

- the principle of action and reaction: action exerted on a system S_1 by a system S_2 is the opposite, at a same point, of action exerted by S_1 on S_2:

$$F_{S_1 \to S_2}^P = -F_{S_2 \to S_1}^P \tag{4.3}$$

Principle of virtual works

This mechanical formalism (Bamberger 1981; Germain 1986) can easily be applied to "general multibody systems" (Schielen 1984; Wittenburg 1977) involving holonomics and nonholonomic constraints, open and closed chains, and makes it possible to automatically derive their motion equations from their geometric, kinematic and dynamic constraint descriptions.

Let $q = (q^i)_{i=1;n}$ be the Lagrangian parameters of one multibody system (S). The principle of virtual work states that there exists at least one reference frame in which, for all virtual displacement of (S) and at any moment, the amount of virtual work that acts upon (S) is zero. It can be expressed by:

$$\delta W_d + \delta W_l + \delta W_j = 0 \tag{4.4}$$

where:

δW_d is the virtual work of given effects,
δW_l is the virtual work of binding effects,
δW_j is the virtual work of inertia effects.

For a system (S) with the generalized coordinates $q = (q^i)_{i=1;n}$, the principle of virtual work can be written as:

$$Q_i + L_i + J_i = 0, \quad i = 1, 2, \ldots, n \tag{4.5}$$

where Q_i (resp. L_i, J_i) is the generalized given (resp. binding, inertia) effect relative to q^i.
Now, let C be the kinetic energy of (S). By using Lagrange's formula we get:

$$J_i = -\frac{\mathrm{d}}{\mathrm{d}t}\left(\frac{\partial C}{\partial \dot{q}^i}\right) + \frac{\partial C}{\partial q^i} \quad i = 1, 2, \ldots, n \tag{4.6}$$

The introduction of L_i is shown in the section about the constraint equations. This formalism can also be used to derive the motion equations for deformable objects leading to a quite different formulation.

4.3   Articulated rigid objects

4.3.1   Articulated rigid object modeling

An articulated rigid system is composed of a set of rigid objects linked together by

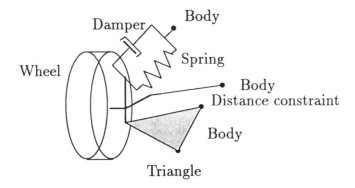

Figure 4.1. *MacPherson suspension.*

mechanical joints. In a general multibody system, this mechanical system gives a kinematic graph where nodes are rigid objects and links are joints. Let us consider a part of a vehicle as an example (see Figure 4.1) of such a system.

For the given mechanism, the kinematic graph is presented in Figure 4.2.

Parameters

The first step in building the motion equations consists of choosing the parameters (the unknowns of the problem). Two methods can be employed:

- We can consider that each object could be represented as a free object, so 6 degrees of freedom describe its motion (3 degrees for translation and 3 degrees for rotation). If n is the number of objects, we obtain $6n$ motion equations. The joints are treated as

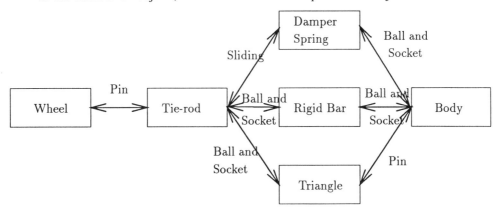

Figure 4.2. *Kinematic graph for a multibody system.*

constraints restraining motion between objects. To the $6n$ motion equations we add constraint equations for each joint. As an example, for a ball and socket joint, 3 scalar equations express that the coordinates of a point in each object are equal. In the vehicle part example, we obtain 36 motion equations plus many constraint equations.

- We can also consider that the system parameters can be the joint degrees of freedom. A problem arises if there are some kinematical loops in the system, with the result that the joint degrees of freedom are not independent and do not represent the mechanism's degrees of freedom. In this case we have to convert the previous graph into a tree by cutting some joints (see Figure 4.3). Then, we can build the motion equations according to the tree joint parameters. The last step consists of treating the cutting joint by adding the constraint equations to close the cutting loops. In the vehicle part example, we obtain only 15 motion equations plus 6 constraint equations to close the two broken loops.

To represent the position of an object, a Cartesian representation is generally used. Some well known methods are used to express the orientation parameters (Wittenburg 1977): Euler angles, Bryant angles, quaternions, Euler parameters (normalized quaternions), etc. The choice leads to a different transformation matrix between local frames. As an example, the transformation matrix used to transform the coordinates of a 3-D point from a frame R_1 to a frame R_2 when the transformation is given by the 3 Euler angles (ψ, θ, and ϕ), assuming that $c_\phi = \cos \phi$, $s_\phi = \sin \phi$ (and so on for the other angles), is given by:

$$M = \begin{bmatrix} c_\psi c_\phi - s_\psi c_\theta s_\phi & s_\psi c_\phi + c_\psi c_\theta s_\phi & s_\theta s_\phi \\ -c_\psi s_\phi - s_\psi c_\theta c_\phi & -s_\psi s_\phi + c_\psi c_\theta c_\phi & s_\theta c_\phi \\ s_\psi s_\theta & -c_\psi s_\theta & c_\theta \end{bmatrix} \tag{4.7}$$

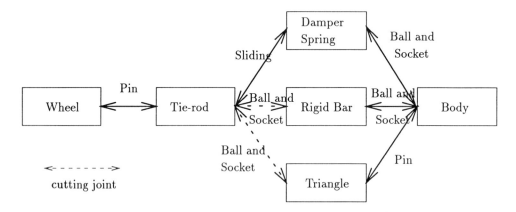

Figure 4.3. *Kinematic tree with additional constraints.*

Table 4.1 *Library of joints.*

No.	Joint	Rot.	Trans.	Dofs
1	Embedding	0	0	0
2	Pin	1	0	1
3	Sliding	0	1	1
4	Twist sliding	1	1	1
5	Cylindrical	1	1	2
6	Plane on plane	1	2	3
7	Ball and socket	3	0	3
8	Cyl. on plane	2	2	4
9	Ball in a cyl.	3	1	4
10	Ball on plane	3	2	5
11	Free object	3	3	6

Mechanical joints

During the geometric modeling phase, the animator can be provided with a library of joints. This library is described in Table 4.1 where for each joint type, different degrees of freedom are available.

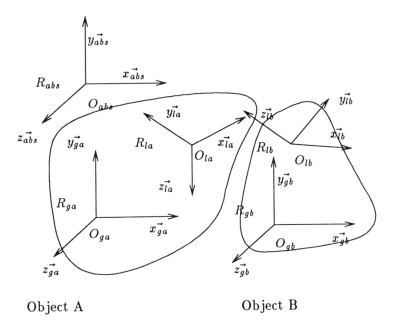

Object A   Object B

Figure 4.4. *Description of joint reference frame.*

The objects are parametrized in their inertial reference frame. The joint reference frames R_l introduced to define the joint location with respect to the local (inertial) reference frames R_g of the associated objects (see Figure 4.4). For instance, the pin joint, parametrized by α_1, is (partially) defined by its transformation matrix in the local (inertial) reference frame of object A, $M_{la \to ga}$ which is a constant matrix.

Efforts

To the multibody system, we add some kinematic or dynamic constraints such as:

- gravity (direction and module);
- springs, dampers, thrusts, forces and torques applied on joint degrees of freedom (dof) or forces applied on specific points, the parameters of which (given in Table 4.2) may evolve over time and therefore may be described by a trajectory with respect to time or obtained from the user via an input device (mouse, trackball, etc.). Effects such as motor, springs, and dampers may be applied to the dof, which may furthermore be constrained by thrusts. A summary of these given effects is presented in Table 4.2, where l is the degree of freedom value and f is the amount of force.
- punctual forces applied to objects;
- nonholonomic constraints such as rolling without sliding (for a wheel);
- kinematic constraints to restrain motion along a specific path (see Section 4.4 about motion control);
- for a specialist, hand-written constraint equations if needed.

4.3.2   Mechanical properties

The mechanical properties of each object (center of gravity (COG), inertia matrix, principal coordinate system of inertia) are extracted from the object's geometric model. Inertia and mass are integrals on the volume. A discrete integration can be performed by using an orthographic ray tracing algorithm from a regular grid mapped on a face of the object bounding box. The ray tracing technique is applicable to a large variety of solid models. Along each ray, inner parallelepipeds are computed according to the grid resolution and the

Table 4.2   *Dof coefficients.*

Descr.	param.	note	effort
spring	k	rigidity coefficient	$f = k(l - l_0)$
	l_0	rest length of the spring	
damper	ν	damping coefficient	$f = \nu \dot{l}$
motor	F	force or torque	$f = F$

intersection points between the ray and the object boundary. The physical properties of the parallelepipeds are calculated, then the object properties are derived using associativity of COGs and additivity of inertia matrices with respect to the global COG.

4.3.3 Motion equations

Various methods can be used to compute the motion equations, depending on the application field, the kinematic loops, the constraints acting on the system, etc. In order to show different motion equation derivations, we present here two methods corresponding to different formulations and computational models.

Recursive formulation
One of the first implementations of a physically based system in computer animation was made by W.W. Armstrong and M.W. Green (1985) and deals with multibody systems represented by a tree structure using only rotational joints with 3 degrees of freedom. This formulation contains both the way to derivate the motion equations and the way to solve them in a recursive algorithm along the tree structure in linear time according to the link number.

Setting up of symbolic motion equations
Motion equations can be automatically generated in a symbolic form from the data structure of the mechanism by using the principle of virtual works as follows:

- for each object, the COG and the angular velocities are symbolically computed by a tree traversal, according to the joints between objects and the relative locations of local frames. Symbolic names are given to the system parameters during this phase;
- from the previous results, the kinetic energy C of the whole mechanism is computed as the sum of each object's kinetic energy;
- for each object and each joint, the given work W_d (gravity, spring, damper, thrust, force and torque works) is evaluated. Its associated given actions Q_i are derived by performing a symbolic derivation of W_d with respect to the generalized coordinates. For some effects (elastic joints for instance) there exists one potential F such as $\delta W_d = \delta F$, and for the viscous joints one dissipative function D such as $\delta W_d = (\partial D / \partial \dot{q}^i) . \delta q^i$. So Q_i is written as:

$$Q_i = \frac{\partial F}{\partial q^i} + \frac{\partial D}{\partial \dot{q}^i} \tag{4.8}$$

- holonomic constraints ($f_h(q, t) = 0$; $h = 1, 2, \ldots, p$) and nonholonomic constraints ($g_l(q, \dot{q}, t) = 0$; $l = 1, 2, \ldots, p'$) are derived from the geometric and kinematic

constraint specifications;
- the last step consists in expressing the motion equations depending on mechanical formalism.

Lagrange's equations

The introduction of the action of binding effects, L_i, can be done in two ways. If we use the principle of Lagrange's multipliers, by introducing $\lambda^h (h = 1, 2, \ldots, p)$ and $\mu^l (l = 1, 2, \ldots, p')$, we obtain the following set of equations:

$$
\begin{cases}
Q_i = \dfrac{\mathrm{d}}{\mathrm{d}t}\left(\dfrac{\partial C}{\partial \dot{q}^i}\right) + \dfrac{\partial C}{\partial q^i} + \displaystyle\sum_h \lambda^h \dfrac{\partial f_h}{\partial q^i} + \sum_i \mu^i a_{l_i} = 0, & i = 1, 2, \ldots, n \\[2ex]
f_h(q, t) = 0, & h = 1, 2, \ldots, p \quad\quad (4.9) \\[1ex]
g_l(q, \dot{q}, t), & l = 1, 2, \ldots, p'
\end{cases}
$$

This system is a non-linear differential equation system. Solving it gives, for each time step, the values of the generalized coordinates and those of the Lagrange's multipliers which are directly related to the forces exerted by links on parameters. The system is solved for each of the $n + p + p'$ variables. Therefore, if we do not need to compute these forces, this method induces extra computation. Furthermore, if links are linearly dependent, the system becomes singular.

When there is no need to calculate the constraint forces, we use a penalization method to take the links into account. With this method we obtain the system:

$$
Q_i - \frac{\mathrm{d}}{\mathrm{d}t}\left(\frac{\partial C}{\partial \dot{q}^i}\right) + \frac{\partial C}{\partial q^i} + k \sum_h f_h \frac{\partial f_h}{\partial q^i} + k \sum_l a_{l_i} g_l = 0, \qquad i = 1, 2, \ldots, n \qquad (4.10)
$$

where k is a chosen penalization constant.

This is a non-linear differential equation system of order n which can be solved more quickly than the previous one. It leads to the same results and becomes equivalent to the previous one when k tends towards infinity. No singularity occurs when binding equations are dependent. Furthermore, the penalization method allows mechanical inconsistencies to be ignored: the constraint violations, for instance, are detected on the graphic output. This is a more convenient detection method for an artist.

4.3.4 Computational scheme

When we write the motion equations using a given formalism, we have to consider the computational model: the way the computer handles these equations. Indeed, the motion equations described in the previous section use a mathematical abstraction not directly suited to computers. So we can deal with these equations in a pure numerical manner or using a symbolic computation scheme.

Before explaining these two schemes, we have to consider the synoptic structure of an animation system which can deal with physical models. Figure 4.5 describes such a system.

In this figure, the first two blocks (*input module* and *formalism computation*) can read and pre-compute internal information depending on the mechanical formalism. Then, a main loop has to numerically compute the object motion. This main loop is divided into two parts. The first part consists of numerically evaluating the system of differential motion equations while the second solves these equations.

- In a purely numerical computation scheme, for each loop, all the mechanical structures must be analyzed to evaluate the numerical matrix representing the differential motion equations. Then this matrix system is solved to obtain the effective motion.
- In a symbolic computation scheme, the mechanical structure analysis is performed once. The result is a symbolic representation of the motion equations as a multi-tree whose nodes are arithmetical operators and leaves are the parameters and constants. The evaluation bloc in Figure 4.5 is now dedicated to the evaluation of the trees associated with the motion equations.

Table 4.3 gives a summary of these two methods according to the blocks of figure.

System solving
For a mechanical system, the set of motion equations is a non-linear differential system of order 2:

$$f_i(\ddot{q}, \dot{q}, q, t) = 0, \qquad i = 1, n \tag{4.11}$$

where:

f_i: ith motion equation;

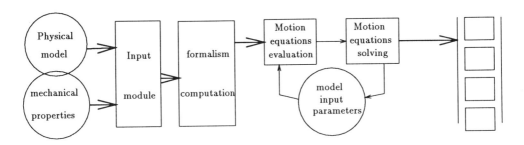

Figure 4.5.   *Animation system.*

Table 4.3 *Numerical versus symbolic computation.*

	Numerical	Symbolic
formalism computation	• mechanism structure traversal • constant value pre-computation	• mechanism structure traversal • symbolic matrices and velocity computation • motion equation derivation • equation preprocessing
equation evaluation	• mechanism structure traversal • numerical transformation matrix computation • numerical velocity computation • etc.	• numerical motion equation evaluation

q: system parameters;
n: number of parameter;
t: time.

In a matrix notation we have:

$$M\ddot{q} + C\dot{q} + Kq + D = 0 \qquad (4.12)$$

where:

M: mass matrix;
C: damping matrix;
K: stiffness matrix;
D: given forces vector.

Three different methods depending on the application field can be used to solve this motion equation system.

state vector
The first method, used in robotics or physical simulation processes, is to convert the differential system of order 2 into a one order differential system by rewriting the motion equation with a state vector composed of parameters and velocities as new unknowns:

$$r = \begin{bmatrix} \dot{q} \\ q \end{bmatrix} \qquad (4.13)$$

The new motion equation system becomes:

$$\dot{Pr} + Qr + S = 0 \tag{4.14}$$

In order to solve this system, Runge-Kutta or Adams-Moulton algorithms (Enright 1984) are often used. In this case the size of this system becomes $2n$, where n is the number of degrees of freedom.

position solving

Another method is to substitute in each equation the velocities and accelerations by finite differences:

$$\dot{q} = \frac{q_n - q_{n-1}}{\Delta t}, \quad \ddot{q} = \frac{q_n - 2q_{n-1} + q_{n-2}}{\Delta t^2} \tag{4.15}$$

The new motion equation system becomes:

$$f_i'(q,t) = 0, \qquad i = 1 \ldots n \tag{4.16}$$

This leads to a non-linear system which can be solved by an iterative method such as Newton–Raphson (Arnaldi et al. 1989). The Jacobian matrix J, used for numerical resolution, can be symbolically computed by using:

$$a_{ij} = \frac{\partial f_i'}{\partial q_j} \tag{4.17}$$

where a_{ij} is the element of J (f_i' is the ith equation and q_j is the jth coordinate). The symbolic computation is performed only once.

acceleration solving

The last way consists in solving the system for the acceleration by writing:

$$M\ddot{q} = -(C\dot{q} + Kq + D) \tag{4.18}$$

assuming that the right side of the equation is directly computable, by taking the values of $\dot{q}$ and q at the previous time step. Then, it is possible to solve this linear system for example by a LU decomposition. Haug (1989) says that this approach may be satisfactory for regular system dynamics and small intervals of time and may lead to substantial violation of position and velocity for constraint equations. The direct integration of equation (4.18) then involves integrating $\ddot{q}$ in order to compute $\dot{q}$ and q (ex Runge-Kutta algorithm).

4.3.5 Simulation results

As an example, we give here a 3-D vehicle model for simulation purposes. Here, the scope is to define a model as completely as possible in order to take into account all the phenomena

involved in a vehicle driving situation. The goal of the simulation is to be able to analyze a driver's behavior in a real time simulation loop with visual restitution of the environment coupled with an effort restitution by a moving platform.

For this simulation application, the complete model is described in Figure 4.6. Adding to the kinematic structure of bodies and joints we find:

- an engine model;
- a gearbox model;
- a differential model;
- an analytical tyre model;
- an analytical aerodynamic model;
- a brake model.

From the driver's point of view, the vehicle can be seen as a black box where 3 inputs allow the control of the mechanism: the brake torques applied on the wheels, the steering arm deviation controlling the vehicle direction and the engine torque applied for example on the front-wheel drive (Figure 4.7).

Figure 4.8 describes the geometrical relationships between the components of a 5 point suspension. The motion induced by this suspension on the wheel is complex. Indeed, the rotation axes for the 2 triangles are not parallel and, coupled to the distance constraint forced by the rigid bar, impose a specific orientation of the wheel when this suspension is active.

In order to check the accuracy of the results, using real vehicle parameters, we can compare simulation values to measurements done on a real vehicle. The measurements contain both the positions, velocities and accelerations of the vehicle and the input values for the brake pressure, the steering arm deviation and the throttle position controlling the engine

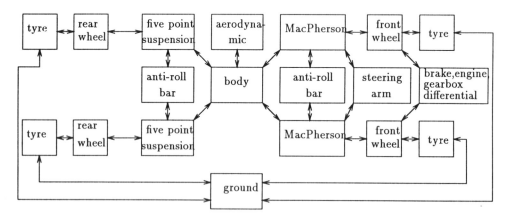

Figure 4.6. *Simulation model.*

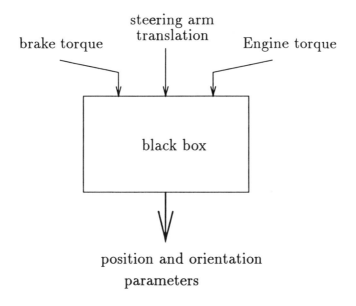

Figure 4.7.   *Black box input model.*

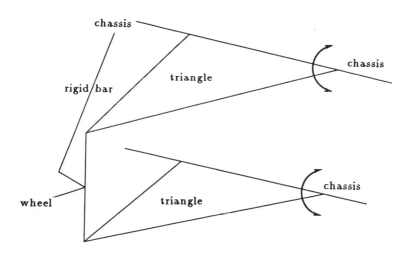

Figure 4.8.   *Five point suspension.*

torque. Figure 4.9 shows the simulation results while Figure 4.10 shows measurements on the real vehicle.

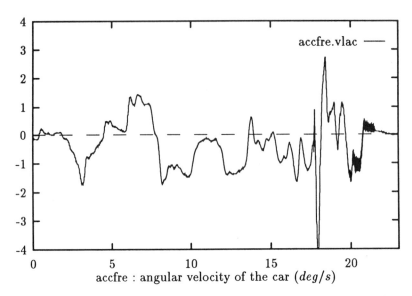

Figure 4.9.   *Simulation results.*

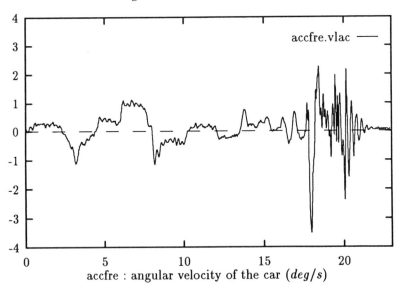

Figure 4.10.   *Real measurements.*

4.4 Motion control

4.4.1 Control techniques

Aims of the motion control

In a physically based animation system, the main difficulty arises when the animator wants to specify the motion of a mechanical structure so that it carries out given tasks. A mechanical model can be considered as a black box where inputs are the forces and torques applied to the system and where outputs are the positions and orientations of the object. Finding forces and torques to ensure the right dynamic behavior of the object is beyond human capabilities. Three kinds of basic tasks are distinguished to describe a motion in automatic control (Samson et al. 1991):

- positioning consists in reaching a given goal: in Figure 4.11, the desired configuration of the double-pendulum is indicated by a dotted line;
- trajectory tracking is usually a generalization of the positioning task (Figure 4.12) when the goal is moving;
- minimization of an *objective* function is useful to describe more complex motions. For instance one could find the trajectory of a mobile robot avoiding obstacles by minimizing a potential.

The task can be described in the configuration space of the mechanism which is the space of parameters $(q^i)_{1 \ldots n}$ (Figure 4.11) or in the Cartesian space which is our usual work space (x, y, z) (Figure 4.12). Of course, each of the three tasks can be considered in each parameter space.

Basic control

In theory, two approaches are possible to control a dynamic system (Figure 4.13). On the one hand, in an open loop, control actions $a(t)$ are computed in advance with the aim of

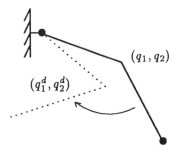

Figure 4.11. *Positioning in configuration space.*

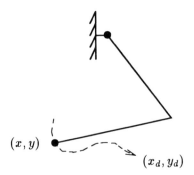

Figure 4.12.   *Trajectory tracking in Cartesian space.*

realizing a given task. On the other hand, in a closed loop, control actions $a(q, \dot{q})$ are expressed as a function of the dynamic system current state which is measured by sensors.

In robotics, state feedback control is always preferred to open loop control because the robot modelling errors as well as sensor errors can thus be balanced, and because the state feedback control allows reaction to external perturbations.

In computer animation the mechanism model has no strong relation with the real world. The mechanical models are considered to be **perfect**. Therefore open loop control as well as closed loop control are usable in this case.

As the distinction between open and closed loops has no practical meaning in computer animation we prefer to point out a more appropriate criterion: the possibility for the animator to interact with the models will be related to **on-line** control techniques. Otherwise we talk about **off-line** control techniques. We now present these two types of methods with their features.

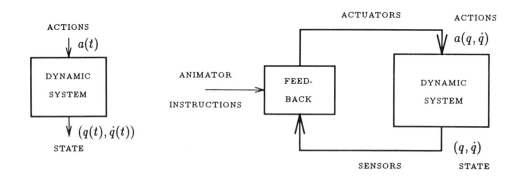

Figure 4.13.   *Control with open and closed loop.*

4.4.2 On-line techniques

On-line techniques allow the animator to act upon the animation evolution while it is simulated. Of course the time criterion has to be considered: the interest of such techniques only appears when the dynamic model is simulated in real time.

Let us recall the motion equations of a mechanism with geometric constraints:

$$
\begin{cases}
M(q)\ddot{q} + N(q,\dot{q}) = a + \left(\dfrac{\partial f}{\partial q}\right)^{\mathrm{T}} \lambda + \left(\dfrac{\partial g}{\partial \dot{q}}\right)^{\mathrm{T}} \lambda' & (n \text{ equations}) \\[2mm]
f(q,t) = 0, & (p \text{ equations}) \\[2mm]
g(q,\dot{q},t) = 0 & (p\prime \text{ equations})
\end{cases}
\qquad (4.19)
$$

q is a set of parameters which represent the mechanism configuration, $M(q)$ and $N(q,\dot{q})$ are respectively the mass matrix and a vector gathering inertial terms and given actions. On the right side a is the vector of control actions. The constraints are treated with Lagrange parameters λ and λ'.

State feedback control (Brady et al. 1982) is the most common technique since it is usually used in robotics. In principle, the actions applied to the mechanism take into account its current state $(q, \dot{q})$. Consider the case of a positioning task in the configuration space. The purpose is to compute the actions so that the current position q coincides with the goal q^d that makes the positioning error $(e = q - q^d)$ vanish. For instance the positioning task of Figure 4.11 would use the error: $e = (q_1 - q_1^d \ \ q_2 - q_2^d)^{\mathrm{T}}$. A basic control would compute the actions as a proportion of the error: $a = K_p e$. Unfortunately the efficiency of the control is not only evaluated on its ability to reach the goal but also on its stability. For this reason and if necessary, the error variation and its integral have also to be considered:

$$
a = K_v \dot{e} - K_p e - K_i \int e \, \mathrm{d}t \qquad (4.20)
$$

where K_v, K_p and K_i are positive matrices. The so-called **PID (proportional integral derivative) control** obtained in this way is very simple. Nevertheless, it does not take into account the mechanical coupling between parameters and acts upon each of them as if they were independent. In the double-pendulum case, moving the first bar (q_1) is not without influence on the second one (q_2): the coupling effect has to be considered for efficient control. Besides, the PID control acts on light bodies in the same way as on heavy ones. In other respects, its application is limited to the configuration space.

Improving this control is possible by taking into account the model (4.19) of a mechanism without links. In Cartesian space, positioning consists in leading a function $\chi(q)$ of the configuration parameters to a desired value $\chi^d(t)$. As for the extremity of the double-pendulum, the error is written as: $e = (x(q_1,q_2) - x^d, \ y(q_1,q_2) - y^d)^{\mathrm{T}}$. The error to be removed can be defined by $e = \chi_q - \chi^d(t)$. On the assumption that the rank of the Jacobian

$J = (\partial\chi/\partial q) = (\partial e/\partial q) \, n$, it is then possible to prove that the **dynamic control** which computes the actions is as follows:

$$a = MJ^{-1}(-K_v\dot{e} - K_pe - \dot{J}\dot{q} + \ddot{\chi}^d) + N \qquad (K_v \text{ and } K_p \text{ are positive matrices}) \qquad (4.21)$$

provides an error evolution with a stable convergence within a second order behavior:

$$\ddot{e} + K_v\dot{e} + K_pe = 0 \qquad (4.22)$$

It is easy to obtain this result carrying over equation (4.21) to equation (4.22) and noting that $\ddot{e} = J\ddot{q} + \dot{J}\dot{q} - \ddot{\chi}^d$. Although the mechanical model is wholly included in this control law, there is the advantage of specifying the goal in Cartesian space which is more natural for the animator. On the other hand kinematic links are not taken into account either in PID control or in dynamic control. Furthermore, the difficulty of tuning the gains K_v, K_p and K_i is common to both methods.

For these two feedback methods common in robotics, the main feature is that they balance the errors and the perturbations. For instance, they allow the animator to move the goal during the simulation. Since the feedback control computes the actions applied to the mechanism, the related techniques are called **control by actions**.

On the other hand **control by constraints** proceeds in a very different way (Stewart and Cremer 1992). The idea is to modify the dynamic system so that its behavior leads to the desired motion. In Cartesian space, the error $e = \chi(q) - \chi^d(t)$ can be made to vanish by following the law (4.22). Thus, forcing such a behavior for the error is done by giving a new constraint. The dynamic system (4.19) becomes:

$$\begin{cases} M(q)\ddot{q} + N(q,\dot{q}) = a + \left(\dfrac{\partial f}{\partial q}\right)^{\mathrm{T}}\lambda + \left(\dfrac{\partial g}{\partial \dot{q}}\right)^{\mathrm{T}}\lambda' + \left(\dfrac{\partial e}{\partial q}\right)^{\mathrm{T}}\lambda'' & (n \text{ equations}) \\ f(q,t) = 0, & (p \text{ equations}) \\ g(q,\dot{q},t) = 0 & (p\prime \text{ equations}) \\ \ddot{e} + K_v\dot{e} + K_pe = 0 & (l \leq n \text{ equations}) \end{cases} \qquad (4.23)$$

The unknown quantities are q, λ, λ' and λ'', where λ'' is Lagrange's multipliers associated with the new constraint which is called a **control constraint**. Using such a constraint is a generalization to the second degree of the constraints already used in the simulator to represent kinematic constraints so far of 0 or 1 degree. As a result, Figure 4.14 shows two positioning motions concerning the extremity of the double pendulum with the same goal starting from two different configurations. These animations are produced with control by constraints but the same motions would be obtained through dynamic control.

Comparing control by constraints and dynamic control leads to the conclusion that they are equivalent. However the use of constraints makes several differences.

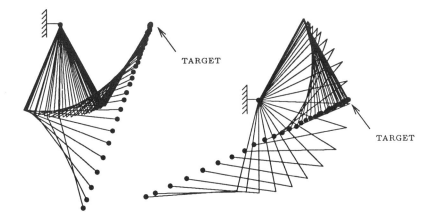

Figure 4.14. *Extremity positioning.*

1. The first one is related to the fact that the Jacobian $J = (\partial e/\partial q)$ does not need to have an n rank. That was a necessary condition for the dynamic control to quantify the fact that the problem is well stated and has one and only one solution. With control by constraints, the condition is weaker so that partial goals (not requiring all the degrees of freedom of the mechanism) are managed more easily for the animator: the animation system will find one of the possible solutions. That is why the error e can have only l values: the mechanism is then redundant with relation to the task in hand. For instance the animator may wish only to force the value of x: $e = x - x^d$.
2. Kinematic links are also treated easily by this method as opposed to state feedback. The nature of the new control constraint is the same as the control of constraints for kinematic links: all of them are satisfied in the same way.
3. To go further, it is possible to use the kinematic links of the mechanism to express more easily the control constraint. For instance, to describe a car moving in a straight line to reach a new position, the feedback control would use the engine torque (Figure 4.15). If using a control constraint the straightforward idea is to force the parameter on which the engine torque acts, that is the rotation of the wheels θ. But it is more intuitive to use the internal link which exists between the rotation of the wheels and the car motion, that is to say the rolling of the wheels on the ground without sliding ($\dot{x} = R\dot{\theta}$) where R is the radius of the wheels. The motion is then described by giving a constraint on the coordinate x. But it is not always possible to express the control by constraints in any set of parameters. Besides, control constraints can be irrelevant with kinematic links: it is necessary to check their validity.

The limitations of control by constraints are mainly due to the controllability of the

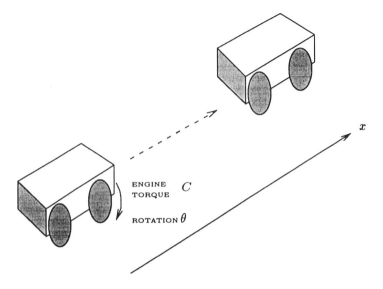

Figure 4.15.   *Constraints for a car.*

mechanism (Isidori 1985).

State feedback control and control by constraints may be implemented together. Their fields of application are complementary:

- in the simulation of mechanisms such as robots or autonomous machines, state feedback control is more realistic. Furthermore, control laws which are actually used can be known.
- for other applications (in particular complex issues such as the animation of a human body) the common use of state feedback control, control by constraints and interactive driving of actions will probably give the most convenient features. For instance, the body balance will be considered as a constraint to be satisfied, as much as limb cooperation, though a grasping task will be done by driving actions or by a state feedback control.

The **control box** (Figure 4.16) realizes the cooperative implementation of the three means of control available on-line, according to the animator's choice:

- control constraints are symbolically included in the dynamic system;
- interactive driving of the actions is done with visual feedback and concerns actuators chosen by the animator;
- state feedback control is realized by computing actions used as input by the simulator.

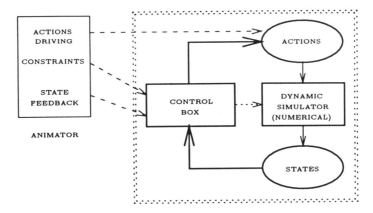

Figure 4.16. *On-line simulation.*

The control box can itself undertake the realization of the animator wishes since the previously described methods are entirely automatic. Besides one can think of tools such as a library of classic control laws. Finally the validity of the animator's specifications is the object of a checking process concerning mainly:

- the constraint's validity;
- the controllability of the mechanism;
- the field of application of the required control techniques.

The principles concerning on-line techniques have been validated by the implementation of prototypes: for example the control of very different mechanisms is presented in Section 4.4.4.

4.4.3 Off-line techniques

Animator interactions are no longer possible: this is the main feature of off-line control. This is due to the following two reasons. First, a time-consuming simulation is unable to allow real-time external interactions. Secondly, a previously fixed scenario cannot allow for interactions during the simulation.

Optimal control (Bryson and Ho 1975) features these two drawbacks and is therefore considered as an off-line technique. Its aim is to realize a positioning task while minimizing a cost function which may show various forms: consumed energy, time needed to reach the goal, function of the distance to obstacles, etc. (Witkin and Kass 1988; Brotman and Netravali 1988). In robotics, optimal control is used in trajectory planning. The results are then taken as a goal for a trajectory tracking step which is achieved through closed loop control.

The interests of optimal control in animation are numerous:

- compared to closed loop techniques, open loop control needs weaker controllability assumptions. Therefore, positioning tasks which are rejected by on-line techniques can be solved here.
- the specifications related to optimal control are more qualitative than quantitative: "fast", "far", or " heavy" are concepts difficult to use but "as fast as possible" is both accurate and close to a natural language (Witkin and Kass 1988).
- some behavior principles refer to efficiency ideas such as speed or energy saving (Chow and Jacobson 1971; Hatze 1976). In particular some principles of biomechanics now being studied can find an experimental frame through optimal control in robotics or in animation.
- finally optimal control uses iterative searching rules which enable it to produce positioning trajectories which are not intuitive for the animator. For instance animating a vehicle parking sequence seems far more difficult in animation than in reality (van de Panne 1989).

Formalizing the problem requires a previous step which consists of using state parameters:

$$\begin{cases} x_1 = q \\ x_2 = \dot{q} \end{cases} \tag{4.24}$$

The dynamic system may then be expressed by two sets of first order equations:

$$(S_1)\begin{cases} \dot{x}_1 = x_2 \\ M(x_1)\dot{x}_2 + L(x_1, x_2, a) = 0 \qquad \text{(2n equations)} \end{cases} \tag{4.25}$$

We formalize the optimal positioning problem which consists of driving the dynamic system from a state $x(t_i)$ to a state $x(t_f)$ within the time interval $[t_i, t_f]$ minimizing a cost function C as follows:

Finding the trajectory x(t) and the related actions a(t) which minimize the criterion

$$J = \int_{t_i}^{t_f} C(x_1, x_2, a)\mathrm{d}t \tag{4.26}$$

within the constraints

$$\begin{cases} \dot{x}_1 - x_2 = 0 \\ M(x_1)\dot{x}_2 + L(x_1, x_2, a) = 0 \end{cases} \tag{4.27}$$

where:

    C is a positive function,
    $[t_i, t_f]$ are given,

$x(t_i)$ is given,

$x(t_f)$ is given.

It is possible to prove that the solutions of this problem satisfy a necessary condition. By introducing additional parameters (ψ_1, ψ_2), so-called **dual variables** associated with (x_1, x_2), this condition states that the two following dynamic systems must be satisfied:

$$(S_2)\begin{cases} -\dot{\psi}_1 - (Mx_2)^{\mathrm{T}}_{x_1}\dot{\psi}_2 - (\dot{M}x_2)^{\mathrm{T}}_{x_1}\psi_2 + L^{\mathrm{T}}_{x_1}\psi_2 + C^{\mathrm{T}}_{x_1} = 0 \qquad\qquad (4.28)\\[2mm] -M\dot{\psi}_2 - \psi_1 - (\dot{M}x_2)^{\mathrm{T}}_{x_2}\psi_2 + L^{\mathrm{T}}_{x_2}\psi_2 + C^{\mathrm{T}}_{x_2} = 0 \qquad (2n \text{ equations}) \end{cases}$$

$$(S_3)\left\{ C^{\mathrm{T}}_a + L^{\mathrm{T}}_a\psi_2 = 0 \right. \qquad\qquad\qquad\qquad\qquad (n \text{ equations})$$

(S_1) is the dynamic model of the mechanism, (S_2) represents the desired evolution of adjoint variables ψ introduced above, and (S_3) is the necessary condition for optimization. To solve the optimization problem we propose two complementary methods. Both of them have a long computational time since they use iterative searching rules:

- the **gradient** method computes variations of $a(t)$ simulating (S_1) and (S_2) so that (S_3) is satisfied in the best way. Its convergence field is very large but its evolution is slow near the solution.
- the so-called **generalized Newton–Raphson method** (NRg) solves (S_1), (S_2) and (S_3) together, given that the related differential equations have 2-point boundary-values. The convergence process is fast around the solution but does not occur elsewhere.

Therefore, it is profitable to apply the gradient method at first and then the NRg method. Usually there are several solutions minimizing the criterion locally, but identifying them is not straightforward. The animator remains the only person qualified to decide about the interest of a given solution. Both these optimization methods are used for positioning the double pendulum in the configuration space within a motion which minimizes the criterion: $C = \frac{a_1^2}{2} + \frac{a_2^2}{2}$ as shown in Figure 4.17.

A particular interest of these optimization methods is that it is possible to generalize them to mechanisms with kinematic constraints (Bunks and Nikoukhah 1990): a vehicle driving example is an opportunity for implementing optimal control with rolling without sliding conditions. A slightly different approach is proposed in Nougaret et al. (1994) to modify trajectories by optimizing a criterion.

4.4.4 Applications

In this section we show two examples of complex models which could hardly be animated without automatic control and definitely not without physically based animation. The first one is a hopping one-legged robot and the second one is a vehicle.

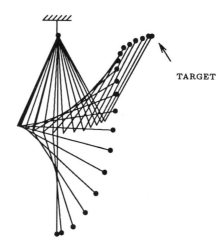

Figure 4.17. *Energy saving positioning.*

Hopping one-legged robot

This machine was designed by Raibert (1986) and Raibert and Hodgins (1991). It consists of a body and a unique articulated telescopic leg, mainly acting as a spring. The leg is provided with two actuators to change its direction, and another one to change its length in order to give thrust (Figure 4.18). For maintaining balance, hopping is necessary. The leg is continuously given an accurate position in order to compensate the falling process. It is also possible to make the robot move by controlling its speed as shown in Figure 4.19.

We implemented a mechanical model and Raibert's PID control according to our control by actions. The detection of events occurs when the leg lands and takes off, because the mechanical model has to be modified. Figure 4.20 shows the trajectory of the body and its projection on the ground when moving first to the (20; 20) coordinates point and switching to the (0; 20) coordinates point.

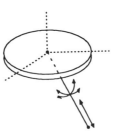

Figure 4.18. *Articulations of the hopping robot.*

Figure 4.19. *Motion of the robot.*

Vehicle

We have considered in this case the model of a car-like vehicle. The trajectories of 5 bodies (the 4 wheels and the body) are described by 14 parameters and 9 constraints, in particular non-sliding conditions. The model allows the operator to apply an engine torque and a direction torque on the wheels. It is therefore possible to drive the car in a natural way with visual feedback but it remains difficult to follow a given trajectory.

We proposed control by actions to drive the car on a road. The animator specifies a desired speed v_d, then the control box computes the torques to apply in order to follow the road at the given speed (Figure 4.21). To control the velocity v of the car a proportional control produces realist results:

$$a_v = -K_{p1}(v - v_d) \tag{4.29}$$

where K_{p1} defines the strength of acceleration and braking.

The tracking of the road can be achieved by using a goal point to reach located on a trajectory at a distance d in front of the car. The direction from the front of the car and the goal point determines the angle β^d to reach for the lock β. A proportional-derivative control is used:

$$a_\beta = -K_{v2}(\dot{\beta} - \dot{\beta}^d) - K_{p2}(\beta - \beta^d) \tag{4.30}$$

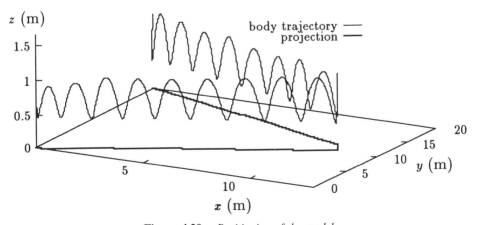

Figure 4.20. *Positioning of the model.*

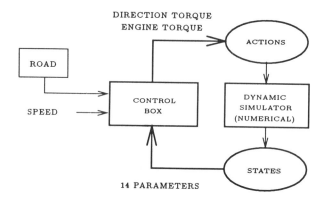

Figure 4.21. *Vehicle control.*

4.5 References

Armstrong W.W., Green M. (1985) "The dynamics of articulated rigid bodies for the purposes of animation", The Visual Computer, 1(4):231–240, December 1985, also in: Proc. Graphics Interface '85.

Arnaldi B., Dumont G., Hégron G. (1989) "Dynamics and unification of animation control", The Visual Computer, 4(5):22–31.

Bamberger Y. (1981) "Mécanique de l'ingénieur 1 : systèmes de corps rigides", Volume 1, Hermann, 293 rue Lecourbe, 75015 Paris.

Brady M., Hollerbach J.M., Johnson T.L., Lozano-Perez T., Mason M.T. (1982) "Robot Motion: Planning and Control", The MIT Press, Cambridge, Massachusetts and London.

Brotman L.S., Netravali A.N. (1988) "Motion interpolation by optimal control", Proc. SIGGRAPH '88, Computer Graphics, 22(4):309–315.

Bryson A., Ho Y. (1975) "Applied optimal control: optimization, estimation and control" (Rev. printing). Hemisphere Publ., New York, London.

Bunks C., Nikoukhah R. (1990) "Optimal control of constrained mechanical systems". In Proc. 8th IFAC Workshop, Paris.

Chow C., Jacobson D. (1971) "Studies of human locomotion via optimal programming", Mathematical Biosciences, 10:239–306.

Enright W.H. (1984) "Numerical methods for systems of initial value problems — the state of the art", in: E.J. Haug, editor, Computer Aided Analysis and Optimisation of Mechanical System Dynamics, pages 309–322, Springer-Verlag, Heidelberg.

Germain P. (1986) "Mécanique", Volume 1, Ecole Polytechnique, 91128 Palaiseau Cedex.

Hatze H (1976) "The complete optimization of a human body", Mathematical Biosciences, 28:99–135.

Haug E.J. (1989) "Computer Aided Kinematics and Dynamics of Mechanical Systems", Volume 1: Basics Methods. Allyn and Bacon, 160 Gould Street, Needham Heights, Massachusetts 02194.

Isidori A. (1985) "Nonlinear Control Systems: An Introduction", Lecture Notes in Control and Information Sciences, 72, Springer-Verlag, Heidelberg.

Luciani A., Jimenez S., Raoult O., Cadoz C., Florens J.L. (1991) "An unified view of multitude behavior, flexibility, plasticity and fractures balls, bubbles and agglomerates", in: Modeling in Computer Graphics, IFIP Working Conference 91 (TC 5/WG5. 10), Springer-Verlag, pp. 55–74.

Nougaret J.L., Arnaldi B., Cozot R. (1994) "Optimal motion control using a wavelet network as a tunable deformation controller'', Proc. Fifth Eurographics Workshop on Animation and Simulation, G. Hégron and O. Fahlander, eds, Oslo, Norway.

Raibert M.H. (1986) ''Legged Robots that Balance'', The MIT Press series in artificial intelligence, Cambridge, MA, London.

Raibert M.H., Hodgins J.K. (1991) ''Animation of dynamic legged locomotion'', Proc. SIGGRAPH '91, Computer Graphics, 25(4):349–358.

Samson C., Le Borgne M., Espiau B. (1991) ''Robot Control: the Task–Function Approach'', Clarendon Press, Oxford Science Publications, UK.

Schielen W.O. (1984) ''Computer generation of equations of motion'', in: E.J. Haug, ed., Computer Aided Analysis and Optimisation of Mechanical System Dynamics, pages 183–215, Springer-Verlag, Heidelberg.

Stewart A.J., Cremer J.F. (1992) ''Beyond keyframing: an algorithmic approach to animation'', Proc. Graphics Interface '92, pp. 273–281.

van de Panne M. (1989) ''Motion Synthesis for Simulation-Based Animation'', PhD thesis, University of Toronto.

Witkin A., Kass M. (1988) ''Spacetime constraints'', Proc. SIGGRAPH '88, Computer Graphics, 22(4):159–168.

Wittenburg J. (1977) ''Dynamics of Systems of Rigid Bodies'', Teubner, Stuttgart.

CHAPTER 5

Choreographers as Animators: Systems to Support Composition of Dance

Tom Calvert and Sang Mah

Graphics and Multimedia Research Laboratory, Simon Fraser University

Abstract

Choreographers are animators who work with live human figures. A dance is composed and choreographed by working out the movement phrases for each figure and directing the interaction between the figures. Until recently there have been no technical tools to assist choreographers, and dances have been composed by working with a group of dancers in a studio, often for weeks or months. This chapter discusses the principles involved in the design of computer based tools to support the choreography of a dance and describes the *Life Forms* system which has been implemented on the Apple Macintosh and Silicon Graphics Inc.'s Indigo families of computers. *Life Forms* is being used by a number of choreographers around the world, most notably Merce Cunningham in New York. The chapter also discusses lessons learned in developing a system for choreographers. This is based on several case studies and on more controlled experiments where protocol analysis is used to analyze video and computer log file records of the physical actions and verbalizations of choreographers composing a dance using a computer based system. An annotation script of the video tape is combined with the log file of user actions and used to deduce the strategies and mental models adopted by the choreographer. Understanding these strategies and mental models allows the design of better tools to support composition and choreography. We believe the same approaches will be useful for the design of animation systems.

5.1 Composition and choreography in dance and animation

5.1.1 Choreographic process

There are many similarities and some differences between the ways in which a choreographer composes a dance and an animator composes a sequence of human animation. After conceiving the original theme and possibly roughing out the ideas with a few notes or sketches, the choreographer usually works with a group of dancers in a studio to develop the outline of the movement sequences and to define the detailed choreography. This process is extremely time consuming, frequently taking many multi-hour sessions spread over weeks or months. Thus, a choreographer usually creates only one or two new choreographies in a year. The process is also expensive in its use of space and the time commitments of the dancers. Few dance companies have resident choreographers and often an independent choreographer would have to add the task of finding dancers to develop new work. After the complete dance has been refined to the satisfaction of the choreographer, it is ready for performance.

Major dance companies usually develop a score to record the completed composition using a notation system such as Labanotation, Benesh notation or Eshkol–Wachman notation (Hutchinson-Guest 1984). Use of these scores is still not standard practice; making the score is tedious and there are relatively few notators who can write and read the notation. In any case, the notation is used only to record the dance and is not useful in the original composition.

Figure 5.1. *Merce Cunningham with his dancers. Photo by Lawrence Ivy, 1991.*

5.1.2   Animation process

The composition of a sequence of human animation starts similarly. The theme is conceived and some rough sketches are made. However, borrowing from film and video production, the animator will usually develop a detailed storyboard showing the important scenes in the sequence and the correspondence to a sound or voice track. This has traditionally been done with pen and paper, but graphic tools on a 3-D workstation provide an obvious way to support this planning. After completing the storyboard, the animator goes to work, but unlike the choreographer the animator must first model the figures to be used (Magnenat Thalmann and Thalmann 1990). State of the art animation systems provide the tools for the animator to ''work-out'' the detailed movements on an interactive 3-D workstation in a way very similar to that in which the choreographer develops a dance with live dancers. The animator must specify the position and posture of each figure for each step in time. Some simple interpolation may be possible, but there is only limited support for developing movement sequences for complex articulated figures (see Bruderlin et al. 1994 for example). Just as with the live dance, a complicated animation of articulated figures can take weeks or months to complete.

In the rest of this chapter we explore our understanding of the compositional and choreographic processes and we describe how some computer based tools have been developed to support the process. A discussion of methods used to study how choreographers use these tools is then presented. This chapter concludes with an overview of work in progress and future research related to enhancing existing tools and designing new tools for movement composition.

5.2   A review of computer based tools for dance

Any discussion of the use of computer based tools to support the choreography and composition of movement must start with a review of work on notation systems. A wide variety of movement notation systems has been developed to describe many aspects of human movement. For example, a notation system to describe movement in psycho-social processes has been developed by Scheflen (1972), and Birdwhistell (1970) has developed a complex system to describe the movements used in inter-personal communication. However, these and other special purpose systems are unsuited for general application. Of the many general notation systems, the only three in common use are Benesh Notation (Benesh and Benesh 1956), Eshkol–Wachman Notation (Eshkol and Wachman 1958) and Labanotation (Hutchinson, 1960). All three have been used to record dance, Benesh being the most popular in the U.K. and Labanotation in North America.

The strength and the weakness of all notation systems is that they rely on an intelligent human observer. Thus, they provide a way to objectively record the analysis of a movement which has been deduced by the skilled notator. Because of the difficulty in acquiring these skills there is a shortage of notators – thus there is a real need to use pattern recognition techniques to automatically develop a movement score from data describing the movement. Although a system which would recognize all the possible subtleties of human movement might be difficult to develop, it should be quite possible to automatically derive a score for most movements. Although Michael Noll suggested the development of such a system in 1966 (Gray 1984) this problem has received little or no attention – probably because of the difficulty and expense involved in acquiring the 3-D data.

5.2.1   Editing and interpreting notation

A number of systems have been developed to prepare and edit notation scores (Gray 1984;

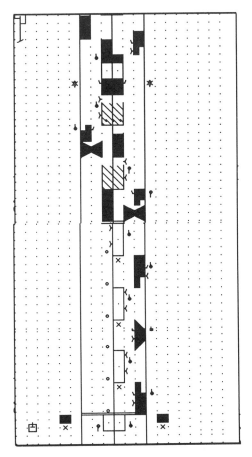

Figure 5.2.   *An example of a Labanotation score created by Hall-Marriot's DANCE system (Hall-Marriot 1995).*

Calvert et al. 1980; and Hunt 1988). However, the only widely used systems for composing and editing notation have been developed for the Apple Macintosh. The MacBenesh system developed by Professor Rhonda Ryman and her colleagues at the University of Waterloo allows development of scores in Benesh notation (Ryman et al. 1984) and the LabanWriter system developed by Professor Lucy Venables and Mr. Scott Sutherland at Ohio State University allows development of scores in Labanotation (Gray, 1984).

Interpreters for a restricted set of Labanotation commands have been developed by Zella Wolofsky and others at Simon Fraser University (Barenholz et al. 1977) and by Smoliar and Weber at University of Pennsylvania (Smoliar and Weber 1977). Other interpreters were developed for Messine notation by Savage and Officer (1984), for a restricted set of Benesh notation by Herbison-Evans (1979) and Politis (1987). It has been suggested that movement notation can be used as a script for input to an animation system, but application has been limited (Calvert et al. 1982).

5.2.2   Tools to support composition

John Lansdown developed a computer based system which stored a library of body stances and used a random process and some constraints to combine them into movement sequences (Lansdown 1977). Print-outs of these sequences were then given to live dancers as the basis for a performance. Eddie Dombrower developed a system to notate, edit and compose dances on an Apple II computer (Gray 1984). Unfortunately, this early system was limited by its computer and by the fact it used DOM notation developed by Dombrower. Since that time the only comprehensive approach to support composition has been the *Life Forms* system which is the main focus of this chapter.

A very interesting recent development is the *DANCE* system (Designing, Animating and Notating Classical Enchainments) developed by Natalie Hall-Marriot at the University of Technology, Sydney (Hall-Marriot 1992, 1995). *DANCE* accepts a slightly formalized version of Ballet French as input and translates this into both a Labanotation score and a script which can be read into *Life Forms* to produce an animation of the dance. This is a very useful development since Ballet French is a well known way to describe classical dance and allows a composer to write a script in familiar language and then see it animated.

5.3   The creative process in choreography and animation

5.3.1   General principles

Creation as it occurs in choreography, animation and design is a progression from chaos to order, from ideation (conceptualization) to implementation (Blinn 1990). An animation or composition system should support this process. While each choreographer takes a somewhat individualistic approach and although the same choreographer may use different approaches from time to time, there do appear to be some underlying general principles. These may be summarized as:

1. The choreographer usually develops the general framework for the composition on the basis of some specific stimuli as well as on the general contextual environment. This stage of the process, which we call Composition, results in the shape of the piece.
2. The shape or framework of the piece must then be fleshed out with the detailed choreography for the individual dancers. This stage we call Choreography.
3. The individual differences between choreographers result largely from the ways in which they switch back and forth between the Composition and Choreography phases of the process. It is clear that in most cases the processes are highly interactive and that the creative artist will switch back and forth in unpredictable ways (Jetha 1993).

The normal way in which many choreographers develop a piece first involves the generation of the conceptual framework and then intensive work (often over many months) with a company of live dancers. As noted above, this is expensive in terms of the time commitment of the dancers and the need for rehearsal space. If a compositional tool could be developed which would allow the choreographer to compose the outline of the piece without live dancers, it might be possible to dramatically shorten the process. We envisage the choreographer working out the shape of the piece at a computer workstation (possibly at home), and then going to the rehearsal studio with live dancers and confirming that the shape "works" before going on to develop the detailed choreography.

Although we know of no detailed model for composition, we have proposed a general framework for such a model (Schiphorst et al. 1990). Our proposal has been particularly influenced by Simon (1969), but also by Koenig (1980), Brightman (1984) and Laske (1989). Their ideas have been confirmed by our own experience (Calvert et al. 1991).

5.3.2   Framework for composition

The framework which we propose sees composition as a goal oriented hierarchical process. But, in artistic composition, creative solution is part of the goal. "A creative solution to a problem may interpret requirements differently or find an answer that involves some entirely different set of objects or patterns" (Pylyshyn 1989). In working within this hierarchical process, artists move back and forth between abstract concepts and detailed specification, seeking alternate ways to look at the composition as it develops. Most compositions draw on knowledge of previous work (by the artist and others), self imposed and external constraints must be taken into account and it is important to be able to visualize the composition as it develops. The elements of our proposed framework, then, are as follows.

5.3.3   Hierarchy of abstractions

Composition starts with a general outline of the piece – a simple sketch or idea. This high level conceptualization of the shape, energy flows and timing of the composition is inherently an abstraction, and is the most difficult to represent. The composition then becomes successively more concrete as details are added and the process moves to lower levels of abstraction. The lowest level in the abstraction hierarchy is a complete physical realization of the dance. An important element of the creative process is the need to move flexibly back and forth between levels. Successive refinement of the low level details may reveal the need to change the high level theme.

Alternate views

The importance of alternate representations is in the juxtaposition of different frames of reference which allow the choreographer to think in various (perhaps unconventional) ways about the composition. For example, in music the score provides a way to lay out and review a piece at the same time as listening to a rendition.

Use of knowledge

Composing involves selecting a compositional process as well as movement materials. The knowledge or expertise of a choreographer is context dependent, and that context is not only socio-cultural but also based on expertise and prior training in the physical kinesthetic experience of dance and movement, and in the forming and structuring practice of choreography.

Working with constraints

Any choreographer works within self imposed or externally imposed constraints in developing a composition. A creative solution is often the result of coming to the boundary or limits of the solution space. It is now either the limits or constraints, or the problem itself, that must be redefined. This meeting with the obstacle or barrier often results in ''the truth that comes riding into history on the back of an error'' (Niebuhr 1949).

Visualization of the composition

Normally the only true evaluation of a composition is to view the physical realization of the final result, i.e. a live performance. However, if the representation is good enough, a composition viewed in simulation or viewed from different abstractions may allow the composer and others to evaluate the work. The animation which results should be as realistic as possible. It is also important for the composer to be able to interact with the animation and view it from any angle.

5.4 *Life Forms* – a tool for composition and choreography

In the years before starting the development of a tool for composition in 1986, we had acquired considerable experience in working with dancers and choreographers and in the development of computer based systems for editing and interpreting dance notation (Calvert et al. 1980, 1982, Calvert 1986). Although systems for editing and interpreting notation have an important role in recording dance, archival tools are not very useful for composition. In order to address the goal of supporting the compositional process we began the development of a completely new system which would directly assist the working choreographer in creating movement. Merce Cunningham noted when he began working with *Life Forms*, "The thing that interested me most, from the very start was not the memory – it wasn't simply notation – but the fact that I could *make* new things" [*LA Times* May 15 1991].

The design and development was carried out by an interdisciplinary team made up of users such as choreographers, as well as systems architects and implementers. The process of designing the interface has been highly iterative – beginning from a very simple concept many, many alternatives have been suggested and evaluated while only a few have been implemented. At times the introduction of a new concept or approach has required a discontinuous design shift to occur in the otherwise incremental process.

Life Forms was initially developed on Silicon Graphics workstations and this remains the platform for our research. However, to provide a version which would be more accessible to working dancers and choreographers we have also developed a version for the Apple Macintosh.

The distinct activities within the compositional process which should be supported in the computer based tool include:

- planning the concept;
- defining stances and/or movement sequences;
- combining multiple dancers in space and time;
- performance of the completed or partially completed piece.

These activities and their implementation in *Life Forms* will now be discussed in turn.

5.4.1 Planning the concept

The initial concept for an animation, just like any other creative composition, starts as an abstraction in the mind of some individual. There may be a text or even a screenplay, but frequently the ideas are first written down in the form of a crude storyboard. This storyboard consists of a series of annotated sketches of the key scenes in the animation (storyboards are widely used in film and video production). Most computer based animation systems give little support to the creator at this stage – they are much like the computer-aided design

(CAD) systems for engineering design which allow the designer to produce detailed drawings but only after all design decisions have been made. Thus, in developing our system to support composition and choreography we have given particular attention to the need to allow the creator to plan and experiment with alternate movements at an early stage.

Implementation in *Life Forms*

In *Life Forms*, the concept can be blocked out following a storyboard-like metaphor using the Stage. Bodies for the dancers are selected from menus and placed on the stage in appropriate positions and with appropriate facings. Initially, it does not really matter what body shapes are used as long as they can be distinguished – indeed in testing an initial concept the characters can be represented by simple tokens distinguished by color or a label. However, many choreographers prefer a body model with a somewhat realistic stance. After a key scene has been set up it is stored and the process is repeated for all key scenes. Simple scenery can be added to the scenes if desired. The result is a storyboard-like series of 3-D key scenes which can be viewed interactively with rotation, translation and zoom controls to plan the animation – an example is shown in Figure 5.3.

Interpolation is used to calculate intermediate frames between the key scenes and the result can be displayed as a crude animation. However, the sequence of key scenes frequently represents widely separated points in time and the animation may not make much sense – the intent at this stage is to refine the concept and plan the dance, not to visualize the details.

5.4.2 Defining stances and/or movement sequences

Detailed movement sequences must be choreographed for each dancer – the individual movement sequence is the building block for the piece. We distinguish between this choreography of individual dancers and the composition of the combined movement of multiple dancers. In animation the classic approach to movement specification is keyframing, i.e. the choreographer captures each important position in a keyframe and interpolation is used to generate the "in-betweens". Any computer based animation system will incorporate keyframing, but this can be supplemented by movement captured from live action (see Chapter 2) as well as procedural movement generated by dynamic simulation (see Chapter 4) and other approaches.

Implementation in *Life Forms*

In *Life Forms*, movement sequences are assembled in the Sequence Editor. As shown in Figure 5.4, the main window displays a user selected projection of a 3-D model of a human figure and along the side there are three small orthogonal views (front, side and top) each of which can be selected as the main view. The different limb segments of the body can be selected directly by clicking on the part or by selection from a menu. Once selected, the

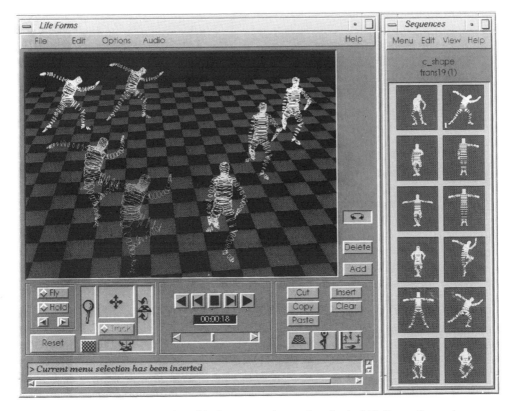

Figure 5.3.   *A key scene from blocking out a dance piece in the* Life Forms *Stage view.*

orientation of the segment can be adjusted either by direct manipulation (click and drag) or by using linear or hemi-spherical potentiometers. Constraints have been built in to limit limb orientation to what is anatomically possible – but the constraints are complex functions and are only approximate. Using a forward kinematics approach (see Chapter 3) a body stance is built up by first orienting the ''root'' segments, and then successively adjusting the more distal segments – for example if support is on the right foot, this would be set first, followed in succession by the lower right leg, the upper right leg, the pelvis, and then the components of the left leg, the torso and the neck/head and arms.

The forward kinematics approach allows a particular body shape to be set up very accurately, but it does not lend itself very well to accurate placement of ''end effectors'' such as hands. Using constrained inverse kinematics (see Chapter 3), any joint can be dragged interactively to a desired position while the joint angles in the chain are adjusted automatically (Figure 5.5 shows the highlighted leg being dragged to a new position). Examples of the kinds of constraints that might be specified are ''do not move torso'', ''do

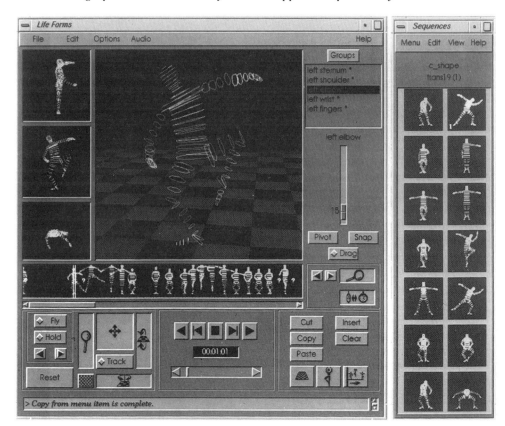

Figure 5.4. *Designing body stances in the* Life Forms *Sequence Editor.*

not move left leg'' or ''do not move foot''. Thus if the hand is reaching for an object and it is close by, the torso does not need to move; on the other hand for a more distant object the only constraint might be that the supporting foot should not move. This very powerful technique is computer intensive but can be performed with little noticeable delay on graphics workstations.

Once a body stance has been satisfactorily defined, it is added to the movement sequence which is being assembled. The sequence consists of a string of key stances and is displayed on a strip like window below the main display. Any stance in the sequence can be selected and brought up in the window for editing. A new stance is often developed most quickly by starting with an existing stance and modifying it. All or part of the sequence in the strip display can be played through at a speed selected by the user – the animated display is based on an interpolation between the key stances specified for the sequence. In interpolating articulated figures the use of quaternions (Shoemake 1985) can produce more realistic results.

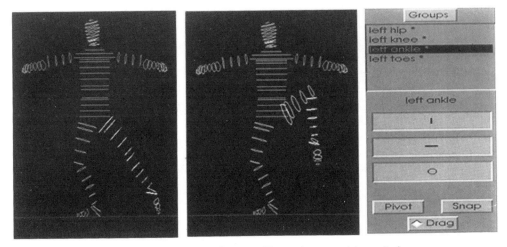

Figure 5.5. *The use of inverse kinematics to position a limb.*

The sequence can also be edited much like text in a word processor using selection, copy, cut and paste commands, and in addition, the timing can be adjusted by moving individual stances in time, and stretching or squeezing selected sections. Playing through the animation of a sequence is helpful, but new insights can be obtained by looking at the development over time, just as a musical score shows how a piece of music develops over time. This feature has shown that it can be very helpful in capturing the dynamics of movement realistically – one of the most difficult parts of keyframe animation.

Sequences can also be generated procedurally for certain classes of movement. This powerful approach avoids the tedious work involved in building each sequence frame by frame. The obvious candidate for implementation procedurally is locomotion since it is repetitive and very tedious to animate frame by frame. Bruderlin has developed procedural approaches to walking (Bruderlin and Calvert 1989, 1993) and running (Bruderlin 1995) – his procedural approach can generate a wide variety of walks and runs which can be used in building sequences. The interface shown in Figure 5.6 allows the user to interactively customize the walk to match the character being animated – an older person, a child, a tired person, etc. Sliders allow the user to adjust such parameters as ''bounciness'', ''torso sway'', ''pelvic list'' and ''step length''. The interface for procedural running shown in Figure 5.7 has a number of different parameters since running is a distinctly different motion. A procedural approach to grasping has also been developed. The output of a procedural generator can be read into the Sequence Editor for further customizing and for integration with other movement.

It is also possible to include the movements performed by a live dancer as part of a sequence. The movement can be captured or rotoscoped in a number of ways; for example if landmarks are placed on the body it is fairly straightforward to digitize the movement from

Figure 5.6.   *Procedurally generated walks are defined in terms of 3 parameters and 15 attributes.*

film or video – at least two simultaneous views are needed to capture the movement in 3-D. Another approach available from several manufacturers is based on multiplexed light or infra-red emitting diodes which are placed on the body and sensed by CCD cameras. This is a good way to capture limited movements and may still be the best way to capture the movements of a particular person. These digitized sequences can then be read into the Sequence Editor of *Life Forms*.

5.4.3   Combining multiple dancers in space and time

When movement sequences have been assembled for each of the dancers being choreographed they are combined in a composition process which involves adjusting the sequences relative to each other in space and in time. Each dancer has been choreographed with detailed movements of its own at the same time as moving through space relative to other dancers and to the environment. If the dancers are to interact closely with each other, then very careful choreography of the interaction may be necessary. Careful coordination of musical accompaniment may also be necessary.

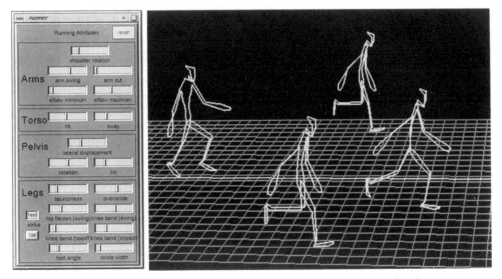

Figure 5.7.   *The interface for creating a running sequence procedurally.*

Implementation in *Life Forms*

In *Life Forms* composition in time is performed on the Timeline and composition in space on the Stage. In the Timeline, the sequences assigned to each dancer are shown as boxes which can be edited as a unit using the select, move, copy, cut or paste commands (Figure 5.8). Using these word-processor-like commands, the choreographer can not only adjust the relative timing of sequences but also very quickly build up complex movement for each dancer by building on the sequences developed in the Sequence Editor.

When a particular frame of the animation is displayed on the stage, the dancers are shown in their appropriate spatial positions for that frame, but in addition, the path for the complete sequence can be displayed (Figure 5.9). The orientation of the path can be adjusted interactively, as can its shape. The dance can then be played through in whole or in part. A soundtrack for digitized sound can also be synchronized to the movement using a separate sound window.

Because of the need to compose the dance in both space and time, users found it helpful if the Timeline was displayed on top of a Stage so that both aspects could be viewed simultaneously (Figure 5.8).

5.4.4   Performance of the completed or partially completed piece

It is important that the choreographer be able to review the composition at any stage in its development. Full visualization implies that the composer can move quickly and flexibly between views of all of the activities discussed above.

Implementation in *Life Forms*

In the Sequence Editor the choreographer can visualize either an entire sequence or any portion of it that is selected on the timeline strip at the bottom. The dancer can be viewed from any direction and the playback is selected with a control panel similar to that on a VCR. In the Stage and Timeline views the movement of the multiple dancers can be visualized in a similar way, showing either the entire piece or a selected portion. In addition, the ''camera'' can be controlled to give any desired view or sequence of views. This feature has proved useful in planning the camera angles to be used in shooting a dance video from a live performance.

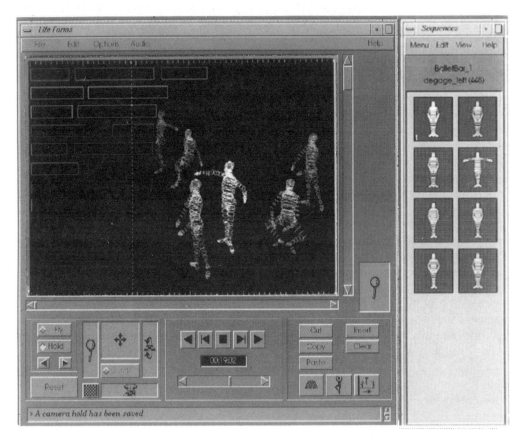

Figure 5.8.   *The Timeline display is used to set up the temporal relationships between dancers. Each row corresponds to a dancer (e.g. Row #1 shows red boxes for sequences for the first red dancer).*

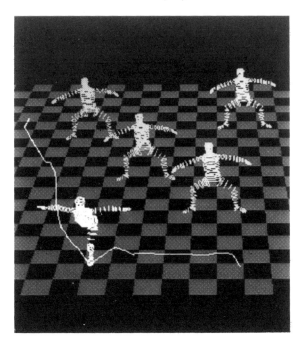

Figure 5.9.   *Spatial relationships are worked out on the Stage.*

5.5   Studying user interactions with *Life Forms*

5.5.1   Case studies

We have been fortunate to be able to study the use of *Life Forms* in compositions by New York choreographer Merce Cunningham. Thecla Schiphorst from our research team has maintained a close liaison with Mr. Cunningham and has developed a case study based on his experience (Schiphorst 1992). Other observations of a less formal nature have been obtained from individual choreographers, from students and from a workshop taught at York University in 1992. These studies are useful in refining our model of the compositional process but it has also become clear that many artists have found that the use of *Life Forms* has changed the way they approach composition. Some comments from choreographers include the following: "I was able to work more directly with internal imagery. It freed me from my own personal movement bias. I was able to have dancers on the screen take on movements that I wouldn't have dreamed of attempting on my own"; or, "Working with the system inspired me in new ways simply because of the visual nature of working with it"; and "I found my choreographic process with *Life Forms* to be more intuitive, more 'out of body', not hampered by my own limitations or concerns for dancers' well-being, nor even

concerned with the outcome necessarily.'' [York University Choreographic Workshop, Summer 1992].

5.5.2   Controlled studies

In order to optimize the design of an interactive composition system we must understand the strategies and techniques adopted by the choreographers in using the systems. In contrast to simple interfaces, basic knowledge of experimental psychology and human factors is quite inadequate for optimal design (Green 1990; Ackermann and Tauber 1990). Psychophysics routinely deals with single-cue tasks; this gives us valuable insight into how information from a small number of similar sensory channels is processed and evaluated, and may tell us how users are likely to behave when they utilize simple graphical and textual displays (Shneiderman 1992). When using modern high-immersion multimedia interfaces, however, users must bring a larger number of disparate sensory channels to bear on the more complex display items.

In studying such interfaces the objectives are twofold:

- to model and understand the strategies of users in learning and problem solving with high-immersion multimedia interfaces and to use this knowledge to design optimal interfaces; and
- to develop new experimental methodologies to assist in understanding user strategies and evaluating complex interfaces.

Formal studies of how composers and animators work with the system are underway. The interface has been modified so that all user actions are automatically recorded by the computer and stored with the timecode from a simultaneous video-recording of user actions and vocalization. The University of Toronto VANNA and Timelines systems (Harrison and Baecker 1992) for annotating video records are used by the experimenters to add observations and notes. Based on this data, protocol analyses are developed (Ericsson and Simon 1980). Studies are being conducted using naive and movement literate subjects.

A problem with all such studies is the definition and communication of the task the subjects are asked to perform. If the task is completely defined, we can study the details of how the tools support the task, but by the same token, such tasks do not allow us to study how choreographers and animators use these tools as part of the creative process. Zeenat Jetha has conducted two studies of the use of *Life Forms* (Jetha 1993) to address the two types of task. In the first, a group of dance students was asked to recreate in *Life Forms* the movements of three human figures from a short video segment. The task was designed in such a way as to encourage the subjects to utilize all of the main tools provided by *Life Forms*. As a result, this design task was suitable for evaluating the functionality of the interface. However, the task limited the creativity of the choreographers as they were merely replicating a video clip of simple movements.

In light of the first experiment, a new video clip was developed, which used an abstract animation of three shapes to suggest movement to the subjects. In this way, subjects could freely interpret the animated shapes into their own movement idea and use this as a basis for a composition. All subjects were given seven training sessions and subjects not familiar with computers were given extra time to develop their skill. For the study the subjects were asked to compose a short dance involving three figures based on the ideas presented in the abstract shapes animation. The choreography had to be completed in less than two hours.

The visual experimental result (the computer screen that subjects were working with) was video-taped, while computer human interactions were captured in a UNIX log file. The subjects were encouraged to verbalize their intentions and actions. Subsequently, all the video tapes were annotated using the Macintosh Timelines application program. Timelines captures the VCR counter of particular events or intervals displayed on the TV screen when the corresponding event or interval button is clicked in the Timelines window on the Macintosh screen.

The first annotation pass for each subject simply marked the time spent in the three main views of *Life Forms*: the sequence editor, the stage view and the timeline. Figure 5.10, below, presents the results of all eight subjects. Each bar signifies the amount of time spent in each view and the order in which the intervals and events occur. For example, subject 6

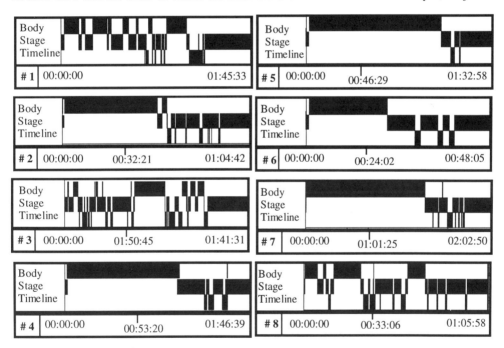

Figure 5.10. *Timelines display of the score for all 8 subjects.*

initially started in the stage view then entered the body editor. After spending some time there, he returned to the stage view, then moved into the timeline, and so on. All subjects started in the stage view because *Life Forms* always opens in the stage view. Further analysis on all graphs reveals that all subjects also end in the stage view, where sequences can be combined together, positioned and played.

Even this high level analysis revealed two quite different strategies. One group of subjects (2, 4, 5, 6 and 7) moved through the views linearly, essentially completing their design of body stances and movement sequences for each dancer before moving to the stage to combine the movements of the different dancers. The second group of subjects (1, 3 and 8) alternated frequently between the three views, splitting their attention between composing sequences and coordinating multiple figures in space and time. More detailed annotation of the video record and the log files reveals other elements of the strategies and mental models of the different subjects. Based on this analysis we are redesigning the system to better support these different approaches.

5.6   Future work and projects in progress

As our understanding of movement composition for dance choreography and animation grows, and as technology facilitates greater control and interaction, our tools for choreography and animation must also evolve. Building on feedback from users, observations from informal case studies, experimental findings and implementation experience (Calvert et al. 1993a), current and future projects aim for a deeper understanding of the creative process and an enhanced tool for movement composition. The areas where there is a particular need for development include: better control of interaction between dancers, better control of interactions with the environment, tools to allow the choreographer to specify movements for groups of figures – possibly utilizing techniques from flocking or behavioral animation – and techniques for modeling more realistic figures.

5.6.1   Body models for choreography

In the past, realistic rendering has been a primary focus in computer graphics, and today as we move closer to lifelike computer-generated images of the human body, the success of this research is clearly evident. However, the closer we come to modeling the human body with eerie accuracy, the greater our sensitivity to minute flaws. For animation, realistic representation of the figure during creation greatly aids the complex task of bringing a computer character to life since the animation is the final form of visualization. For dance choreography, the final form for viewing is the live performance with human performers.

Currently in *Life Forms*, a number of different figure representations are available (see Figure 5.11). The user is given a choice in body models to complement personal preferences

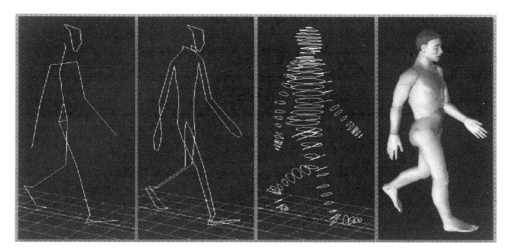

Figure 5.11.   *A selection of different body models for movement composition. From the left: 5.11(a) stick figure; 5.11(b) outline figure; 5.11(c) contour figure; 5.11(d) 3D figure. From Viewpoint DataLabs Intl.*

and the task at hand. During planning and stance/sequence definition, a more complete 3-D representation is often distracting to the choreographer since the simplicity and cleanness of the movement being created can be lost in the complexity of a full 3-D model (such as that shown in Figure 5.11d). For the traditional animator, using the same model as the final viewing model eliminates the time required to map the finished movement to another body model later. There is an ongoing exploration to find better 3-D representations and modeling techniques for the human body to provide real-time display and interaction.

Other related research is aimed at improving the structural representation of the human body. The complex structure of the human body with over 400 joints is a challenge to model, particularly for interactive systems. It is impossible for a user to handle all 400+ joints. For feasible user interaction, knowledge of the underlying structure must be built into the system. Such knowledge is already present in *Life Forms* in the structure of torso and spine, and in the use of inverse kinematics. The *Life Forms* spine has 22 joints which can be moved as a single entity by selecting the torso group directly. Though the trade-off is additional computation time, this detailed representation of the spine significantly enhances the quality of the motion. A current research project by Ph.D. candidate B. Sawatzky at Simon Fraser University will further define the spine to give greater articulation and response for animation control.

Procedural representations for specialized movements with embedded knowledge provide ease of specification to both choreographers and animators. For example, procedural modeling of the hand and grasping (Bruderlin et al. 1994) enables simultaneous and coordinated motion of the joints in the hand. Conventional animation techniques require that

each joint or each finger be tediously positioned individually. Procedural grasping allows a natural way of specifying hand movement, and leads towards incorporating task-oriented capabilities in *Life Forms*.

5.6.2   Multi-joint coordination and interacting figures

Inverse kinematics and procedural algorithms can be used to develop facilities needed to coordinate multiple joints or groups of joints of different body parts. Each one of us has an inherent understanding of how a human body moves because we are all "animators" of our own body. Existing animation systems, including *Life Forms*, have no notion of natural coordination between user-selected joints or groups of joints. For example, a user cannot arbitrarily select an arm and a leg of a figure and manipulate them simultaneously to coordinate their movements. This kind of control is similar to puppetry, and can be implemented with an inverse kinematics algorithm that handles multiple constraints (Bawa 1995).

Other desirable interaction features include inter-figure coordination and multi-figure manipulation. Specifying constraints between joints of different figures is useful for composing movement for interacting figures as in ballroom dancing where the hands of the partners are constrained to move together. Multi-figure manipulation refers to extending the *Life Forms* Sequence Editor to handle a number of figures to animate intricate interactions between the figures. This is currently done with the Stage view and the Timeline in *Life Forms*, but can be facilitated for difficult interactions such as one figure lifting a second figure.

5.6.3   Movement composition in relation to an environment

Though dance usually requires little more than open space for performance, there are choreographers interested in exploring the relationship between movement and the environment (physical objects and architectural spaces). More often than not, "place holders" representing the environment are sufficient for the choreographic process, and the objects in the environment do not require detailed representation. Figure 5.12 shows an animation created with *Life Forms* using chairs as part of the performance space. Though scenery is permitted on the stage view, the sequence editor is not capable of importing objects or part of a performance space. The challenge is to design the interface to supply necessary visual cues of the performance space to aid movement composition. This may include cues such as a floor plan of objects in the performance space, bounding boxes of objects to show volume and height, and 3-D wall grids.

Figure 5.12. *Diane Le Duc's "Chairs": a* Life Forms *choreography exploring the composition of movement as interaction with an environment.*

5.6.4 Higher level functions for group composition

Experience with choreography of contemporary and classical dance emphasizes the different needs placed on a compositional tool by different dance forms. The creation of movement in a classical form identified the lack of functionality to support group composition. For example, groups of dancers repeating the same movement may enter from different directions on the stage. The movement is expressed in terms of patterns across the floor of the performance space. A tool that supports composition as movement patterns will provide powerful functionality. There is presently no control for rotating the entire animation of a single dancer or a group of dancers. Furthermore, as the direction of the general movement for a group of figures is changed, the individual figures of the group must be altered accordingly (see examples in Figure 5.13 on page 122 and the plate section between pages 152 and 153, from "D Symphonies" choreographed by Jimmy Gamonet of the Miami City Ballet Company).

Another area related to higher level functions for group animation is the integration of behavioral animation techniques such as flocking (Reynolds 1987) and techniques from artificial intelligence research (Magnenat Thalmann et al. 1988; Morawetz and Calvert 1990; Ridsdale and Calvert 1990; Mah et al. 1994; and Maes et al. 1994). An important research issue related to autonomous behavior capabilities in an animation tool is the provision of control for the user. As a tool for a choreographer or animator, a system must yield final

Figure 5.13.   Life Forms *animation showing the need for tools to support movement patterns for a group of dancers with repeated movement sequences. D Symphonies (1995). Miami City Ballet (Miami). Photo by Louis Jay.*

direction to the human user. Though it is not clear how to best incorporate this along with autonomous techniques for movement composition, exploratory work has started with the initial integration of *Life Forms* with the agent programming language RTA (Wavish and Graham 1995). More details on behavioral animation may be found in Chapter 11.

Interpolation control
Better control over the interpolation process between keyframes or key stances is needed. Though it is possible to influence interpolation through keyframe positioning, it is necessary to provide greater control over the process at a higher level. The linear and spline interpolation options in *Life Forms* need to be supplemented by ''ease in and ease out'' capability common in traditional character animation systems. Research is in progress to implement ways to provide more natural human movement and better techniques for specification. This research is undertaken by Leslie Bishko, an animator and dancer who is evaluating Laban's effort-shape analysis as a basis for expressing movement quality (Bishko 1994). There is also work under way for gesture-based control of movement composition and keyframe interpolation which builds on compatible research for gesture-based music composition (Mulder 1995).

5.6.5   The role of motion capture in composition

As already discussed in Chapter 2, motion capture is again of interest to the animation industry. Though suggested for dance education and training (Mahoney 1995), it is currently of limited value for dance composition because of the same difficulties experienced in animation. Though the captured motion has the nuances associated with realistic human motion, the data set is large and dense, and not easily modified. Figure 5.14 shows the density of the captured data as represented in the frameview of the *Life Forms* Sequence Editor.

However, with recent advances toward dataset reduction and keyframe extraction, motion capture technology has the potential for adding full body movement recording to a movement composition tool. The motion capture equipment is currently still too expensive and difficult to use for most choreographers. Furthermore, once the data is recorded, techniques are required for data manipulation and blending with keyframed animation to maintain consistent style. One research interest involving motion capture is to extract emotional characteristics from the data of an enacted movement, and apply it to other movement sequences for high level composition (Amaya et al. 1995).

5.6.6 Studies of the compositional process

The approaches we are using to better understand how choreographers use the computer based tools in *Life Forms* are described above. However, these initial studies barely scratch the surface. For example, one of our studies showed that a choreographer was moving rapidly through a composition, first "auditioning" dancers by playing stored sequences and then assembling these sequences into the makings of a piece. This went well for the first two dancers but while working on the third, the choreographer became confused and mixed up the sequences intended for the second dancer with those for the third. The result was that the two dancers' sequences became hopelessly intermixed and the choreographer gave up and started again. This indicated that there was a need for a summary display which would assist the user in keeping track of the way the different sequences were being used. Although such a summary could be deduced from the Timeline display, obviously it was not adequate. A progressive "undo" command which allows a user to backtrack would also have been useful. This example indicates the kind of information that can be derived from these studies

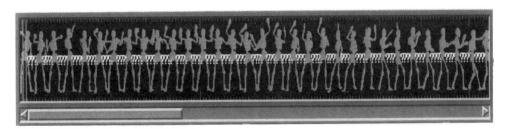

Figure 5.14.   Life Forms *frameview of motion capture data from Viewpoint DataLabs Intl. The question marks in the frameview indicate keyframes that are not displayed.*

and suggests that as the system evolves, each new version should be tested and the results used to guide further evolution.

5.7 Discussion and conclusions

In this chapter we have described how a system which is very much like a computer animation system can be used to support the composition and choreography of dance. However, the motivation is different, since the goal of the choreographer is to create a piece for live dancers to perform. We believe that the *Life Forms* system has already proved that tools of this type can be highly successful, although much more can be done.

It is significant that when Merce Cunningham in New York started to use *Life Forms*, reviews of his work usually couched their critiques in terms of "work created on the computer"; this led to a lot of hype and often ill-informed comment. It is a measure of the success and maturity of *Life Forms* as a tool, that current reviews of Mr. Cunningham's work often do not even mention "the computer" and instead focus on criticism of the aesthetics of the work.

5.8 Acknowledgment

The authors gratefully acknowledge support from the Social Sciences and Humanities Research Council of Canada, the Natural Sciences and Engineering Research Council of Canada, the PRECARN-IRIS Network of Centres of Excellence and Kinetic Effects Inc. (Seattle, WA).

5.9 References

Ackerman D. and Tauber M.J. (eds) (1990). "Mental Models and Human-Computer Interaction 1", Amsterdam: North-Holland.
Amaya K., Bruderlin A. and Calvert T. (1995) "Emotion from Motion: Transformation of 3D Kinematics", Proc. of the Western Computer Graphics Symposium, pp. 104–105.
Barenholz J., Wolofsky Z., Ganapathy I., Calvert T.W. and O'Hara P. (1977) "Computer Interpretation of Dance Notation", in Computing in the Humanities, Proc. 3rd Int. Conference on Computing in the Humanities, pp. 235–241, Waterloo, Ont.: Univ. Waterloo Press.
Bawa S. (1995) "Interactive Control of Animations: An Optimization Approach to Real-Time Inverse Kinematics", M.Sc. Thesis, School of Computing Science, Simon Fraser University.
Benesh R. and Benesh J. (1956) "An Introduction to Benesh Dance Notation". London: A.C. Black.
Birdwhistell R.L. (1970) "Kinesics and Context: Essays on Body Movement Communication", Univ. of Pennsylvania Press, Philadelphia.
Bishko L. (1994) "Expressive Technology: The Tool as Metaphor of Aesthetic Sensibility", Animation Journal, Fall 1994, pp. 74–91.

Blinn J. (1990) ''Jim Blinn's Corner: The Ultimate Design Tool'', IEEE Computer Graphics & Applications, November, pp. 90–92.

Brightman P. (1984) ''Making Dances with Algorithms: Towards a Theory of Choreography, Based on the Use of Computer Programs and Laban Concepts'', M.A. Thesis, Columbia University.

Bruderlin A. (1995) ''Procedural Motion Control Techniques for Interactive Animation of Human Figures'', Ph.D. Thesis, School of Computing Science, Simon Fraser University.

Bruderlin A. and Calvert T.W. (1989) ''Goal-Directed, Dynamic Animation of Human Walking'', Computer Graphics (SIGGRAPH 89), vol. 23, pp. 233–242.

Bruderlin A. and Calvert T.W. (1993) ''Interactive animation of personalized human locomotion'', Proc. Graphics Interface 93, pp. 17–23.

Bruderlin A., Teo C.G. and Calvert T.W. (1994) ''Procedural movement for articulated figure animation'', Computers and Graphics, vol. 18, no. 4, pp. 453–461.

Calvert T.W. (1986) ''Towards a language for human movement'', Computers and the Humanities, vol. 20, no. 2, pp. 35–43.

Calvert T.W., Chapman J. and Patla A. (1980) ''The integration of subjective and objective data in animation of human movement. Computer Graphics'', vol. 14, pp. 198–203.

Calvert T.W., Chapman J. and Patla A. (1982) ''Aspects of the Kinematic Simulation of Human Movement'', IEEE Computer Graphics and Applications, vol. 2, pp. 41–50.

Calvert T.W., C. Welman C., S. Gaudet S., T. Schiphorst T. and C. Lee C. (1991) ''Composition of Multiple Figure Sequences for Dance and Animation'', The Visual Computer, vol. 7, pp. 114–121.

Calvert T.W., Bruderlin A., Mah S., Schiphorst T. and Welman C. (1993) ''The evolution of an interface for choreographers'', Proc. InterCHI Conference, pp. 115–122, Amsterdam, April.

Ericsson K.A. and Simon H.A. (1980) ''Verbal Reports as Data''. Psychological Review, vol. 67, pp. 215–251.

Eshkol N. and Wachmann A. (1958) ''Movement Notation'', London: Weidenfeld and Nicholson.

Gray J.A. (1984) ''Dance in Computer Technology: A Survey of Applications and Capabilities, Interchange'', vol. 15, no. 4, pp. 15–25.

Green T.R.G. (1990) ''Limited Theories as a Framework for Human-Computer Interaction'', in Mental Models and Human–Computer Interaction I, D. Ackermann and M.J. Tauber (eds), pp. 3–39, New York: Elsevier.

Hall-Marriot N. (1992) ''Ballet in Bits and Bytes'', Proc. First Dance and Technology Conference, Univ. Wisconsin, pp. 25–28.

Hall-Marriot N. (1995) ''DANCE: Describing, Animating and Notating Classical Enchainements'', Ph.D. Thesis, University of Technology, Sydney.

Harrison B.L. and Baecker R. (1992) ''Designing Video Annotation and Analysis Systems'', Proc. Graphics Interface '92, Vancouver, pp. 157–166, May.

Herbison-Evans D. (1979) ''A Human Movement Language for Computer Animation'', in Language Design and Programming Methodology, J. Tobias (ed), New York: Springer-Verlag, pp. 117–128.

Hunt S.E. (1988) ''An Interactive Graphical Editor for Labanotation'', Honours Thesis, Basser Dept. of Computer Science, University of Sydney.

Hutchinson A. (1960) ''Labanotation'', New York: Theatre Arts Books, second edition.

Hutchinson-Guest A. (1984) ''Dance Notation: The Process of Recording Movement on Paper'', London: Dance Books.

Jetha Z. (1993) ''On the Edge of the Creative Process: An Analysis of Human Figure Animation as a Complex Synthesis Task'', B.A.Sc. Thesis, School of Engineering Science, Simon Fraser University.

Lansdown J. (1977) ''Computer Choreography and Video'', Computing in the Humanities, S. Lusignan and J.S. North (eds), pp. 241–252, Waterloo, Ont.: University of Waterloo Press.

Maes P., Darrell T., Blumberg B and Pentland S. (1994) ''Interacting with Animated Autonomous Agents'' in Working Notes AAAI Spring Symposium on ''Believeable Agents'', Stanford, CA.

Magnenat Thalmann N., Thalmann D., Wyvill B. and Zeltzer D. (1988) ''Synthetic Actors: The Impact of Artificial Intelligence and Robotics on Animation'', Siggraph Course Notes #4, Boston.

Magnenat Thalmann N. and Thalmann D. (1990) "Computer Animation: Theory and Practice", Tokyo: Springer-Verlag.

Mah S., Calvert T.W. and Havens W. (1994) , "A constraint-based reasoning framework for behavioural animation", Computer Graphics Forum, vol. 13, no. 5.

Mahoney D.P. (1995) "Motion Capture Gives Athletes an Edge", Computer Graphics World, January, pp. 17–18.

Morawetz C.L. and Calvert T. (1990) "A framework for goal-directed human animation with secondary movement", Proc. Graphics Interface '90, pp. 60–67, May.

Mulder A.G.E. (1995) "Gesture in a Musical Performance Context", to be published in the CHI 95 Workshop Notes for Gesture at the User Interface.

Niebuhr R. (1949) "Nature and Destiny of Man", New York: Scribner.

Politis G. (1987) "A Computer Graphics Interpreter for Benesh Movement Notation", Ph.D. thesis, Dept. of Computer Science, University of Sydney.

Pylyshyn Z. (1989) The design process: lecture notes, Precarn Workshop.

Reynolds C.W. (1987) "Flocks, Herds and Schools: A Distributed Behaviour Model", Proc. ACM Siggraph 87, Computer Graphics, vol. 21, no. 4, pp. 25–34.

Ridsdale G. and Calvert T. (1990) "Animating Microworlds from Scripts and Relational Constraints", Computer Animation 90, N. Magnenat Thalmann and D. Thalmann (eds), pp. 107–117.

Ryman R., Singh B., Beatty J.C. and Booth K.S. (1984) "A computerized editor for Benesh movement notation", CORD Dance Research Journal, vol. 16, no. 1, pp. 27–34.

Savage G.J. and Officer J.M. (1984) "CHOREO: An Interactive Computer Model for Dance", Intl. Journal for Man–Machine Studies, pp. 1–17.

Scheflen A.E. (1972) "Theory of Body Language and the Social Order", Englewood Cliffs, NJ: Prentice Hall Inc.

Schiphorst T. (1992) "A case study of Merce Cunningham's use of the LifeForms computer choreographic system in the making of Trackers", M.A. Thesis, Simon Fraser University.

Schiphorst T., Calvert T., Lee C., Welman C. and Gaudet S. (1990) "Tools for Interaction with the Creative Process of Composition", Proc. CHI'90, Seattle, April, pp. 167–174.

Shneiderman, B. (1992) "Designing the User Interface: Strategies for Effective Human–Machine Interaction", second edition, Baltimore, Md: John Hopkins University Press.

Shoemake K. (1985) "Animating Rotation with Quaternion Curves", Proc. SIGGRAPH '85, Computer Graphics, vol. 19, no. 3, pp. 245–254.

Simon H.A. (1969) "The Sciences of the Artificial", Cambridge, MA: MIT Press.

Smoliar S.M. and Weber L. (1977) "Using the Computer for a Semantic Representation of Labanotation", in Computing and the Humanities, S. Lusignan and J.S. North (eds), pp. 253–261, Waterloo, Ont.: University of Waterloo Press.

Wavish P. and Graham M. (1995) "A Situated Action Approach to Implementing Characters in Computer Games", to be published in Applied A.I. Journal, Summer.

Warp Generation and Transition Control in Image Morphing

Seung-Yong Lee and Sung Yong Shin

Department of Computer Science, Korea Advanced Institute of Science and Technology

Abstract

This chapter summarizes the warp generation and transition control methods in image morphing techniques. Warp generation methods are classified as mesh-based and feature-based approaches, and the basic ideas of the methods are explained. Then, the method proposed by the authors which considers the one-to-one property of warps is summarized in more detail. An effective method for controlling transition behavior proposed by the authors is also described in this chapter.

6.1 Introduction

Recently, an animation technique called morphing has attracted much attention because of its astonishing effects. Morphing deals with the metamorphosis of an object into another object over time. While three-dimensional object modeling and deformation is a solution to the morphing problem, the complexity of objects often makes this approach impractical. Realistic modeling and rendering of complex objects such as humans require too much time and may be impossible.

The difficulty of the three-dimensional approach can be effectively avoided with a two-dimensional technique called image morphing (Wolberg 1990, Morrison 1993). Image morphing manipulates two-dimensional images instead of three-dimensional objects and generates a sequence of in-between images from two images. When viewed in a row, the in-between images produce an animation that the objects in the first image change to the objects in the second image over time. Image morphing techniques have been widely used

127

for creating special effects in television commercials, music videos, and movies. Image morphing examples in various applications are listed in Hall (1992).

The problem of image morphing is basically how an in-between image is effectively generated from two given images. A simple way for deriving an in-between image is to interpolate the colors of each pixel between two images. However, this method crumbles away the features on the images and does not give a realistic metamorphosis. Hence, an image morphing technique interpolates the features between two images to obtain a natural in-between image.

The feature interpolation is performed by combining warps with the color interpolation. A warp is a two-dimensional geometric transformation and generates a distorted image when it is applied to an image. When two images are given, the features on the images and their correspondence are specified by an animator with a set of points or line segments. Then, warps are computed to distort the images so that the features have intermediate positions and shapes. The color interpolation between the distorted images finally gives an in-between image. More detailed process for obtaining an in-between image can be found in Wolberg (1990) and Lee (1995).

In generating an in-between image, the most difficult part is to compute warps for distorting the given images. Hence, the research in image morphing has concentrated on deriving warps from the specified feature correspondence. Image morphing techniques can be classified into two categories as mesh-based and feature-based methods in terms of their ways for specifying features. In mesh-based methods, the features on an image are specified by a nonuniform mesh. Feature-based methods specify the features with a set of points or line segments.

This chapter summarizes the warp generation methods in image morphing techniques. We first explain mesh-based methods and feature-based methods. Then, the method proposed by the authors for generating a one-to-one warp from a set of feature point pairs is described. The one-to-one property of a warp is important because it guarantees that the distorted image does not fold back upon itself.

Another interesting problem of image morphing is the control of transition behavior in a metamorphosis sequence. In generating an in-between image, the same transition rate is usually applied over all points on the image. This results in an animation in which the entire image changes synchronously to another image. If transition rates are controlled differently from part to part on an in-between image, a more interesting animation can be obtained.

Methods for controlling transition behavior are provided in mesh-based image morphing techniques. However, the methods perform transition control with the meshes for specifying features and are inconvenient when complicated meshes are taken. The authors have proposed a more convenient method for transition control. The method separates the transition control from feature interpolation and thus can be used with any warp generation methods. We summarize the method in this chapter.

6.2 Mesh-based methods

In mesh-based methods, a warp is generated from two nonuniform meshes. Two meshes have the same size, and each point on one mesh corresponds to a point on the other mesh. One mesh S represents the positions of the features on an image I, and the other mesh D specifies the moved positions of the features in the distorted image I'. Then, the problem is to compute a warp from the meshes S and D which gives the correspondence between all points on the images I and I'. We give two typical mesh-based image morphing techniques, mesh warping in Wolberg (1990) and metamorphosis using Bézier clipping (Nishita et al. 1993).

6.2.1 Mesh warping

In mesh warping, the distorted image I' is derived from the image I and the meshes S and D in two passes. The first pass determines the correspondence between the x-coordinates of points in I and I'. With the correspondence, the image I is distorted in the horizontal direction, generating an intermediate image I''. In the second pass, the mapping between the y-coordinates of points in I'' and I' are derived, and the intermediate image I'' is distorted in the vertical direction, resulting in the distorted image I'.

Let the size of the meshes S and D be $m \times n$. In the first phase of the first pass, an interpolating spline is computed from the x-coordinates of m mesh points on each column of the meshes S and D. Then, these vertical splines are sampled at each row on the images I and I'', partitioning each row to n intervals. Each interval in a row on the image I matches the corresponding interval in the same row on the intermediate image I''.

In the second phase of the first pass, the correspondences between intervals are spread to pixels on the images I and I''. The intervals are normalized, and the normalized index at every pixel boundary in I'' is determined. For a pixel in I'', the index is used to identify corresponding pixels in I, and the color is sampled by box filtering. This results in an intermediate image I'' in which the data in the meshes S and D are nicely propagated in the horizontal direction.

In the second pass, each row in the meshes S and D is fitted with an interpolating spline through the y-coordinates of n mesh points. Each column in the images I'' and I is partitioned to m intervals by sampling the horizontal splines. Then, the intermediate image I'' is sampled in the vertical direction to generate the distorted image I' from the correspondence between the intervals. The image I' shows a proper distortion of the image I in both horizontal and vertical directions as implied by the meshes S and D.

6.2.2 Metamorphosis using Bézier clipping

Nishita et al. (1993) employed two-dimensional free-form deformation and Bézier clipping to generate warps. In the method, a parameter space P is taken as a medium between the image I and the distorted image I'. It is assumed that a uniform mesh of the same size as meshes S and D is overlaid onto the parameter space P. The mapping from the space P to the image I is defined from the meshes R and S by a free-form deformation.

In generating the distorted image I' from the image I, backward mapping is used. For each pixel on the distorted image I', the color sampled at the corresponding pixel on the image I is copied. The problem is then to compute a warp from the meshes S and D which gives the position on I for each point on I'. Because there exists the mapping from the parameter space P to the image I, the warp can be derived if a mapping from I' to P is found.

Nishita et al. employed Bézier clipping to compute the parameter values for each pixel in the distorted image I'. The image I' is considered a set of Bézier patches where the mesh D serves as control points. For a scanline in I', a region on the parameter space P is obtained by Bézier clipping, which generates a subpatch intersecting the scanline. Then, isoparametric curves in the same direction are sampled densely from the region, and the parameter values at the intersections between the curves and the scanline are computed by Bézier clipping. The parameter values of each pixel on the scanline are derived by the linear interpolation of the values at the intersection points.

6.2.3   Discussion

Mesh warping provides a fast and intuitive technique for distorting images. Local deformations explicitly specified by the meshes are properly reflected in the distorted images. Two passes handling horizontal and vertical distortions independently enable an image to be effectively resampled with a one-dimensional box filter. Mesh warping was developed in Industrial Light and Magic and used for creating special effects in many movies including *Willow* and *Indiana Jones and the Last Crusade*.

The method of Nishita et al. can produce various types of warps which are smooth up to the desired degree. When a bilinear Bézier patch is used, the method can handle all affine transformations. The first order continuity is preserved in distorting an image by bicubic Bézier patches. To get the kth order of continuity, Bézier patches of degree $(k+2)$ can be used.

Mesh-based techniques have a drawback in specifying features. The features on an image should be represented by a nonuniform mesh while they can have an arbitrary structure. Complex features on an image may not be exactly controlled by a nonuniform mesh. If the size of the mesh is increased for a complicated image, many mesh points must be properly handled, though most of them do not correspond to features on the image.

6.3   Feature-based methods

Feature-based methods overcome the drawback of mesh-based methods by specifying the features on an image with a set of points or line segments. A warp is generated from the correspondence between two sets of feature points or line segments. For each point or line segment in the feature set on an image, the corresponding point or line segment in the other set specifies the position in the distorted image. Line segments are used in field morphing (Beier and Neely 1992), and there are several methods for deriving warps from feature points.

6.3.1 Field morphing

In field morphing, the distorted image I' is derived from the image I with two sets of line segments S and D. Because the backward mapping is used, the problem is to compute a warp which gives the position on I for each point on I'.

A line segment can define a coordinate system on a plane. The direction of the line segment determines one axis U of the coordinate system, and the other axis V is chosen in the perpendicular direction to the line segment. One end point of the line segment provides the origin. Let p be a point on the plane and q the projection of p to the line segment. The coordinate of p in the U axis is derived by dividing the length of the line segment into the distance of q from the origin. The distance between p and q gives the coordinate in the V axis.

Let the sets S and D contain only one line segment l_S and l_D, respectively. For each point p in the distorted image I', the corresponding position in the image I is derived using the coordinates defined by the line segments l_S and l_D. First, the coordinates of a point p in I' is computed with the line segment l_D. Then, the line segment l_S derives from the coordinates the position in I corresponding to the point p. When the sets S and D contain multiple line segments, a weighted averaging of the transformations from line segments is performed. For a point p in I', the corresponding position in I is computed with each pair of line segments in S and D. Then, the displacements between the positions and the point p are calculated, and a weighted average of the displacements is obtained. The weight is determined from the distance of the point p to each line segment in D. The average displacement is added to the point p to determine the position in I.

6.3.2 Warp generation from feature points

When the features on an image and their distortions are specified by two point sets, a warp should spread the data over all points in the image. The warp is composed of two real valued bivariate functions defined on the image, which determine the x- and y-components, respectively. The components can be represented by surfaces where function values are interpreted as the heights from a plane. If the components are considered independently, the warp can be derived by constructing two smooth surfaces which interpolate scattered points. The interpolated points are obtained from the feature points and their corresponding positions.

There are several methods for generating smooth surfaces from scattered points. They were extensively surveyed in Wolberg (1990) and Ruprecht and Müller (1992) and can be classified into several categories such as the inverse distance weighted interpolation, the triangulation-based method, the regularization method, and the spline interpolation based on radial basis functions. The advantages and disadvantages of the methods are detailed in the surveys, and the spline interpolation is recommended as the best one. However, the computation time of the spline interpolation increases as the cube of the number of interpolated points. When a large number of points are interpolated, the regularization method is a better choice. The authors have applied the regularization method to derive warps from the feature point sets (Lee et al. 1994). In the method, the multigrid relaxation method is used to efficiently generate the numerical solutions of the interpolating surfaces. The resulting warps properly propagate the feature distortions all over the images. Litwinowicz and Williams (1994) also used the regularization method and the multigrid relaxation in generating warps.

6.3.3   Discussion

Field morphing provides an expressive method for specifying the features on an image. Because any structure such as a mesh is not required, it suffices to place line segments only at the features. Adding new line segments increases control in that area with no additional handling of other line segments. Field morphing was used by Pacific Data Images for creating metamorphosis in a music video, Michael Jackson's *Black or White*, and many commercials. Field morphing suffers from unexpected warps referred to as ghosts. This results from the fact that the influences of line segments are blended by simple weighted averaging. The drawback prevents an animator from realizing the precise warps required for complex metamorphoses.

Feature point interpolation based on the regularization method overcomes the drawback while preserving the advantage of field morphing. Line segments can be used for specifying features in these methods through point sampling. The computation time does not increase with densely sampled points because the required computation in the multigrid relaxation method remains nearly constant regardless of the number of interpolated points.

6.4   One-to-one warps

When an image is distorted, a smooth warp is expected to generate no discontinuous parts in the resulting image. However, if the warp is not one-to-one, the distorted image folds back upon itself and contains annoying discontinuous parts. The methods in Section 6.2 and Section 6.3 generate continuous or even C^1-continuous warps but do not consider the one-to-one property.

This section summarizes the warp generation method proposed by the authors which guarantees the one-to-one property. In the method, the features and their distortions are specified by two point sets. A warp is considered a deformation of a rectangular plate which places selected points at the specified positions. The requirements for a warp are represented by energy terms, and the desired warp is derived by minimizing the sum of the energy terms. The energy minimization problem is transformed to a partial differential equation which is solved by a numerical method.

6.4.1 Deformation model

Let Ω be a rectangular thin plate and $p = (u, v)$ a point on Ω. If every point on the plate is placed on the xy-plane, a shape of the plate can be represented by a vector-valued function, $\mathbf{w}(p) = (x(p), y(p))$. The function $\mathbf{w}$ specifies the position of each point p on the plate, lying in the xy-plane. The natural undeformed shape of the plate is a rectangle on the xy-plane.

Suppose that the selected points on the plate are required to move to the given positions on the xy-plane. A C^1-continuous and one-to-one warp which satisfies the constraints can be derived by minimizing the energy functional,

$$E(w) = \int_\Omega \int \left[\left\| \frac{\partial^2 \mathbf{w}}{\partial u^2} \right\|^2 + 2 \left\| \frac{\partial^2 \mathbf{w}}{\partial u \partial v} \right\|^2 + \left\| \frac{\partial^2 \mathbf{w}}{\partial v^2} \right\|^2 \right]$$

$$\mathrm{d}u\mathrm{d}v + \alpha \int_\Omega \int (J - 1)^2 \mathrm{d}u\mathrm{d}v + \beta \sum_k \| \mathbf{w}(p_k) - q_k \|^2 \tag{6.1}$$

J is the Jacobian of the function $\mathbf{w}$, that is, $J = \dfrac{\partial x}{\partial u} \dfrac{\partial y}{\partial v} - \dfrac{\partial x}{\partial v} \dfrac{\partial y}{\partial u}$, q_k is the new position specified for a selected point p_k on Ω, α and β are parameters controlling the relative influences of the terms on the energy functional.

The first term in $E(\mathbf{w})$ integrates the curvature variations of $\mathbf{w}$ over the domain Ω. The function $\mathbf{w}$ which minimizes the term has continuous first partial derivatives (Terzopoulos 1986). The second term concerns the one-to-one property of the function $\mathbf{w}$. Minimizing the term tries to make the Jacobian J one at each point on Ω, which implies the resulting function $\mathbf{w}$ is one-to-one. The positional constraints of the function $\mathbf{w}$ are forced by minimizing the last term.

If a function $\mathbf{w}$ minimizes the energy functional $E(\mathbf{w})$, the first variational derivative of $E(\mathbf{w})$ must vanish all over the domain Ω (Gelfand and Fomin 1963). The condition can be represented by the vector expression,

$$\frac{1}{2} \frac{\delta E}{\delta \mathbf{w}} = \left(\frac{\partial^4 \mathbf{w}}{\partial u^4} + 2 \frac{\partial^4 \mathbf{w}}{\partial u^2 \partial v^2} + \frac{\partial^4 \mathbf{w}}{\partial v^4} \right) + \alpha \left(\frac{\partial}{\partial u} \left(J \frac{\partial \mathbf{w}^\perp}{\partial v} \right) - \frac{\partial}{\partial v} \left(J \frac{\partial \mathbf{w}^\perp}{\partial u} \right) \right)$$

$$+ \beta (\mathbf{w}(p_k) - q_k) = 0 \tag{6.2}$$

Here, $\mathbf{w}^{\perp}$ denotes the vector $(-y, x)$ which is perpendicular to the vector $\mathbf{w} = (x, y)$. The last term appears only at a point p_k on Ω for which its position q_k is specified.

The partial differential equation given in Equation (6.2) is called the Euler–Lagrange equation. Unfortunately, it is in general very difficult to obtain an analytic solution for the Euler–Lagrange equation. This suggests a numerical method applied to a discrete version of the equation.

6.4.2 Numerical solution

We discretize the domain Ω to an $M \times N$ regular grid and represent the function $\mathbf{w}$ by its values at the nodes on the grid. The positional constraints are converted to the constraints on the values of the nodal variables. The standard finite difference approximation (Press et al. 1992) transforms the differential equation given in Equation (6.1) into a system of equations which consists of MN unknown vectors and MN vector equations. If the nodal variables comprising the function $\mathbf{w}$ are collected into an MN dimensional vector, the system can be written in a matrix form,

$$\mathbf{Aw} + \alpha\mathbf{j}(\mathbf{w}) + \beta(\mathbf{I}'\mathbf{w} - \mathbf{q}) = 0 \qquad (6.3)$$

$\mathbf{A}$ is an $MN \times MN$ matrix which contains the coefficients of the nodal variables resulting from the first term in Equation (6.2). $\mathbf{j}(\mathbf{w})$ is an MN dimensional vector which approximates the second term on the nodal variables. $\mathbf{I}'$ is an $MN \times MN$ diagonal matrix in which an element is one only if the positional constraint is assigned to the corresponding nodal variable. The MN dimensional vector $\mathbf{q}$ contains the positional constraints on the nodal variables.

To solve Equation (6.2), we rewrite the equation as a diffusion equation,

$$\frac{\partial \mathbf{w}}{\partial t} = \mathbf{Aw} + \alpha\mathbf{j}(\mathbf{w}) + \beta(\mathbf{I}'\mathbf{w} - \mathbf{q}) \qquad (6.4)$$

An initial distribution $\mathbf{w}$ relaxes to an equilibrium solution as $t \to \infty$. At the equilibrium, all time derivatives vanish and hence $\mathbf{w}$ is the solution of Equation (6.3). When differentiating Equation (6.4) with respect to time, we evaluate the right-hand side at time t rather than time $t - 1$, which results in the implicit Euler scheme. For computing the y- and x-components of $\mathbf{j}(\mathbf{w})$, x- and y-components of $\mathbf{w}$ are assumed constant during a time step, respectively. The assumption makes the nonlinear term $\mathbf{j}(\mathbf{w})$ linear with respect to $\mathbf{w}$. The resulting equations are

$$-\gamma(\mathbf{x}_t - \mathbf{x}_{t-1}) = \mathbf{Ax}_t + \alpha\mathbf{B}(\mathbf{y}_{t-1})\mathbf{x}_t + \beta(\mathbf{I}'\mathbf{x}_t - \mathbf{x}_q) \qquad (6.5)$$

$$-\gamma(\mathbf{y}_t - \mathbf{y}_{t-1}) = \mathbf{Ay}_t + \alpha\mathbf{B}(\mathbf{x}_{t-1})\mathbf{y}_t + \beta(\mathbf{I}'\mathbf{y}_t - \mathbf{y}_q) \qquad (6.6)$$

$\mathbf{x}_t$ and $\mathbf{y}_t$ are the x- and y-component vectors of the function $\mathbf{w}$ at time t. $\mathbf{B}(\mathbf{y}_{t-1})$ and $\mathbf{B}(\mathbf{x}_{t-1})$ are $MN \times MN$ matrices which contain the coefficients of $\mathbf{x}_t$ and $\mathbf{y}_t$ in the linear approximations of $\mathbf{j}(\mathbf{w})$, respectively. $\mathbf{x}_q$ and $\mathbf{y}_q$ denote the positional constraints on $\mathbf{x}$ and $\mathbf{y}$. The parameter γ controls the step size in time.

Equations (6.5) and (6.6) can be arranged in the forms,

$$(\mathbf{A} + \alpha\mathbf{B}(\mathbf{y}_{t-1}) + \gamma\mathbf{I} + \beta\mathbf{I}')\mathbf{x}_t = \gamma\mathbf{I}\mathbf{x}_{t-1} + \beta\mathbf{x}_q \tag{6.7}$$

$$(\mathbf{A} + \alpha\mathbf{B}(\mathbf{x}_{t-1}) + \gamma\mathbf{I} + \beta\mathbf{I}')\mathbf{y}_t = \gamma\mathbf{I}\mathbf{y}_{t-1} + \beta\mathbf{y}_q \tag{6.8}$$

in which $\mathbf{x}_t$ and $\mathbf{y}_t$ can be calculated from $\mathbf{x}_{t-1}$ and $\mathbf{y}_{t-1}$. The multigrid relaxation method (Briggs 1987) efficiently solves Equations (6.7) and (6.8) by exploiting the bandedness of the matrices on the left-hand side.

This method for solving Equation (6.4) takes the implicit Euler scheme for the first and third terms in the equation and the semi-implicit Euler scheme for the second term. Hence, the solution of the equation can be found very robustly and rapidly with a big time step.

Figure 6.1 shows a deformation example in which the grid size is 64×64. In the figures, black spots represent the positions of selected points to which positional constraints are assigned. It takes 1.6 seconds to derive the deformation on a Silicon Graphics Crimson Workstation. When the size of the grid is 512×512, the computation time increases to 26.7 seconds. This example verifies that the proposed method generates a desired deformation very effectively.

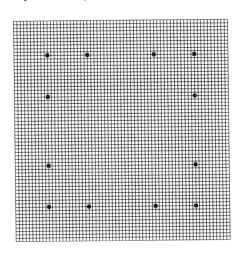

(a) The undeformed shape

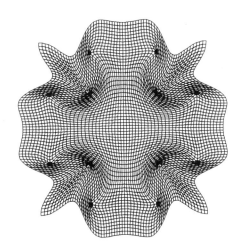

(b) A deformation of the plate

Figure 6.1.   *A deformation example.*

6.5   Transition control

Mesh-based image morphing techniques provide methods for controlling transition behavior in a metamorphosis. In mesh warping, a transition curve is assigned to each point of the mesh for specifying features (Wolberg 1990). These curves determine the transition rates when the positions of features are interpolated in an in-between image. When complicated meshes are employed, it is tedious to assign a proper transition curve to every mesh point. Nishita et al. (1993) mentioned that the transition behavior can be controlled by a Bézier function defined on the mesh for specifying features. However, the details of the method were not given except for one example.

This section summarizes the more effective method for transition control proposed by the authors. In the method, transition control is separated from warp generation with a new metamorphosis framework. Transition functions are included in the framework to facilitate the control of transition behavior. The transition functions can be derived from the transition curves specified at selected points on an image. Procedural transition functions can also be used to generate various interesting in-between images.

6.5.1   Metamorphosis framework

Transition functions specify a transition rate for each point on the given images over time. Let T_0 be a transition function defined on the source image I_0. For a given time t, $T_0(t)$ is a real-valued function defined on I_0. In generating an in-between image $I(t)$, $T_0(t)$ determines how fast each point on I_0 moves to the corresponding point on the destination image I_1. $T_0(t)$ also determines how much the color of each point on I_0 is reflected on the corresponding point on $I(t)$. Let T_1 be the transition function defined on the destination image I_1, which specifies the same transition behavior with T_0. To each point on I_1, $T_1(t)$ should assign the transition rate which $T_0(t)$ gives to the corresponding point on I_0.

Let R denote the identity warp. Let W_0 and W_1 be the warps which specify the corresponding point on I_1 and I_0 for each point on I_0 and I_1, respectively. Let $W \cdot I$ denote the application of a warp W to an image I. The procedure for generating an in-between image $I(t)$ can be described as follows:

$$W_0(t) = (1 - T_0(t)) \cdot R + T_0(t) \cdot W_0$$
$$W_1(t) = T_1(t) \cdot R + (1 - T_1(t)) \cdot W_1$$
$$I_0(t) = W_0(t) \cdot ((1 - T_0(t)) \cdot I_0) \qquad (6.9)$$
$$I_1(t) = W_1(t) \cdot (T_1(t) \cdot I_1)$$
$$I(t) = I + 0(t) + I_1(t)$$

Transition rates are assumed to take values between 0 and 1 such that I_0 and I_1 imply the source and destination images, respectively.

6.5.2 Transition function generation

At a given time, transition functions on images are real-valued functions defined on a rectangular region. If transition rates are considered the heights from the region, transition functions are reduced to surfaces deformed only in the vertical direction. When the transition rates on selected points on an image are given, a transition function can be derived by constructing a smooth surface which interpolates scattered points. The resulting transition function properly propagates the given transition rates all over the image. The thin-plate surface model (Gelfand and Fomin 1963) can be used to derive the interpolating surface.

Let Ω be a rectangular thin plate on the uv-plane and $p = (u, v)$ a point on Ω. If the plate is allowed to be deformed only in the direction perpendicular to the uv-plane, a shape of the plate can be represented by a function $f(p)$. The function f specifies a real value for each point on the plate.

Suppose that the function f should have the given values at selected points on the plate. A C^1-continuous function f which satisfies the constraints can be derived by minimizing the energy functional,

$$E(f) = \int_\Omega \int \left[\left(\frac{\partial^2 f}{\partial u^2}\right)^2 + 2\left(\frac{\partial^2 f}{\partial u \partial v}\right)^2 + \left(\frac{\partial^2 f}{\partial v^2}\right)^2 \right] \mathrm{d}u\mathrm{d}v + \beta \sum_k (f(p_k) - t_k)^2 \qquad (6.10)$$

Here, t_k is the value specified for a point p_k on Ω. If a function f minimizes the energy functional $E(f)$, the first variational derivative of $E(f)$ must vanish all over the domain Ω. The condition can be represented by the expression,

$$\frac{1}{2}\frac{\delta E}{\delta f} = \left(\frac{\partial^4 f}{\partial u^4} + 2\frac{\partial^4 f}{\partial u^2 \partial v^2} + \frac{\partial^4 f}{\partial v^4}\right) + \beta(f(p_k) - t_k) = 0 \qquad (6.11)$$

The last term containing β appears only at a point p_k on Ω for which a value t_k is specified. The solution of the differential equation can be derived by the finite difference approximation and the multigrid relaxation method.

Figure 6.2 shows a surface example in which the grid size is 64×64. In the figure, black spots represent the interpolated values. It takes 0.4 seconds on an SGI Crimson to generate the surface by the multigrid relaxation method. When the size of the grid is 512×512, its computation time is 5.0 seconds. This shows that the multigrid relaxation method is efficient enough for interactive use.

To control the transition behavior in a metamorphosis, an animator selects a set of points on an image and specifies a transition curve for each point. The point set has no relation with the point set used for specifying features in warp generation. The transition curves give the transition behavior of the selected points over time as shown in Figure 6.3.

Let P be a set of points on the source image I_0 for which transition curves are specified. Let $C(p_k)$ be the transition curve for a point p_k in P. For a given time t, the transition function

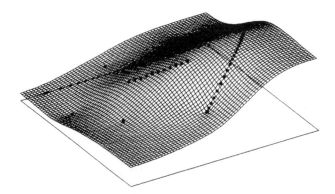

Figure 6.2. *A surface example.*

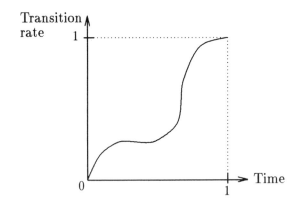

Figure 6.3. *A transition curve.*

$T_0(t)$ should have the transition rate $C(p_k; t)$ at each point p_k in P. With the set of $C(p_k; t)$ as the constraints on values, such a transition function can be derived by the above surface construction method.

The transition function T_1 is specified on the destination image I_1 and should give the transition behavior which is the same with T_0. If a point p on I_0 corresponds to a point q on I_1, the transition rate $T_1(q; t)$ should be the same with $T_0(p; t)$ for each time t. Hence, the transition function $T_1(t)$ can be derived by sampling $T_0(t)$ with the warp function W_1, that is, $T_1(q; t) = T_0(W_1(q); t)$.

The functions in time and positions can be used as transition functions which generate various interesting in-between images. For example, let the transition function T_0 be defined by

$$T_0(x, y; t) = \begin{cases} 2t(1 - x/x_{max}), & \text{if } 0 \leq t \leq \frac{1}{2}, \\ 1 - 2(1 - t)x/x_{max}, & \text{if } \frac{1}{2} < t \leq 1. \end{cases} \qquad (6.12)$$

T_0 generates a sequence of in-between images in which the source image gradually changes to the destination image from left to right. The corresponding transition function T_1 is derived by sampling T_0 with the warp function W_1.

6.5.3 Examples

Figure 6.4 on pages 140–141 shows examples of the transition control (parts (a)–(h) also appear in the plate section between pages 152 and 153). Two face images are given in Figures 6.4(a) and 6.4(b) which are considerably different near the ears. We specify the correspondence of features in Figures 6.4(c) and 6.4(d). Without transition control, the ears and hair are jumbled up in the middle image as shown in Figure 6.4(e). To obtain a better in-between image, we select the parts near the ears in Figure 6.4(f) and assign the transition curve in Figure 6.4(i). The transition curve in Figure 6.4(j) is specified for the line segments in the middle of Figure 6.4(f). Figure 6.4(g) shows the in-between image at time 0.47 where the transition rates are computed from the specified transition curves. In the image, the parts near the ears resemble the first image. Figure 6.4(h) is an in-between image in which a linear function of x-coordinates is used for the procedural transition function. In the image, the man is changed to the woman from the left to the right.

6.6 Conclusions

This chapter summarizes the warp generation and transition control methods in image morphing techniques. Warp generation methods are classified to mesh-based and feature-based approaches, and the basic ideas of the methods are explained. Then, the method proposed by the authors which considers the one-to-one property of warps is summarized in more detail. An effective method for controlling transition behavior proposed by the authors is also described in this chapter.

The most tedious part of image morphing is to establish the correspondence of features between images by an animator. Techniques of computer vision may be employed to automate this task. An edge detection algorithm can provide important features on images, and an image analysis technique may be used to find the correspondence between detected features. One of the most challenging problems in image morphing is to develop an efficient method for specifying features and their correspondence, especially in the morphing between two image sequences.

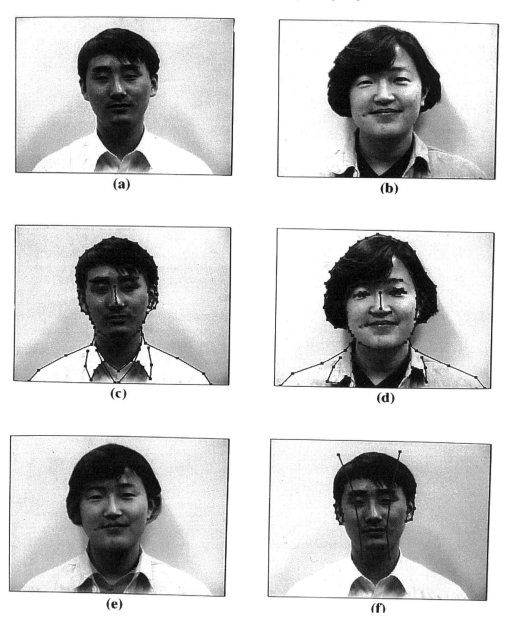

Figure 6.4 (a)–(f).   *Examples of transition control.*

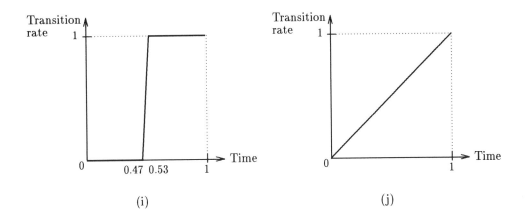

(i)   (j)

Figure 6.4 (g)–(j). *Examples of transition control.*

6.7 References

Beier T. and Neely S. (1992) "Feature-based image metamorphosis", Computer Graphics, Vol. 26, No. 2, pp. 35–42.

Briggs W.L. (1987) "A Multigrid Tutorial", SIAM, Philadelphia.

Gelfand I. and Fomin S. (1963) "Calculus of Variations", Prentice Hall, Englewood Cliffs.

Hall V. (1992) "Introduction to morphing", Manuscript. (Available for anonymous ftp from march.cs.curtin.edu.au(134.7.1.1) in pub/graphics/bibliography/Morph.)

Lee S.Y. (1995) "Image Morphing Using Scattered Feature Interpolations", Ph.D. thesis, KAIST, Taejon, Korea.

Lee S.Y., Chwa K.Y., Hahn J., and Shin S.Y. (1994) "Image morphing using deformable surfaces", In Proceedings of Computer Animation '94, Geneva, Switzerland, IEEE Computer Society Press, pp. 31–39.

Litwinowicz P. and Williams, L. (1994) "Animating Images with Drawings", In SIGGRAPH 94 Conference Proceedings, ACM Press, New York, pp. 409–412.

Morrison M. (1993) ''The Magic of Image Processing'', SAMS Publishing.

Nishita T., Fujii T. and Nakamae, E. (1993) ''Metamorphosis using Bézier Clipping'', In Proceedings of the First Pacific Conference on Computer Graphics and Applications, Seoul, Korea, World Scientific Publishing Co., Singapore, pp. 162–173.

Press W.H., Teukolsky S.A., Vetterling, W.T., and Flannery, B.P. (1992) ''Numerical Recipes in C'', Cambridge University Press, Cambridge, second edition.

Ruprecht D. and Müller H. (1992) ''Image Warping with Scattered Data Interpolation Methods'', Research Report 443, Fachbereich Informätik der Universitat Dortmund, 44221 Dortmund, Germany.

Terzopoulos D. (1986) ''Regularization of Inverse Visual Problems Involving Discontinuities'', IEEE Transaction on Pattern Analysis and Machine Intelligence, Vol. 8, No. 4, pp. 413–424.

Wolberg G. (1990) ''Digital Image Warping'', IEEE Computer Society Press, Los Alamitos.

CHAPTER 7

Visually Guided Animation

A. Pentland, I. Essa, T. Darrell, A. Azarbayejani and S. Sclaroff
The Media Laboratory, Massachusetts Institute of Technology

Abstract
This chapter describes methods to take classic film characters, or video of current-day personalities, and produce computer models and animations of them by automatic analysis of the video or film footage. In this chapter we survey our progress toward producing such automatic modeling and animation systems.

7.1 Introduction

Perhaps the major difficulty in both modeling and animation is the sheer complexity of natural shapes and movement. This complexity can be partially addressed by the use of sophisticated physical models to simulate real world action and interaction. However for many processes it is either too expensive to simulate every detail, or we do not fully understand the underlying physical situation well enough to make an accurate simulation.

These difficulties are particularly acute for animation of human figures. For while we may know the static, passive characteristics of the muscles, there is very little information on the spatial and temporal patterning of human muscle action. Moreover, we know almost nothing about the control and guidance strategies used by people. Consequently, today's best human animation employs very sophisticated geometric and physical models, but only primitive models of muscle control.

Lack of a good, high-level control model is also the limiting factor in production of extended animations. The best animations are still produced by artists who carefully craft keyframes, a time-consuming and laborious process. Even though the key-frame process does not require an explicit control model, it is likely that such a model would help by providing the artist with the right animation "control knobs".

These problems have motivated our research group to take another approach to the problem. Our group is working on automatic animation: driving a computer animation by analyzing images of an actor or situation. We are interested in being able to take classic film characters, or current-day events, and produce computer models and animations of them by automatic analysis of the video or film footage.

The goal of this chapter is to review our work toward automatic animation. We will make no attempt to fully explain the technical underpinnings of our work or to provide full references to the literature; these details are available in referenced articles.

The plan for the first half of this chapter is to illustrate the estimation techniques we have developed for accurate tracking of humans. Note that each technique is aimed at a specific kind of detail and as we go on we will show how we incorporate newer ideas to extract additional detail. Each level of additional detail changes the scope of applications envisioned for extracting human movements.

1. We will start by illustrating our Kalman filter techniques for accurately tracking people.
2. We will then show how by including object dynamics in the estimation process, it is possible to obtain accurate computer models of non-rigid biological motion.
3. If we further include models of muscle control in the estimation process, it becomes possible to obtain accurate estimates of the underlying muscle activations.

Modeling geometry, motion, and muscle control requires making a large number of accurate measurements of image motion. This is because the situations we wish to model have a large number of degrees of freedom. Consequently, such detailed modeling is not currently possible in real-time systems without special hardware.

However in many situations we know in advance that there are a relatively small set of predetermined actions, or setting a relatively small number of "control knobs", that we care about. This is particularly characteristic of interactive systems, which typically have a limited repertoire of behaviors and reactions. In such systems there are relatively few independent geometric parameters, each of which may have a large degree of temporal variation. We have found that it is generally possible to set these parameters using simple, real-time visual measurements, making possible real-time processing using only standard computer workstations. The second half of this paper will focus on the real-time, interactive systems we have built using this methodology.

7.2 Measurement from images

Ideally, we would like to have a real-time system that can recover the shape and motion of objects in a robust and flexible manner. The desire for real-time operation and arbitrary-length sequences strongly favors recursive techniques that integrate information from each new frame with prior accumulated information. The requirement of robustness suggests techniques that explicitly account for measurement noise and modeling uncertainty. These are both strengths of the extended Kalman filter (EKF), which has been the subject of much structure and motion estimation research.

Our work toward recovering geometry and motion, therefore, has been based on use of the EKF. The fundamental notions underlying this class of EKF estimators are the following:

1. For each new image, measure the position or movement of image features.
2. These position or movement measurements are then related back to 3-D coordinates and motions by inverting the standard image projection equations.
3. Because this inversion is underconstrained and noisy, it is necessary to average measurements over time (i.e. to use an EKF).

Because of the particular type of averaging used in the EKF, it is possible to avoid any delay or lag in the system (Friedmann et al. 1992). This makes it possible to build interactive systems that feel much more "real".

We will illustrate the power of the EKF approach by two examples: first, using video analysis to track a person's head as accurately as a Polhemus sensor (but without the use of sensors or markers), and second, creating an accurate model of the scene being observed. Additional detail can be found in Azarbayejani et al. (1993a, 1993b).

7.2.1 Example: tracking objects

In this first example, a person's head was tracked using both the vision algorithm and the Polhemus magnetic sensor (see Chapter 2) simultaneously. Figure 7.1 shows the vision and Polhemus measurements after an absolute orientation was performed to align the estimates properly. The Root Mean Square (RMS) difference in translation is 1.25 cm and the RMS difference in rotation is 1.5 degrees. This accuracy is equal to the observed accuracy of the Polhemus sensor, indicating that the vision estimate is as accurate as the Polhemus sensor, if not better.

In the second example, we extracted a 3-D model from a few second video clip (at 30 frames per second) of a person moving around in front of a camera. Figure 7.2(a) shows one frame of the original digitized video. Features are extracted on the face and tracked through the whole sequence (Figure 7.2(b)). A cylindrical shape of a face is fitted to these feature points and a hat is placed over it (Figure 7.2(c)). Figure 7.2(d) shows a synthesized frame of the sequence where a "virtual" hat has been placed on top of the person's head.

7.2.2 Example: modeling geometry

In this example, we extracted a 3-D model from a 20-second video clip of a walk-around outside the Media Laboratory at MIT. Figure 7.3(a) shows two frames of the original

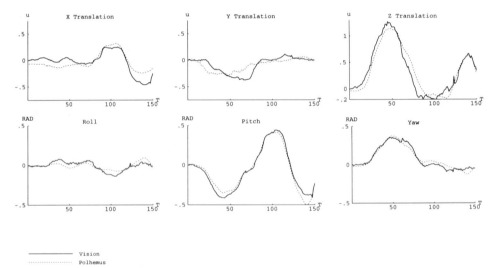

Figure 7.1. *Head tracking. Top: Head being tracked. Graphs: Vision and Polhemus estimates of head position. Much of the observed error is known to be due to Polhemus error. RMS differences are 1.25 cm and 1.5 degrees.*

digitized video. The visible faces of the building include two outside walls, an overhang, and two lower walls under the overhang.

Figure 7.3(b) shows the twenty corner-like features on the building that were tracked automatically. These image feature positions are the input to our extended Kalman filter structure/motion recovery algorithm.

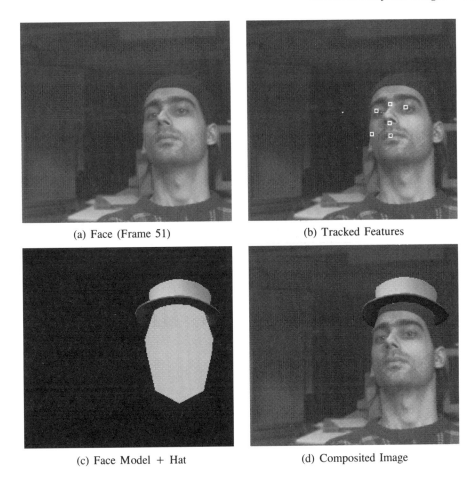

(a) Face (Frame 51)

(b) Tracked Features

(c) Face Model + Hat

(d) Composited Image

Figure 7.2. *Tracking head movement and extracting 3-D shape of the head. Adding a "virtual" hat to the image.*

The recovered 3-D locations of these feature points were then used to compute 3-D polygons for the building surfaces visible in the scene, shown in Figure 7.3(c). The 2-D vertices of the polygons that define each face were manually identified in one video frame and the recovered camera position for that frame is used to back-project the 2-D vertices on to the appropriate 3-D plane, resulting in 3-D vertices for the polygons in scene coordinates.

Texture maps for each polygon were built up by back-projecting twenty-five video frames. Averaging, weighted by the size of the UV projection, was used to combine the texture maps. Figure 7.3(d) shows the final graphical representation of the building.

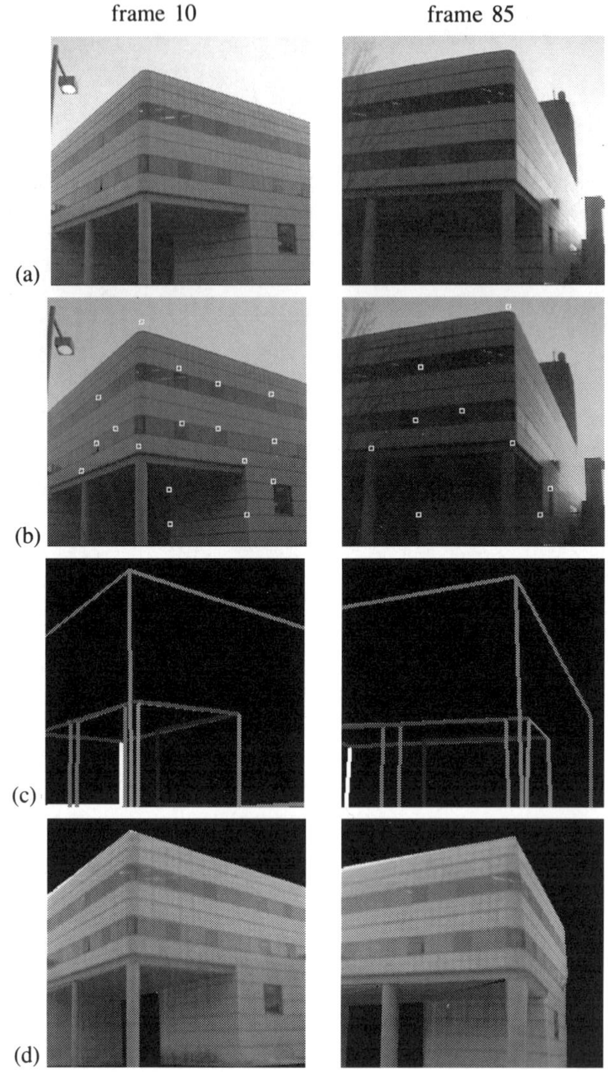

frame 10   frame 85

Figure 7.3. *(a) Original video. (b) The features are tracked in the video sequence using normalized correlation. Features are added and deleted as necessary. (c) 3-D polygons are obtained by segmenting a 2-D image and back-projecting the vertices on to a 3-D plane. The plane for each polygon is computed from the recovered 3-D points corresponding to image features in the 2-D polygon. (d) Texture maps are obtained by projecting the video on to the 3-D polygons to obtain the final model. Note that since multiple frames are used to obtain the texture maps, the lamp post passing in front of the building between frames 10 and 35 is filtered out of texture map.*

7.3 Physical modeling

The EKF can be made more accurate by adding a detailed physical model to help it average measurements in a more physically-meaningful manner. Physical modeling is by now a well-known approach in the computer vision literature; we make use of a variant known as modal analysis (Pentland and Williams 1989, Pentland and Sclaroff 1991, Sclaroff and Pentland 1991, Essa et al 1992). The advantage of using this method is that it allows stable, closed-form solutions, and permits much more efficient physical simulation. For additional details see Sclaroff et al. (1992) and Sclaroff and Pentland (1993).

7.3.1 Recovering shapes and models

The EKF methods of the previous section allow a very sparse recovery of the shape of the object. We can use these physically-based modeling techniques, described in detail in Pentland and Williams (1989), Pentland and Sclaroff (1991), Sclaroff and Pentland (1991), Essa et al (1992), to fit 3-D volumetric models to such point data.

This fitting process is illustrated in Figure 7.4. This figure shows the range data gathered from a 360 degree laser rangefinder built by CYBERWARE corporation. The 3-D model for the head was recovered using our modal shape recovery method and a displacement map

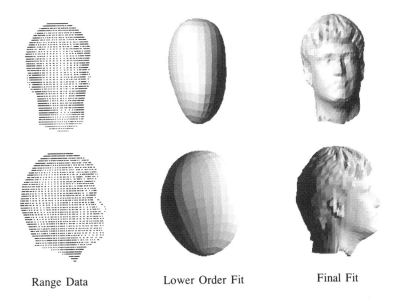

Range Data   Lower Order Fit   Final Fit

Figure 7.4. *Recovery of heads using range data.*

computed and applied to get the fine details (Pentland and Sclaroff 1991, Sclaroff and Pentland 1991). The final recovered model is illustrated in Figure 7.5, which shows two frames from a physically-based animation in which a jello-like head is struck with a wooden mallet.

7.3.2   Tracking nonrigid shapes

In the previous sections we described using the EKF for estimation of static shape and object motion. For nonrigid motion, however, it is necessary to also consider the elastic dynamic properties of the body and of the data measurements. We can do this by incorporating a physical model of the observed object into our extended Kalman filter.

We will describe this work with the aid of an example of tracking a human arm and a whole articulated figure. Additional detail can be found in Pentland and Horowitz (1991) and Pentland (1993).

Figure 7.6 shows an example of tracking an arm. The 3-D shape and motion of a flexing bicep was tracked over time using the image contours extracted from the images. A physical model with the extended Kalman filter is then used to estimate the 3-D rigid and nonrigid motion of the arm and to predict the arm's shape, rotation, and position at the next time step. This prediction uses the fitting process described above. The resulting rigid and nonrigid motions are shown by the 3-D wireframe model overlayed on the original images in Figure 7.6.

Figure 7.7 illustrates an example of using this technique to track an articulated object. This figure shows three frames from a twelve image sequence of a well-known tin woodsman caught in the act of jumping. Despite the limited range of motion, this example is a difficult one because of pronounced highlights on thighs and other parts of the body. The estimated motions for this sequence are illustrated by the bottom row of Figure 7.7. As can

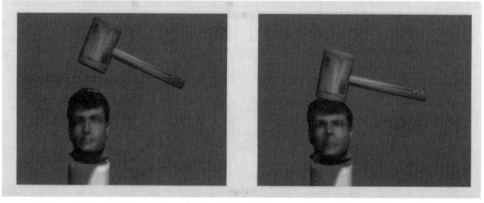

Figure 7.5. *A deformation of a head from Cyberware data, being hit by a mallet.*

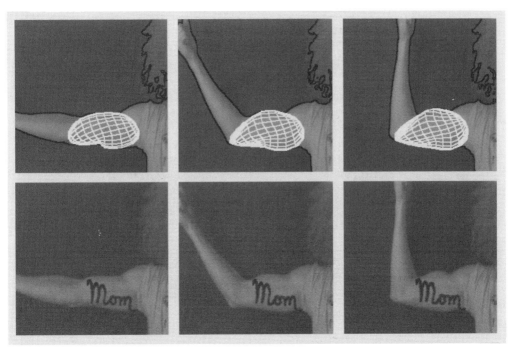

Figure 7.6. *Nonrigid tracking of a flexing arm from image contours found by taking zero crossings in the thresholded image. The resulting model of the moving bicep model was used to apply an artificial tattoo.*

be seen by comparing the 3-D motion of the model with that in the original image, the resulting tracking is reasonably accurate.

7.4 Control models for animation

By incorporating physical models into the EKF, we can obtain accurate estimates of even nonrigid motion. However the descriptions we obtain in this manner are still passive, that is, they do not tell us about muscle activations, but only about the resulting movement and deformation. To obtain estimates of the muscle activations, it is necessary to augment the EKF with a control model, as shown in Figure 7.8. In this figure, the lower loop is the EKF (including the physical model) and the upper loop is the control loop. The output of this second control estimation process is the muscle activations required to account for the observed motion and deformation (Essa and Pentland 1994).

We have applied this methodology to the problem of measuring facial muscle activations. Because facial motion is so complex, the input must be very detailed and dense.

Figure 7.7. *Three frames from an image sequence showing tracking of a jumping man.*

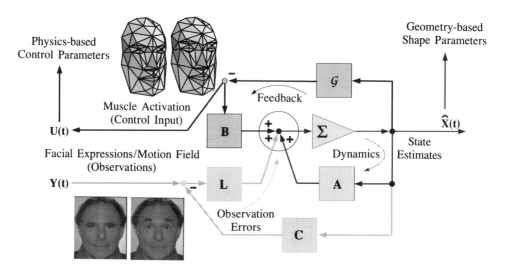

Figure 7.8. *Block diagram of the control-theoretic approach. Showing the estimation and correction loop (bottom), the dynamics loop (right side), and the feedback loop (top).*

Figure 2.1 The fire and ice scene from Peter Gabriel's music video "Steam". Courtesy Homer & Associates.

Figure 2.7 Weldon Pond, a Windlight Studios production for CBS. Courtesy CBS Inc.

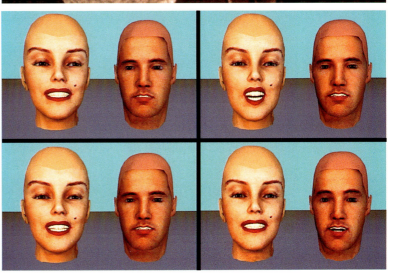

Figure 8.11 Texture mapping of animated faces.

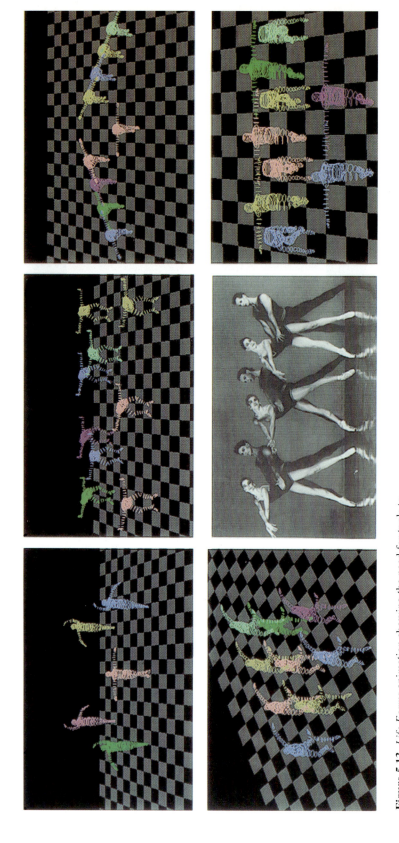

Figure 5.13 *Life Forms* animation showing the need for tools to support movement patterns for a group of dancers with repeated movement sequences. From "D Symphonies" (1995), by the Miami City Ballet (Miami). Photo by Louis Jay.

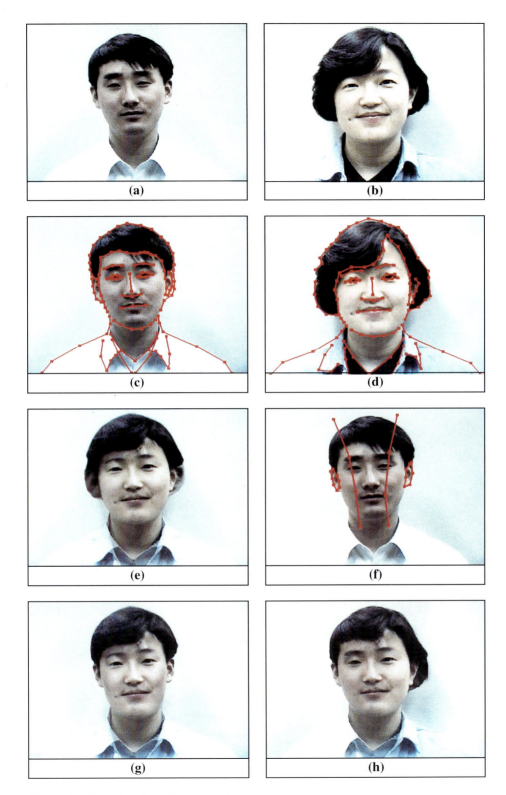

Figure 6.4 Examples of transition control.

Figure 9.11 Synthetic actress with hairstyle.

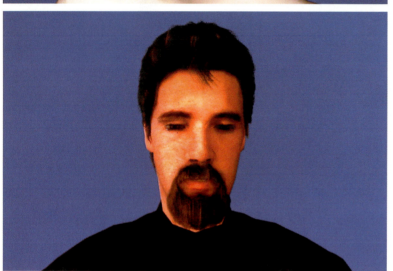

Figure 9.12 Beards and mustaches.

Figure 11.6 Biomechanical model for walking from the film *Still Walking*.

Consequently we use as input, pixel-by-pixel measurements of surface motion (optical flow) as input measurements. These dense motion measurements are then coupled to a physically-based face model and to a muscle control model. The outputs of this modeling process are detailed records of both the displacement of each point on the facial surface, and the muscle control required to produce the observed facial motion. The recovered and muscle control patterns can be used to recognize facial expressions, animate other models, or composed to make new combination expressions.

The advantage of this approach over a priori facial modeling is that we can observe the complex muscle coarticulation patterns that are characteristic of real human expressions. For instance, it has been remarked that a major difference between real smiles and forced or faked smiles is motion near the corner of the eye. We have been able to observe and quantify the relative timing and amplitude of this near-eye motion using our system. Now we will briefly discuss the important aspects of this parameterization. For additional detail see Essa and Pentland (1994).

7.4.1   Spatial patterning

To illustrate that the new parameters for facial expressions are more spatially detailed than FACS, the Facial Action Coding System, comparisons of the expressions of raising eyebrow and smile produced by standard FACS-like muscle activations and our visually extracted muscle activations are shown in Figure 7.9 and Figure 7.10.

The top row of Figure 7.9 shows AU2 (''Raising Eyebrow'') from the FACS model and the linear actuation profile of the corresponding geometric control points. This is the type of spatial-temporal patterning commonly used in computer graphics animation. The bottom row of Figure 7.9 shows the observed motion of these control points for the expression of raising eyebrow by Paul Ekman. This plot was achieved by mapping the motion onto the FACS model and the actuations of the control points measured. As can be seen, the observed pattern of deformation is very different from that assumed in the standard implementation of FACS. There is a wide distribution of motion through all the control points, and the temporal patterning of the deformation is far from linear. It appears, very roughly, to have a quick linear rise, then a slower linear rise and then a constant level (i.e., may be approximated as piece-wise linear).

7.4.2   Temporal patterning

Figure 7.11 shows plots of facial muscle actuations for the smile and eyebrow raising expressions. In this figure the 24 face muscles were combined into seven local groups for purposes of illustration. As can be seen, even the simplest expressions require multiple muscle actuations.

Expression	Magnitude of Control Point Deformation
AU2	
Raising Eyebrow	

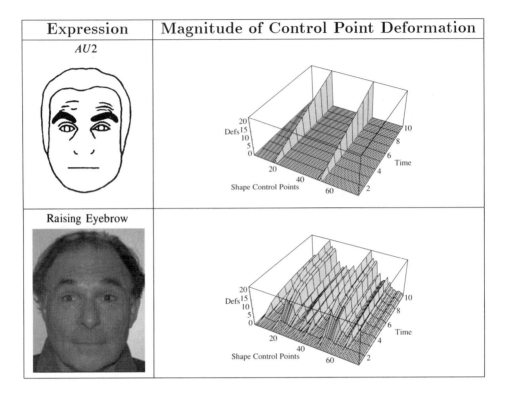

Figure 7.9.   *FACS/CANDIDE deformation vs. observed deformation for the Raising Eyebrow expression. Surface plots (top) show deformation over time for FACS actions AU2, and (bottom) for an actual video sequence of raising eyebrows.*

Of particular interest is the temporal patterning of the muscle actuations. We have fit exponential curves to the activation and release portions of the muscle actuation profile to suggest the type of rise and decay seen in Electro Mio Graphy (EMG) studies of muscles. From this data we suggest that the relaxation phase of muscle actuation is mostly due to passive stretching of the muscles by residual stress in the skin.

Note that Figure 7.11(b) also shows a second, delayed actuation of muscle group 7 about three frames after the peak of muscle group 1. This example illustrates that coarticulation effects can be observed by our system, and that they occur even in quite simple expressions. By using these observed temporal patterns of muscle activation, rather than simple linear ramps, more realistic computer animations can be produced.

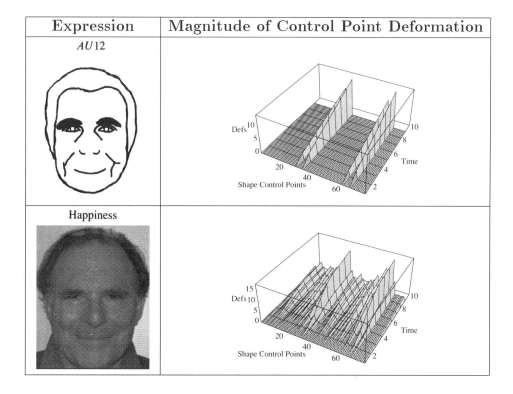

Expression	Magnitude of Control Point Deformation
*AU*12	
Happiness	

Figure 7.10. *FACS/CANDIDE deformation vs. observed deformation for the Happiness expression. Surface plots (top) show deformation over time for FACS actions AU12, and (bottom) for an actual video sequence of happiness.*

7.5   Interactive video environments

In the first half of this chapter we surveyed our work on detailed measurement of shape, behavior, and muscle activation. In the remainder of this chapter we will concern ourselves with real-time interactive tracking. Interactive tracking typically involves relatively few parameters, e.g., sequencing a set of predetermined movements, or control knobs. That is, there are often relatively few independent geometric parameters, each of which may have a large amount of temporal variation. Consequently, we can use fairly simple visual measurements to establish the geometric parameters, but we would like to do this very quickly – in real time if at all possible.

We have constructed a number of real-time systems that we refer to as interactive video environments (IVE). The first of these systems was called ALIVE (Artificial Life Interactive

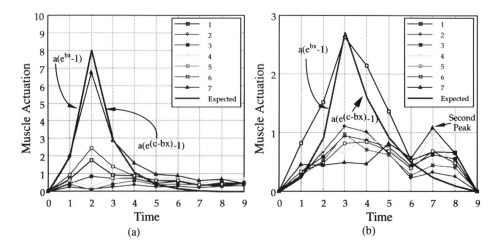

Figure 7.11. *Muscle actuations over time of the seven main muscle groups modeled for the expressions of raising brow and smiling – lip motion. The plots (a) and (b) show actuation over time for the seven muscle groups.*

Video Environment) system, which was demonstrated to over 500 participants at SIGGRAPH 1993 (Maes et al. 1994). This system used active, attention-driven vision to allow simulated ''artificial life'' agents to interact with real people through a video screen. In this environment the agents and the user can ''see'' each other – users can see the agents on the video screen, and the agents can see users through a computer vision system. An image of the user appears on the video screen, effecting a type of ''magic mirror'', in which users see themselves in a different world through the use of a simulated mirror (Figure 7.12).

Developing vision routines for such an interactive system offers several challenges relative to traditional image processing, and in particular calls for active/situated vision techniques. We have used a behavior-based approach to model both the action selection of the agents and their perception of the user. This has allowed us to use a large number of specialized image processing modules while still employing only limited processing power. In the following sections we will discuss some of the issues involved in constructing such a visually-guided interactive environment.

7.5.1 Finding the user

Before other processing can occur, the vision system must isolate the figure of the user from the background (and from other users, if present). Our approach is to use low-level image processing techniques to detect differences in the scene, and to use connected-components analysis routines to extract objects.

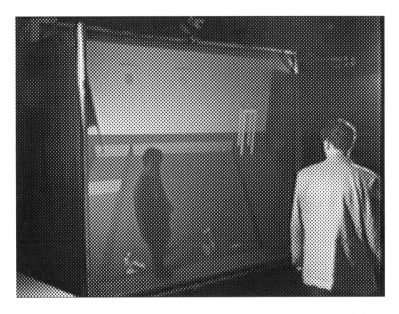

Figure 7.12. *The magic mirror metaphor: the user sees his/her image surrounded by autonomous agents.*

The simplest method of detecting differences is to constrain the background to be a known color, and detect instances of that hue in the input images. Several commercial video image processing boards are available that can automatically isolate figure/ground and perform video compositing based on this approach. A slightly more sophisticated approach is to allow the background to be an arbitrary, but static, pattern. Mean and variance information about the background pattern are computed using samples collected over a specified time-window. Using these statistics to determine thresholds for pixel class membership, accurate figure-ground membership can be determined, as illustrated in Figure 7.13.

7.5.2   Scene projection and calibration

Once the figure of the user has been isolated from the background, we compute its rough location in the world. If we assume the user is indeed sitting or standing on the ground plane, and we know the calibration of the camera, then we can compute the location of the bounding box in 3-D, as illustrated by Figure 7.14.

Establishing the calibration of a camera is a well-studied problem, and several classical techniques are available to solve it in certain broad cases. Typically these methods model the

Figure 7.13. *Binary silhouettes of users after figure-ground processing. Task-dependent vision routines to find hands and pose information use this representation as input.*

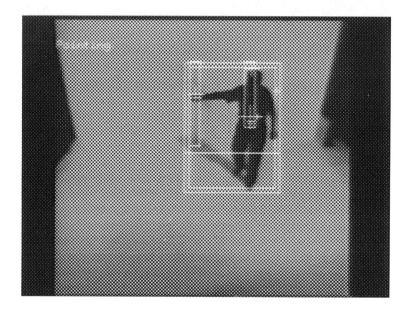

Figure 7.14. *The vision system works off a silhouette of the user. It computes a range of features including the bounding box, which is used to project the user's location in 3-D.*

camera optics as a pinhole perspective optical system, and establish its parameters by matching known 3-D points with their 2-D projection.

Knowledge of the camera geometry allows us to project a ray from the camera through the 2-D projection of the bottom of the bounding box of the user (Figure 7.14 shows the bounding box as found in a real image, in this case the user is at the "back" of the virtual world, i.e., far from the mirror). Since the user is on the ground plane, the intersection of the projected ray and the ground plane will establish the 3-D location of the user's base. The 2-D dimensions of the user's bounding box and its base location in 3-D constitute the low-level information about the user that is continuously computed and made available to all agents in the computer graphics world.

7.5.3   Hand tracking

One of the most salient cues used by the agents in our world is the location of the user's hands. We have implemented a hand search algorithm that uses spatial search patterns to localize hands in the input images. We make heavy use of the domain constraints outlined above, e.g. that people are (mostly) oriented in a fronto-parallel plane with respect to the camera. Figure 7.14 also illustrates the output of the hand recognition system on a real image.

The hand-tracking algorithm we have developed comprises several different context-dependent search heuristics. In general, a normalized correlation search is done along the sides of the upper-torso bounding box to find a strong horizontal edge. The upper-torso bounding box is defined in such a way that it discounts to some degree the effect of shadows and feet in the horizontal dimension: it takes the vertical dimensions from the real bounding box and computes horizontal dimensions from the top 66% of the user's image.

Depending on the current context, different search windows and search patterns are used. The main contextual cue is the size of the bounding box, which provides a rough estimate of overall pose. If the box is narrow, we infer that the user's hands are at his or her side, and we do not attempt to find them in the silhouette. In this case we return the hand position to be located on the side of the bounding box, at the same relative height along the bounding box as it was last reliably seen.

7.5.4   Gesture interpretation

Hands are relevant to the agents in the world both for their absolute position, and for whether they are performing characteristic gesture patterns. We use simple low-level recognition strategies to detect these characteristic patterns.

Our model of gestures is highly reduced, and comprises two possible spatio-temporal hand patterns: pointing and waving. Each is defined in terms of the 2-D motion of the location of the hand in the image plane. Pointing requires a particular relative hand location (an extended arm), and a steady position over time. Waving requires a predominantly side-to-side motion of the hand, while the user is otherwise stationary. These are special cases of our more general work on gesture recognition, which builds space and time separable template patterns for recognition (Darrell and Pentland 1993). However this work assumed a high-resolution image of the object performing the gesture. As we have as yet no high-resolution camera to provide a foveated image of the hands (or face) of the user, we presently only model gesture as change in position (or lack thereof) over time.

Using this training we are able to use temporal context to actively focus our visual routines, thus allowing us to recognize a large class of hand gestures. Recently we have used this approach to recognize hundreds of sentences in American Sign Language (ASL), using a base vocabulary of 40 word gestures (Starner and Pentland 1994).

7.5.5   Facial animation

Because face models have a large number of degrees of freedom, facial modeling requires dense, detailed geometric measurements in both space and time. Currently such dense measurement is both computationally expensive and noisy; consequently it is more suitable to off-line analysis of discrete facial movements rather than real-time analysis of extended facial action.

Facial animation, in contrast, typically involves temporally sequencing between a fixed set of predefined facial actions. For instance, an animation sequence might consist of the lip movements associated with speech plus a few eye motions plus eyeblinks and eyebrow raises. More details may be found in Chapter 8.

Because the full range of facial motion is typically not present in any particular animation sequence, the number of degrees of freedom required for the animation is limited. One can think of the animation as having a fixed, relatively small set of "control knobs", one for each type of motion, and then producing the animation by moving these control knobs appropriately. As described in the previous sections, the muscle parameters associated with these control knobs are determined by the off-line modeling of each individual type of facial action.

The major question, of course, is when and how much to move each control knob (face control parameter). In our system the setting of each muscle control parameter is determined using sparse, real-time geometric measurements from video sequences. One way to obtain these measurements would be to locate landmarks on the face, and then to adjust the control parameters appropriately. The difficulty with this approach is first that landmarks are difficult to locate reliably and precisely, and second that there are no good landmarks on the cheek, forehead, or eyeball.

An alternative method is to teach the system how the person's face looks for a variety of control parameter settings, and then to measure how similar the person's current appearance is to each of these known settings. We have found that a fast, reliable similarity metric is the correlation of stored 2-D intensity templates with the new data. We take views corresponding to each trained expression for which we have obtained detailed force and timing information using the method outlined above. By constraining the space of expressions to be recognized, we can match/recognize existing expressions rather than derive new force controls for the input video, and dramatically improve the speed of the system.

When the input image matches one of the trained examples, the corresponding previously stored motor controls are actuated in the facial model. If there is no match between the image and the existing expressions, an interpolated motor actuation is generated based on a weighted combination of expressions. The mapping from vision scores to motor controls is performed using piecewise linear interpolation implemented using a Radial Basis Function (RBF) network. (We have also implemented a Gaussian RBF and obtained equivalent results.)

The RBF training process associates the set of view scores with the facial state, e.g. the motor control parameters for the corresponding expression. If we train views using the entire face as a template, the appearance of the entire face helps determine the facial state. This provides for increased accuracy, but the generated control parameters are restricted to lie in the convex hull of the examples. View templates that correspond to parts of the face are often more robust and accurate than full-face templates, especially when several expressions are trained. This allows local changes in the face, if any, to have a local effect in the interpolation.

For each incoming frame of video, all of these 2-D templates are matched against the image, and the peak normalized correlation score is recorded. Note that the matching process can be made more efficient by limiting the search area to near where we last saw the eye, mouth, etc.

Figure 7.15 illustrates an example of real-time face animation using this system. Across the top, labeled (a), are five video images of a user making an expression. Each frame of video is then matched against all of the templates (eye, mouth, etc), and normalized correlation scores are measured. A plot of the normalized correlation score for each template is shown in (b). These scores are then converted to state estimates and fed into the muscle control loop, to produce the muscle control parameters shown in (c). Five images from the resulting animation sequence are shown in (d). Some snapshots of the working system are shown in Figure 7.16. Also shown are bounding boxes which define the templates. For additional details, see Essa et al. (1994) and Darrell and Pentland (1993).

7.6   Conclusion

We have developed a range of automatic modeling and animation tools. These tools allow users to produce accurate models and animations of situations pictured in either film or video. Technical details are contained in the following references; these papers and software implementing some of these algorithms are available by anonymous FTP from whitechapel. media.mit.edu, or by sending email to the authors.

7.7   Acknowledgments

The authors would like to thank Thad Starner, Brad Horowitz, Martin Friedmann, Pattie Maes, Bruce Blumberg, and Ken Russell.

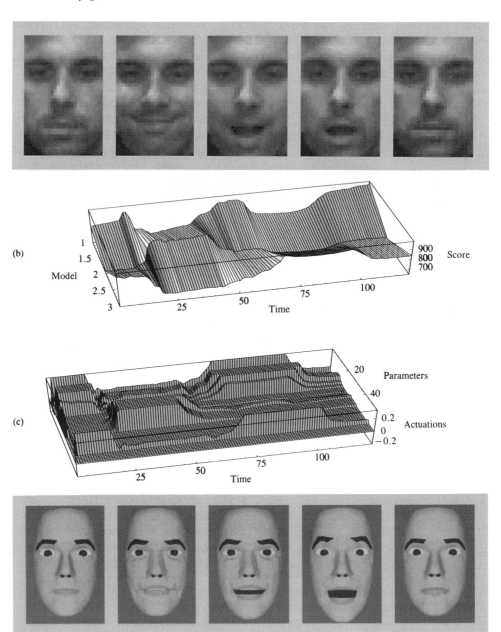

Figure 7.15.   *(a) Face images used as input, (b) normalized correlation scores for each 2-D template, (c) resulting muscle control parameters, (d) images from the resulting tracking of facial expressions.*

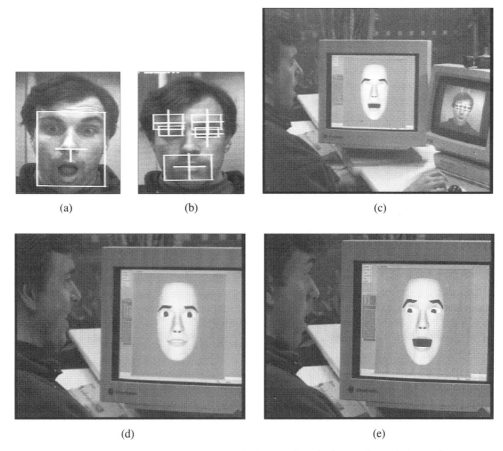

(a)   (b)   (c)

(d)   (e)

Figure 7.16. *(a) Face with single template, (b) face with multiple templates, (c) complete system tracking eyes, mouth, eyebrows, (d) tracking a smile and (e) a surprise expression.*

7.8 References

Azarbayejani A., Starner T., Horowitz B. and Pentland A. (1993a) "Visually Controlled Graphics", IEEE Trans. Pattern Analysis and Machine Vision, special issue of computer graphics and computer vision, Vol. 15, No. 6, pp. 602–604.

Azarbayejani A., Horowitz B. and Pentland A. (1993b) "Recursive Estimation of Structure and Motion using the Relative Orientation Constraint", IEEE Conference on Vision and Pattern Recognition, New York, June. Also available as: M.I.T. Perceptual Computing Technical Report No. 243.

Darrell T. and Pentland A. (1993) "Space–Time Gestures", Proc. IEEE Conf. on Computer Vision and Pattern Recognition, New York, June.

Essa I., Sclaroff S. and Pentland A. (1992) "A Unified Approach for Physical and Geometric Modeling", Computer Graphics Forum, Vol. 2, No. 3, pp. 129–138. also appears: Eurographics, Cambridge, England, Sept 7–11.

Essa I., Darrell T. and Pentland A. (1994) ''Modeling and Interactive Animation of Facial Expressions using Vision'', IEEE Conf. Computer Vision and Pattern Recognition, Seattle, WA, June. Also available as: M.I.T. Perceptual Computing Technical Report No. 256.

Essa I. and Pentland A. (1994) ''A Vision System for Observing and Extracting Facial Action Parameters'', IEEE Conf. Computer Vision and Pattern Recognition, pp. 76–83.

Friedmann M., Starner T. and Pentland A. (1992) ''Synchronization in Virtual Realities'', Presence: Teleoperators and Virtual Environments, Vol. 1, No. 1, pp. 139–144.

Maes P., Darrell, T., Blumberg B. and Pentland, A. (1994) ''The ALIVE System: Full-body Interaction with Animated Autonomous Agents'', SIGGRAPH-93 Tomorrow's Realities Track, M.I.T. Media Laboratory Perceptual Computing Technical Report No. 257, January.

Pentland A. (1993) ''Modal Descriptions for Recognition and Tracking'', IEICE Trans. Information and Systems, Vol. j76-D-II, No. 8, 1489–1496.

Pentland A. and Horowitz B. (1991) ''Recovery of Non-Rigid Motion and Structure'', IEEE Trans. Pattern Analysis and Machine Intelligence, Vol. 13, No. 7, pp. 730–742.

Pentland A. and Sclaroff S. (1991) ''Closed-Form Solutions For Physically Based Shape Modeling and Recognition'', IEEE Trans. Pattern Analysis and Machine Intelligence, Vol. 13, No. 7, pp. 715–730.

Pentland A. and Williams J. (1989) ''Good Vibrations: Modal Dynamics for Graphics and Animation'', ACM Computer Graphics, Vol. 23, No. 4, pp. 215–222.

Sclaroff S. and Pentland A. (1991) ''Generalized Implicit Functions for Computer Graphics'', ACM Computer Graphics, Vol. 25, No. 2, pp. 247–250.

Sclaroff S. and Pentland A. (1993) ''A Modal Framework for Correspondence and Recognition'', Int'l Conference on Computer Vision, Berlin, Germany, May 1993. Also available as: M.I.T. Perceptual Computing Technical Report No. 201.

Sclaroff S., Essa I. and Pentland A. (1992) ''Vision-Based Animation: Applications of a Unified Approach for Physical and Geometric Modeling'', Eurographics Workshop on Physically-Based Modeling, Cambridge, England, Aug 31.

Starner T. and Pentland A. (1995) ''Real-time Reading of American Sign Language'', Int'l Symposium on Computer Vision, pp. 265–270, Miami, FL, Nov. 22–25.

CHAPTER 8

Human Facial Animation

Prem Kalra
MIRAlab, University of Geneva

Abstract

The face plays a very important role in human communication. We consciously or even at times unconsciously use the visual cues from faces to understand people's intentions. The communicative and visual sensory power of the face may be well exploited today using computers. Facial communication can definitely offer a new dimension for the man–machine interaction and interface. This, however, demands creation of a 3-D virtual face which can exhibit emotions, can speak, react and communicate. To realize this, there are several issues to be addressed. At the lowest level, one needs to establish the representation and construction of a face for its conformity and deformability. Subsequently, it requires a model to generate convincing movements, encapsulating different levels of abstractions. It may also involve the mode and means for specifying and controlling the facial motion. In this chapter, some of these issues have been considered, and treated for the design and development of our prototype facial animation system.

8.1 Introduction

A face holds numerous clues to identification, personality, emotions, aesthetic, race, etc. It is the most communicative component of the human figure. People tend to read the subtle variations in a face to infer or draw perceptions. The complexities of face modeling, dynamics and behavior provide a challenge for research in the computer graphics world. Furthermore, faces are interesting and challenging because of our everyday familiarity with faces and facial expressions. Recognizing faces and understanding facial expressions are

among the earliest skills we as human beings develop (Parke 1991). We have a very highly developed ability to distinguish and recognize very subtle differences in facial expressions. This dexterity imposes a further challenge for those who want to model and synthesize the face's characteristics.

The computer generation of faces has attracted a number of recent investigations and applications: speech synthesis for the deaf and hard of hearing, computer synthetic facial surgery, low bandwidth speech phones, video telepresence, models for the analysis of facial expressions of non-verbal communication by psychologists, and criminal investigations. The applications cover a large range of disciplines from entertainment to medicine and demonstrate the versatility and ubiquitous nature of the face. The common challenge, however, has been to develop facial models that not only look real but which are also capable of synthesizing the various nuances of facial motions quickly and convincingly.

The task of human face modeling and animation is very complex as its understanding comes only from a complete knowledge of what happens in reality. The difficulties are due to not only the complex physical structure of the human face but also the dynamics that are involved as well as psychological and behavioral aspects. The nature of the problem therefore demands a multi-disciplinary approach that exploits specialized knowledge about the psychology of human expressions, the anatomy of facial muscle structures, the histology of facial tissues, the physics of deformations, the geometry of its shape and the realism of graphical visualization.

Many factors prompted the continuous research in facial modeling and animation: the global interest in these models, their importance and relevance, underlying problems, inter-disciplinary research strategies, and the numerous and varied applications. This chapter provides the current state of the art in facial animation systems, approaches and techniques, and presents the development of our approach toward facial modeling, animation and control, rendering and interaction.

8.2 Background

Though natural and realistic facial animation is a difficult task, there have been many successful research efforts in this area. This section provides a brief review of the main existing methods for facial animation with their salient characteristics. In order to address the major issues involved in the development of a facial animation system, three questions need to be answered: HOW to move, WHAT to move and WHEN to move (Patel 1992). The first part refers to the deformation mechanism employed to distort the facial mesh, the second part instructs the need for a specification or notation scheme to decide what different regions of a face should move, and finally the last part shows the necessity of temporal control and synchronization for the different parts moving simultaneously.

8.2.1 Basic facial animation models

Various models of creating movement and/or deforming a face have been developed over the years. Some of them are based merely on the production of believable visual effects and do not use physical and structural laws, and some are based on the physical structure of the face and use the anatomical fact that a face is deformed as a result of muscular contractions. The following sections present the different classes of existing models and the approaches used for deforming a face.

Interpolation
One of the earliest approaches for animating faces is the use of interpolation of a few expressive poses of a face. Parke (1972) used this method and demonstrated the viability of this approach for producing convincing animation. The basic idea is very simple, and is similar to shape or key frame interpolation (see Section 1.3). This involves collection of geometric data describing the face in different poses of expression. An interpolation parameter then provides the change of the face from one pose to another as a function of time. The range of expressions obtained is, however, restricted. In addition, each pose needs an explicit data set, which amounts to handling of large data for creating a reasonable length of animation.

Parameterization
The limitations and restrictions of interpolation techniques led to the development of the parametric model by Parke (1974, 1982). The basic intention was to obtain a fairly large range of faces by specifying a small set of appropriate parameters. The model allows manipulation and control of both facial expressions and facial conformations. Such a parametric model is more flexible than the models using key frame interpolation, and users can manipulate faces more easily (DiPaola 1990). The parameterization used is ad-hoc, based on observation and common knowledge of the underlying structure. The model is dependent on the facial topology, which curtails the generality of the model. In addition, a complete set of such parameters is difficult to obtain which would define a complete range of faces and possible expressions. Pearce et al. (1986) extended the model to include an abstract notation for specifying expressions in terms of key words describing the part of the face to be moved, the type of movement and the parameter value.

Simulation of muscles
Attempts have also been made to create models which are based on simplified structures of bones, muscles, skin and connective tissues. These models provide the ability to manipulate facial expressions based on simulating the characteristics of the facial muscles. The major advantage of this approach is that it has generality since all human faces have the same set of muscles. Most simulations have used the Facial Action Coding System (FACS) (Ekman and Friesen 1969) as a scheme for describing the muscle actions. The scheme is briefly described

in the ensuing sub-section followed by the different major muscle models proposed in the literature.

FACS

The Facial Action Coding System (FACS), a comprehensive system for coding facial expressions, was developed by Ekman and Friesen (1969) where facial activity can be described in terms of a group of small basic actions. These basic actions or action units (AUs) are based on the anatomy of the face and occur as a result of one or more muscle actions. The system was developed in view to encode all possible facial expressions by the action units. FACS identifies about sixty AUs which separately or in various combinations are able to characterize any expression (Ekman and Friesen 1975). The system, though not developed for computer animation, has been widely used as a descriptive scheme for specifying and controlling facial animation.

Network of arcs

Platt and Badler (1981) developed a face model where a simplified representation of skin, muscle and bone structure are modeled. The skin, which is interconnected elastic mesh, is connected to the inflexible bone by muscle arcs. Facial expressions are manipulated by applying forces to the skin mesh through the muscle arcs. When a simple fiber contracts, a force is applied to muscle point in the direction of its tail (bone point). This force causes a displacement of the muscle point. The force is then reflected along all the adjacent arcs, which enable propagation of it to the neighboring parts. FACS is used as the notation scheme for the muscle actions. The limitations of this method are that it is time consuming and does not characterize the type of functionality of the underlying muscles.

Geometric vector operators

Waters (1987) developed a muscle model where he considered two types of muscles: linear that pull and sphincter that squeeze. A simple spring and mass model is used for skin and muscle. The muscles are defined as geometric operators having vector properties and are independent of the underlying structure. Each muscle vector has a zone of influence as a function of radial distance from the muscle point. Positioning of muscles is achieved through identification of key nodes on the face and enabling correspondence of these points to the 3-D model. The control parameters for animation are based on FACS. The approach has limitations in that it requires specific parameters such as muscle tension and elasticity to drive it. Such measurements are difficult to both acquire and use as a basis for expression synthesis. The model was used for the facial animation of Bill's head in the film *Tin Toy* (Reeves 1990). Patel and Willis (1991) have also used this model in their system FACES.

Abstract muscle procedures

A procedural model was developed by Magnenat Thalmann et al. (1988) where the ''Abstract Muscles Action'' (AMA) procedures control the animation. These AMA procedures are similar to the action units of FACS. An AMA is a specialized routine which simulates the specific action of a face muscle. The procedures operate on specific areas of the face, each of which must be defined at the time of face construction. Each AMA procedure is responsible for a facial parameter corresponding to a muscle action. Thus, the user is provided more accurate control. However, the model lacks a natural conception of muscular characteristics which may be applicable in a general way.

Physically based simulation
Extensions to the Waters model (Waters 1987) have been made by Terzopoulos and Waters (1990). The facial tissues are modeled using three layer deformable lattice structure. The three layers correspond to the skin, the subcutaneous fatty tissue, and the muscles. The bottom surface of the muscle layer is attached to the bone. Each layer is in fact a mesh of points. The models offer subtle facial movements using point to point control and a physically based technique to compute the deformations. The technique produces realistic results; however, there are some inherent problems with such approaches. The equations included tend to become complex and computationally intensive. The dynamic equations use numerical methods to solve and are iterative and expensive; numerical instability of equations may give undesirable results. The tri-layer structure has been simplified by Waters and Terzopoulos (1991) to gain computation speed. Pieper (1989) studied the physical properties of skin and used finite element mesh for the physical model of the skin.

Others
There have been several other attempts to simulate muscle actions using different techniques. For example, using B-spline surfaces for facial models, muscle movement of face is produced by changing the control points of the B-spline surface (Waite 1990, Nahas et al. 1988). The model uses FACS as a notation scheme. B-spline surface representation provides a smooth surface to the face, but integration of other facial features such as eyes, eyelids, lips, etc., is not obvious.

Viaud and Yahia (1992) have used a cardinal spline representation with a spring network. Muscular activity is simulated by applying forces to the spring network. Hierarchical splines and springs are used by Wang (1993) for modeling and deforming a face.

In another approach Guenter (1989) has proposed a method of attaching muscle and wrinkle lines to any part of the face. Muscles can have different shapes, the contraction is computed in 2-D and then mapped onto 3-D. Muscles can be specified for one or more AUs. The skin is modeled as a linear elastic rectangular mesh. Muscles are assumed to be force vectors applied at the vertices of the facial mesh. The model needs to solve the global stiffness matrix which is computationally expensive.

Spatial mapping and transformation method
There are some models used particularly for performance-driven animation (explained in Section 8.2.3) which are not based on the underlying model of bones, muscles or skin. Here

deformations are accomplished by local deformations of textures and geometry.

As already mentioned in Section 2.4.2, Patterson et al. (1991) used such an approach for animating the head of a dog in the film *The Audition*. The motion is created by placing some marks on the real face and tracing over a period of time. These marks have designated points on the 3-D model and describe the center of a cosine window basis function. When the designated points on the model are displaced, the neighboring geometry is moved by some fraction of the displacement depending on the distance from the dot. This approach is rather similar to that used by Williams for his model (Williams 1990).

Kurihara and Arai (1991) proposed a transformation method for deriving an individual model from a canonical model. This transformation method is also used for animating a face. A set of control points is selected and the transformation method gives the displacements of these control points. The displacements of other points are computed using a linear interpolation method in a triangular domain. The displacement of some control points of the face model, as used in the transformation method, is also used to create animation in another approach with winged edge polyhedral model of the head (Elson 1990). Here, the modeling of the object and the animation potential are inseparably intertwined.

These models lack intuitive mapping of face deformation as there is no implicit definition of muscles.

8.2.2   Speech, emotion and synchronization

Most facial movements result from either speech or display of emotions; each of these has its own complexity. However, both speech and emotions need a higher level specification of the controlling parameters. The second level parameterization used in speech animation is usually in terms of phonemes. These phonemes in turn control the lower level parameters for the actual deformations. Similarly, emotion is a sequence of expressions, and each expression is a particular position of the face at a given time. In order to have natural manipulation of speech and emotion there is a need for some synchronization mechanism. It is important that the parameterizations for speech and emotion are orthogonal to each other. The same conversational signals may have different emotional overlays; i.e. a sentence may be said in different emotional states with joy, sadness or anger.

For automatic lip-synchronization to be feasible, the position of the lips and tongue must be related in some identifiable way to characteristics of the speech sound (Lewis 1991). Parke (1974) used the basic low level parameters to produce speech. The idea of having a second level of parameterization in terms of phonemes has been used by several researchers (Bergeron and Lachapelle 1985, Hill et al. 1988, Lewis and Parke 1987, Magnenat Thalmann et al. 1988) to produce speech. Efforts for lip synchronization and speech automation have been reported in the study of Lewis and Parke (1987). In their approach, the desired speech is spoken and recorded. Linear prediction method is used for analyzing the spoken text, the result of which is the sequence of phonemes with their respective timings.

Hill et al. (1988) have introduced an automatic approach to animating speech using speech synthesized by rules. Lip-reading techniques (Jeffers and Barley 1971) are used for creating lip positions corresponding to speech. About 40 sounds and 10 corresponding facial expressions are distinguished for speech production. For automation, an acoustic entry is added in the table of parameters.

Magnenat Thalmann et al. (1988) have used lip synchronization based on AMA procedures. A collection of multiple tracks is used, where each track is a chronological sequence of key frames for a given facial parameter. Tracks are independent but can be mixed in the same way as sound is mixed in a sound studio. This approach was used in the film *Rendez-vous à Montréal* (Magnenat Thalmann and Thalmann 1987). However, the process of synchronization is manual and must be performed by the animator.

In another approach, Cohen and Massaro (1990) designed a system to study visual speech. The effort was to investigate the visual and auditory influence on speech perception. They used the articulatory gesture model of Löfqvist (1990), where a speech segment has dominance over vocal articulation which increases and decreases over time during articulation. For the adjacent segments having overlapping dominance functions, a blending over time was done for the articulatory commands related to these segments. The model has been further extended to include coarticulation of the tongue (Cohen and Massaro 1993).

Pelachaud et al. (1991) included linguistic issues in facial animation. One of their main goals is to build a system of 3-D animation of facial expressions with emotion correlated with the intonation of the voice. With a given utterance, how a message changes depends on the context. The facial movements are characterized by separating them into phonemic, intonational and emotional components. The coordination of various facial motions with intonation is done by a set of rules.

In another scheme of lip-synchronization, Benoit et al. (1994) analyzed real human faces to extract parameter that drive continuous functions that fit the shape of the lips. The coefficients for the continuous functions are predicted from three parameters: the horizontal width, the vertical height of the internal lip contour and the distance between a vertical profile reference and the lip contact protrusion.

8.2.3   Driving mechanisms

Animating the face manually for every action is a very tedious task and may not even yield the desired results. Faces have their own language where facial actions may express emotions, illustrate speech, comment on feelings or show attitude. Knowledge of such a language and its interaction with the face is essential to improve any facial animation system. In addition, understanding the gesture motions of the head and eyes which accompany speech and amplify the communication process is very important.

There are presently three main types of facial animation systems in terms of driving mechanisms or animation control. One type of system uses a script or command language for specifying the animation (Kaneko et al. 1992, Magnenat Thalmann et al. 1988, Pelachaud et al. 1991). These systems are simple but non-interactive and thus not very appropriate for real time animation. In addition, fine-tuning an animation is difficult when merely editing the script, as there exists a non-trivial relation between textual description and animation results.

Another type of system is performance-driven where motion parameters are captured from live performance (deGraf 1989, Terzopoulos and Waters 1991, Williams 1990). Here, the motion is captured by tracking some feature marks (Williams 1990) or snakes (Terzopoulos and Waters 1991) from video and then used to offer a manner of control to the computer simulation. This type of system provides the plausibility of real time animation. These types of motion copying systems are non-flexible and the external control on animation is quite limited. Though it provides high accuracy for timings, it is extremely difficult to edit.

Systems driven by speech (Hill et al. 1988, Lewis 1991) focus on lip-synchronization and speech decomposition into phonemes. Parameters defining facial models are grouped to represent the mouth shape of each phoneme. These are adequate when animation involves only speech. The animation is accomplished in two separate steps, the first step performs recording and analysis of speech spoken and the second is to establish the correlation of the spoken speech with the necessary facial movements. It has limitations for real time animation.

Despite the fact that natural and realistic facial animation is not an easy task, the research efforts made are very encouraging. In general, a facial model should incorporate answers to the questions ''How to deform the facial mesh'', ''what portion or region is to be moved'' and ''when a particular part should move with respect to the others''. In the next section, the overview of our proposed system of facial animation encapsulating these aspects is presented.

8.3   System overview

Facial movements, like other body movements, rely on perception-driven behaviors. Cognitively, these can be understood as externalization or manifestation of verbal or non-verbal communication agents on a face. These agents activate certain channels of a face associatively. Each activated channel in turn triggers the relevant muscles. Activation of muscles eventually deforms the face. In a computational model, such behavior can be interpreted as translating behavioral or cerebral activity into a set of functional units which embody the necessary activity-information. The resulting actions are then combined or merged in a sequence of discrete actions which, when applied, cause the necessary movements on the face. Our proposed system (Kalra 1993) for facial animation resolves the difficulty of manually manipulating the face model by offering a multi-level structure to the system, where each level is independently controllable. The different levels encompass information from the various levels of abstraction from sentences and emotions to the facial geometry and image visualization. In our system we model such behavior by separating facial animation into three major components, namely face model, animation controls and composer.

The face model primarily describes the geometric structure of the face, deformation controller and muscle actions. The model receives streams of actions to perform. These actions are decomposed into the required muscle actions and a new instance of the face is derived for each frame.

The animation controls specify animation characteristics (Magnenat Thalmann and Thalmann 1991). A facial animation system needs to incorporate adequate knowledge about its static and dynamic environments to enable animators to control its execution with a possible predefined, yet flexible set of commands. The system's structure should therefore embed such a know-how in a natural way. In order to satisfy this need, the system employs a hierarchical structure and modular design. Commands to the top level of the system need not be detailed descriptions of movement, instead these are like task description – for example: SAY ''I won't go'' while LOOKING left–right. The levels underneath are like functional synergy (Zeltzer 1982) where the task description is processed after having been decomposed into relevant low level motion parameters. The task description may contain higher level abstraction entities such as emotion, head motion and speech. Different types of input components may be used to specify these abstract entities.

A composer is required which acts like a multiplexer and permits integration of the animation controls coming from different sources. The input to the composer is a set of basic units of action from the input components, and the output is a timed sequence of these basic actions to the facial model.

The rendering module, though considered separate, communicates with the high level controls to control some of the rendering attributes during the execution of a facial expression and eventually affect the facial model.

Figure 8.1 shows the overview of the design of such a system. The sources of stimuli for facial motion may be encapsulated in the different abstraction levels like emotions, head movements and sentences, or expressions or phonemes. Different input components may be used to contain and process the information about these abstract entities. The composer performs actions like blending or filtering, to the incoming basic units of action and produces an array of the elementary actions to feed to the facial model where the actual deformation occurs. The feedback loop and global control for the composer can help regulate the overall intensity of the basic actions. Finally, each instance of the face is rendered using the rendering module.

In the following sections, we present the different modules of the system. First, the deformation controller is described, where the activities of muscles are simulated. Animation of a face with higher level abstract entities specification is then presented. Different input methods for animation are given followed by the rendering module.

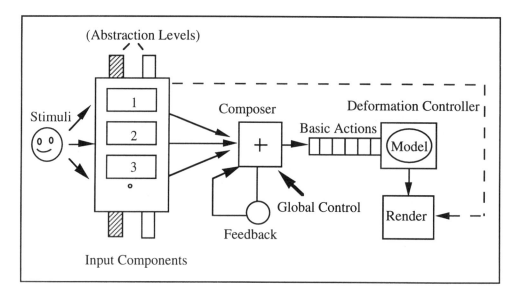

Figure 8.1.   *The overview of the system.*

8.4 Simulation of muscles

There have been several efforts for modeling the muscle process as mentioned earlier. It is evident that the skin supported by bone and multiple layers of muscle produces thousands of movement combinations. With all the muscle forms it is clear that they have a highly complex three dimensional structure endowed with viscous, elastic and other mechanical properties that result in skin displacement. The simulation of such interactions would be formidable. What is in fact needed is not the exact simulation of neurons, muscles, joints, veins, but a model with a few dynamic parameters that emulate just the primary characteristics. We have considered a different approach to model muscle processes based on rational free form deformations (Kalra et al. 1992). The main considerations in deciding the type of model for muscle action simulation are:

- Simple and easy to perform.
- Natural and intuitive to apply.
- Interactive and rapid to use.

Free form deformations (FFDs) fit the above requirements. FFDs have already been successfully used for deforming geometric models (Sederberg and Parry 1986). Its further extensions EFFD (Extended Free Form Deformation) and AFFD (Animated Free Form Deformation) (Coquillart 1990, Coquillart and Jancene 1991) have been proposed to enhance the scope of its use. Some generic muscular actions like squashing, stretching and pulling can easily be associated with the movement of the control points of the control lattice. In the context of articulated figures, they have been used in the Critter system (Chadwick et al. 1989). FFDs provide the flexibility of general free form spline control coupled with sculptural flexibility of deformations. For purposes of animation, a key advantage to abstracting deformation control from that of the actual surface description is that the transition of form is no longer dependent on the specifics of the surface itself.

8.4.1   Free form deformations

Free form deformation (FFD) is a technique for deforming solid geometric models in a free form manner (Sederberg and Parry 1986). It can deform surface primitives of any type or degree, for example, planes, quadrics, parametric surface patches or implicitly defined surfaces. Physically, FFDs correspond to deformations applied to an imaginary parallelepiped of clear, flexible plastic in which are embedded the object(s) to be deformed. The objects are also considered to be flexible so that they are deformed along with the plastic that surrounds them. The scheme provides the designer with an intuitive appreciation for its effects.

FFD involves a mapping from R3 to R3 through a trivariate tensor product Bernstein polynomial. Mathematically, imposing a local coordinate system (S,T,U) on a parallelepiped region with origin at X_0, a point X has (s,t,u) coordinates in this system such that

$$X = X_0 + sS + tT + uU \tag{8.1}$$

A grid of control points P_{ijk} ($i = 0$ to l, $j = 0$ to m, $k = 0$ to n) is imposed on the parallelepiped. The location of these points is defined as

$$P_{ijk} = X_0 + \frac{i}{l}S + \frac{j}{m}T + \frac{k}{n}U \tag{8.2}$$

For any point interior to the parallelepiped, $0 < s < 1$, $0 < t < 1$, $0 < u < 1$, the deformation is specified by moving the control point(s) from their undisplaced latticial position. The deformed position X' of a point X is computed from the following equation:

$$X' = \sum_{i=0}^{i}\sum_{j=0}^{m}\sum_{k=0}^{n} P_{ijk}B_i^l(s)B_j^m(t)B_k^n(u) \tag{8.3}$$

where $B_i^l(s)$, $B_j^m(t)$, $B_k^n(u)$ are the Bernstein polynomials.

The distortion of the solid inside follows the configuration of the outside control box. One of the major advantages of FFDs is that they can be applied in different representations. For example, for the polygonal representation of the model, one can still use this layer of specifying the deformations which follow the free form paradigm. The versatility and its

intuitive appreciation primarily suggests its application for design of our muscle model. In addition, these are not as computationally expensive as the physically based deformation techniques. This makes them viable for interactive and quick response, typical needs for real time systems. In our model, we have found that the use of only a parallelepiped structure for control lattice was adequate.

8.4.2   Rational free form deformation

As an extension to basic FFDs, we provide the option of including rational basis functions in the formulation of deformation (Kalra et al. 1992). The rational basis functions allow incorporation of weights defined for each control point (W_{ijk}) in the parallelepiped grid. With the new formulation equation (8.3) changes as follows:

$$X' = \frac{\sum_{i=0}^{l}\sum_{j=0}^{m}\sum_{k=o}^{n} P_{ijk} W_{ijk} B_i^l(s) B_j^m(t) B_k^n(u)}{\sum_{i=0}^{l}\sum_{j=0}^{m}\sum_{k=0}^{n} W_{ijk} B_i^l(s) B_j^m(t) B_k^n(u)} \tag{8.4}$$

The advantage of using rational FFDs (RFFDs) is that it provides one more degree of freedom when manipulating the deformations by changing the weights at the control points. When the weights at each control point are unity, the deformations are equivalent to the basic FFD. Figure 8.2 shows an illustration where the deformations are accomplished by changing the position of the control point (Figure 8.2(b)) and by changing the weight at the control point (Figure 8.2(c)). It is possible to combine the two types.

8.4.3   Region-based approach

To simulate the muscle action on the skin surface of human face, we define regions on the face mesh which correspond to the anatomical descriptions of the facial regions on which a muscle action is desired. A parallelepiped control unit then can be defined on the region of interest. The deformations which are obtained by actuating muscles to stretch, squash, expand and compress the inside volume of the facial geometry, are simulated by displacing the control point and by changing the weights of the control points of the control-unit. The region inside the control-unit deforms like a flexible volume, corresponding to the displacement and the weights of the control points. Displacing a control point is analogous to adding a muscle vector to the control-unit. As opposed to the Waters model (Waters 1987) where the animator has to specify the muscle vectors in the form of some geometric operators, here the displacement of the control points gives rise to similar effects. Specifying

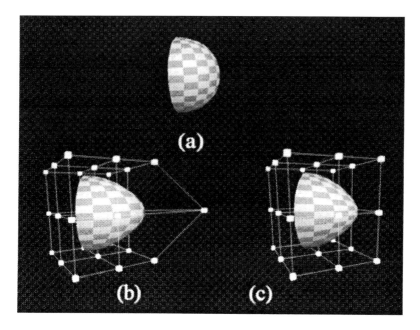

Figure 8.2. *Rational free form deformation.*

the displacement of the control point is, however, more intuitive and simpler than simulating the muscle vectors. In addition, the result matches the natural notion of muscles acting on that region. For example, a depressor muscle would need to squash the control point inside the control-unit, and a pulling muscle would pull the control points away from the control-unit.

In order to propagate the deformations of regions to the adjoining regions, linear interpolation can be used to decide the deformation of the boundary points. Although higher order interpolation schemes can also be used, movements in the face are rather small and any higher ordered discontinuities arising may not affect the visual aspects so much. The computation involves first finding the neighboring boundary points of a region, computing a weight factor depending on the length of the incident edge, and then calculating the resulting deformation. As the whole process slows down the calculations for the overall deformations, we propose defining a larger region and using a stiffness factor associated with the points in the region to control the deformation (see Section 8.4.4). In a dynamic approach using a physically based technique muscle pulls can be transmitted a great distance through the mesh unlike real skin where muscle pulls tend to have local effects. Use of a geometric approach avoids such propagation and does not need any restoring force to delineate the pulling effect.

8.4.4 Physical characteristics of skin

Skin as such is difficult to model as it has a non-linear, anisotropic stress–strain relationship. It is also viscoelastic, which means that the stress–strain relationship is time dependent. In addition, facial skin is under tension even when no expression is present on the face and this tension is difficult to measure experimentally. There is extensive literature on the mechanical properties of skin (Larrabee 1986) but even very sophisticated skin models are greatly simplified. In our model, physical properties of the skin surface such as mass, stiffness and elasticity can also be incorporated when applying the deformations. The deformed point in that case can be given as:

$$X'' = (X' - X) \cdot p + X \qquad\qquad (8.5)$$

where X'' is the final deformed position of the point,
  X' is the position obtained after the FFD,
  X is the undeformed position,
  p is the factor for the surface properties.

Association of physical properties provides a means of further controlling the deformations in a more natural way. Mostly we use a factor which may be considered as a stiffness factor of the skin which linearly changes the deformation intensity for the node point.

8.5 Animation of faces

Animation in a literal sense refers to bringing life, though in the context of synthesis it can be considered as generating the illusion of life. This illusion in a simplified form may be due to providing motion, evolution or a change of state over a period of time. Nevertheless, it involves critical issues related to ''how to specify what to move when''. Evidently, manual specification for each frame is a formidable task generating a reasonable length of animation. Motion specification and control, in fact, has to correspond to reality in terms of identifying the sources of movement and their execution.

As it is difficult to create a model for facial animation that is both physically realistic and easy to use, we use a multi-level approach which divides the facial animation problem into a hierarchy of independent levels (Kalra et al. 1991). The upper levels use higher degrees of abstraction for defining entities such as emotions and phrases of speech, allowing animators to manipulate these entities in a natural and intuitive way. From the highest to the lowest, the levels of abstraction in our system are illustrated in Figure 8.3. A synchronization mechanism is provided at the top level that requires animators to specify the highest level entities: emotions, sentences and head movements with their duration. The system provides default values for duration in case they are not specified. These entities are then decomposed into lower level entities and sent through the pipeline of control at the lower levels of the

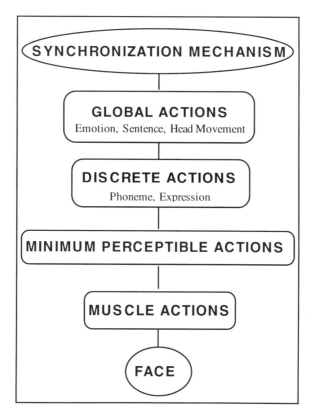

Figure 8.3. *Multi-level structure.*

hierarchy. The temporal characteristics of animation are generally controlled at higher levels and the spatial characteristics are controlled at lower levels in our multi-level system.

We first start with issues related to specification of animation in terms of different entities at different levels of abstraction as defined in the high level control module (Magnenat Thalmann and Kalra 1992, Mangili 1991).

8.5.1 Abstract entities

Specification of animation in terms of muscle actions involves some rather tedious manipulations by the animator. There is a definite need for higher level specification which would avoid setting up the parameters involved for muscular actions when producing an animation sequence. The Facial Action Coding System (FACS) (Ekman and Friesen 1978) has been used extensively to provide a higher level specification when generating facial

expressions, particularly in a non-verbal communication context. In our multi-level approach we define the functional synergy at each level encapsulating the definition of the entities the level beneath. The following sections present these entities.

Minimum Perceptible Action (MPA)

A Minimal Perceptible Action is a basic facial motion parameter. Each MPA has a corresponding set of visible features such as movement of eyebrows, jaw, or mouth and others occurring as a result of muscle contractions and pulls. MPAs also include non-facial muscle actions such as nodding, head turning and eye movement. Each MPA is specified with a normalized intensity between 0 and 1 or −1 and 1. An MPA can be considered an atomic action unit similar to the AU of FACS, execution of which results in a visible and perceptible variation of a face.

The calculation of MPAs from higher level entities is completely independent of the facial model. However, the type of control offered by MPAs is at a lower level from the animator's point of view.

It is possible to create animation at the MPA level. The animator would be required to specify temporal information, which may be just the frame number along with the included MPAs. Many existing systems use this level of specification for animation. However, this approach is still cumbersome and requires considerable manual effort. We therefore include a higher level of abstraction where MPAs can be grouped in a meaningful way. At this level, we define entities referring to discrete actions like expressions and phonemes.

Expression and phonemes

Expressions and phonemes in our system are considered as facial snapshots, i.e., a particular position of the face at a given time. For phonemes, only the lips are considered during the emission of sound. A facial snapshot consists of one or more MPAs with their intensity specified. The set of MPAs included is general enough to account for most possible facial expressions. A generic expression can be represented as follows.

```
[expression <name>
  [mpa <name-1> intensity <i-1>]
  [mpa <name-2> intensity <i-2>]
  . . .
]
```

Example of an expression

```
[expression surprise
  [mpa open_jaw intensity 0.17]
  [mpa puffcheeks intensity −0.41]
  [mpa stretch_cornerlips intensity −0.50]
  [mpa raise_eyebrows intensity 0.40]
  [mpa close_lower_eyelids intensity −0.54]
  [mpa close_upper_eyelids intensity −0.20]
]
```

Example of a phoneme

```
[phoneme ee
  [mpa stretch_cornerlips intensity −0.29]
  [mpa open_jaw intensity 0.50]
  [mpa lower_cornerlips intensity −0.57]
  [mpa raise_upperlips intensity −0.20]
]
```

Facial snapshots representing expressions and phonemes can be built up interactively. Users can construct and save static expressions, and thus build up a library of pre-defined expressions. There are options such as `Add`, `Delete` and `Save`. For example, `Add` enables a user to start interactively and build an expression from the same range of MPAs used in generating an animation sequence. Figure 8.4 shows a working session with the expression editor.

Emotions, sentences and head movement
Using expressions and phonemes to create animation is still not natural enough. The animator would rather like to specify and control animation at the task level where he can describe animation directly in terms of its inherent sources. Thus, in our system we allow the animator to specify animation directly in terms of global actions like emotions, sentences and head movements. Such specification saves an animator from learning the detailed knowledge of lower level entities in the system.

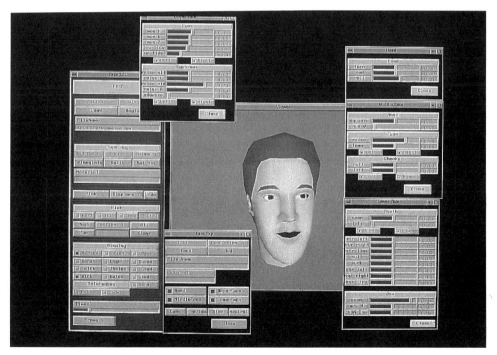

Figure 8.4. *Working session with expression editor.*

Emotion

Emotions are highly personal and complex to understand. Different people often react differently to particular situations. The analysis and study of the cause and perception of emotion is itself a complete research domain of human behavior in the area of psychology. We therefore restrict our concentration in considering a natural and valid definition and specification of emotion for our computational model.

An emotion is considered an expressive episode of a face over a time period. It can be interpreted as evolution of a face over time. For example, when starting from a neutral or background state, an emotion would include all the sequence of visible changes involved in returning to the same neutral or background state. A generic emotion is an envelope consisting of four stages: attack, decay, sustain and release (Ekman and Friesen 1978). Figure 8.5 shows a hypothetical example of emotion illustrating the four stages.

The duration (temporal characteristics) and intensity (spatial characteristics) are context dependent. For example, intensity and duration of a "smile" in a normal situation and in a laughable situation are different. In addition, each stage of emotion is not equally sensitive to the expansion of time. Attack and release stages do not expand proportionally to the scale of expansion for the entire duration. To preserve this non-proportionality of expansion for each stage we incorporate a sensitivity factor associated with each stage of emotion. At any instance the duration for each stage is given as

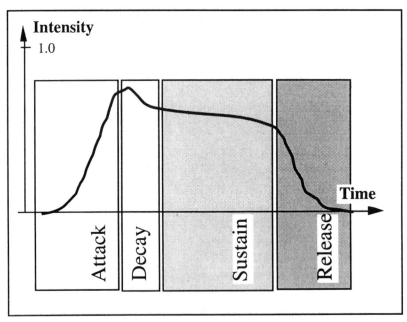

Figure 8.5. *Hypothetical example of emotion.*

$$t' = a \, s_i \, t_i \tag{8.6}$$

where a: scaling factor for the entire duration
   s_i: sensitivity factor for each stage i, with $\sum s_i = 1$
   t_i: average duration for each stage i

The intensity of emotion is determined by the intensities of the sequence of expressions attached to the intermediate stages of emotion. We give as an example the emotion "surprise" that uses three different instances of expression "surprise".

```
[emotion surprise
  [attack duration 12 sensitivity 0.15] [expression surprise1 intensity 0.7]
  [decay duration 12 sensitivity 0.35] [expression surprise2 intensity 0.8]
  [sustain duration 12 sensitivity 0.35] [expression surprise3 intensity 0.7]
  [release duration 12 sensitivity 0.15]
]
```

This parameterization mechanism for both temporal and spatial characteristics also enables us to differentiate and identify what are called "spontaneous" and "deliberate" emotional expressions. The spontaneous or elicited emotions are unmodulated expressions congruent with an underlying emotional state, while deliberate expressions are those intentionally employed by the sender for some purpose. For example, felt (spontaneous) and false (deliberate) smiles can be differentiated in both temporal and spatial nature. For false smiles the attack stage is shorter and the sustain stage is longer than for felt smiles. Furthermore false smiles exhibit no orbiculi activity. These facts help add behavioral attributes to emotions.

Sentences
Delivery of a sentence or word with proper lip-synchronization addresses several issues. Mechanisms to control the intensity, duration and emphasis of each word are provided (Mangili 1991). Pauses (punctuators) are added to control the rhythm and intonation of the sentence. A word is specified as sequence of phonemes. The relative duration of each phoneme in a word is determined according to its placement and neighboring phonemes, and the number of syllables in the given word. For each word the sequence of phonemes is considered as a list of relative expressions with normalized duration (between 0 and 1).

Head movement
Movement of the head plays an extremely important role in natural facial animation. While talking, in addition to using lips for emission of sounds, a person may simultaneously turn or roll his head and move his eyes to accentuate and regulate emphasis for conversational signals. We consider head movement as a separate entity involving non-muscular actions such as a turning of the head and movement of the eyeballs. The sequence of expressions during the span of head movement is represented as a list of relative expressions.

8.5.2   Synchronization

We need a synchronization mechanism to ensure smooth flow of emotions and sentences with head movements. A language HLSS (High Level Script Scheduler) (Mangili 1991) is used to specify synchronization in terms of an action and its duration. The general format of specifying an action is as follows: while <duration> do <action>.

The duration of an action can be a default duration, a relative percentage of the default duration, an absolute duration in seconds or a deduced duration from the other actions preceding or succeeding the present action. The starting time of each action can be specified in different ways, for example, sequentially or parallel using the normal concepts of "fork" and "end" employed in scheduling problems. Figure 8.6 illustrates the sequential and parallel synchronization of actions.

8.6   Input accessories

As the system considers the specification of different input components separately from the animation, we can try various ways of controlling the animation. Also, various input components can be used at the same time. Such an approach provides a platform where we can experiment with new methods of control. This analysis may allow us to identify the kind of access we may require for defining and controlling varying levels of abstractions for computational animation models in virtual environments. These accessing components may

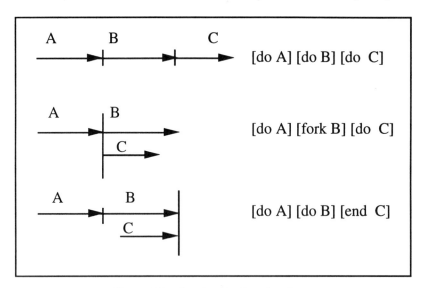

Figure 8.6.   *Synchronization of actions.*

demand different kinds of interaction which may establish the need for experimentation with several types of devices (Kalra et al. 1993). As no single mode of control can give completeness, such a test-bed environment can evaluate what device can be used for which means of control. The possibility of composing and mixing different types of controls further enhances the reconfigurability of the system. This can eventually allow cooperative group tasks for animation, where more than one person can control the animation in real time. We present here four different types of input accessories we have tried.

8.6.1 Script

A script is a standard method of specifying animation that consists of different types of entities. It is like a special language using a few key words for specific operations. Most automated facial animation systems employ this approach.

In our system a language HLSS (described earlier) is used to specify synchronization in terms of an action and its duration. The keywords like "do", "fork" and "end" are used which specify the relationship of an action with the neighboring actions. In addition, they help determine the starting and ending time of an action.

One of the major advantages of such an input accessory is that it is in text form. Users can very conveniently change it by editing a text file. On the other hand, being non-interactive it is not possible to change certain parameters while the script is running. Therefore, it is not very suitable for real-time animation. It is more useful for background animation. Figure 8.7 shows expressions created on a synthetic face using script.

8.6.2 MIDI-keyboard

MIDI-keyboards can be another source for controlling the animation. The keyboard has a number of keys enabling us to associate several parameters with the keys. Activation of each key gives two kinds of information: initial velocity with which the key is hit and the pressure variation. System G (Gross 1991) a real-time, video animation system uses a Korg M1 keyboard to move different parts of the mask of a face. However, the system has special purpose processing hardware to perform the animation.

In our system, this device can be used as a direct manipulator for MPAs. Each key may be assigned to an MPA and the initial velocity of the key may be attached to its intensity. This type of control is at a rather low level. Higher level control can also be obtained by assigning the keys to expressions and phonemes. Here, some of the expressions and phonemes are associated with particular keys of the keyboard. The intensity of the expression or phoneme is governed by the velocity of the key hit. The duration of an expression can be determined by the duration for which the key is pressed. That means an expression starts with the intensity corresponding to the velocity of the key hit and continues until the key is released.

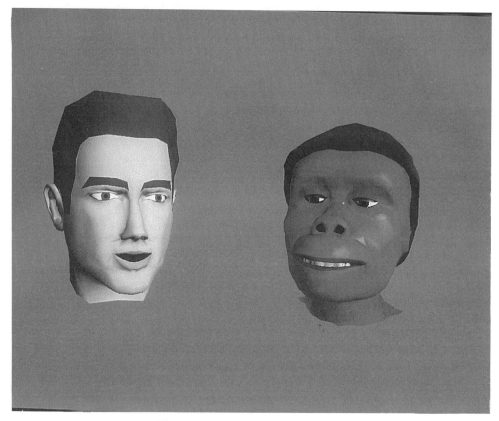

Figure 8.7.   *Expressions using script.*

The pressure variation of the key hit may be used for modulating the intensity of an expression during its execution. It may be interesting to use an array of keys to control a single emotion; here, the mapping of keys would be with the included expression instances or channels. For example, for an emotion containing eye, head and mouth motion, each may be associated with a set of keys respectively.

The advantage of such a device is that it provides a number of keys which can be assigned individually to the motion parameters. This gives simultaneous control on many parameters; but at the same time it demands hardwiring a desired action to a particular key. Each modification or extension in the control method will require reconfiguration of the meaning of the keys. Also, unidimensional arrangement of keys in the keyboard forces a certain type of order in the manner of control. For music the ordering is with respect to frequency. However, it is not evident how to arrange facial expressions in a unidimensional fashion, and this consequently constrains the use of the device in its natural form.

8.6.3 Postures and gestures dialog

The type of control presented in the previous section is directly dependent on the physical structure of the device used: the mapping between a user's actions and animation controls is obtained by associating a meaning to the various key presses. This device dependency is a factor that limits the animator's expressiveness.

The use of devices which simply sense user's motions, and the use of adaptive pattern recognition can overcome these problems. The use of hand-gestures can provide non-verbal cues for a natural human–computer interaction. In our system, we use posture recognition (Gobbetti 1993, Balaguer and Gobbetti 1993) on data obtained from the DataGlove to obtain the categorical and parametric information that drive the facial animation. The recognition technique here is based on multi-layer perceptrons (MLPs) (Rumelhart et al. 1986), a type of artificial neural network which is potentially able to approximate any real function (Cybenko 1989). A multi-layer perceptron consists of several layers of processing units with multiple inputs and a single output which are connected by weighted links. During training each output unit is taught to discriminate between its associated class and all the others by presenting a binary target value equal to $+1$ if the current input is a member of the class and -1 if not. Once learning is completed, the weights are frozen and classification is done corresponding to the most active output unit for each of the patterns presented to the network.

Once a posture is recognized, parametric information can be extracted from the location of the hand and how it moves. This information can then be used to drive the facial animation. The type of posture as the categorical information can be associated with a type of action performed by the face. We experimented with two types of controls: direct control at the expression level and higher level control at the emotion level.

In the first case, putting the hand in a given posture sets the type of expression for face, while the orientation of the hand controls the expression's intensity. We found this way of control to be adequate for facial editing, but inadequate for real-time animation control. Control at a higher level, for example the emotion level, is much more appropriate. In this case, hand posture selects the type of emotion, and orientation of the hand at the beginning of the posture with respect to the absolute vertical direction controls the overall intensity of the emotion. The amount of rotation between the beginning and the end of the posture controls the overall duration. Gesture dialog for facial animation control provides a continuous dynamic interaction. In this approach your own definition of a particular gesture can be specified by training the gesture recognition system and can associate it with one type of emotion or other task-entity. This gives more flexibility and freedom to the user for controlling the animation.

The position of the hand with respect to a fixed reference frame is normally used to control geometric information such as head and eye rotations. A typical use of this kind of control is to have the synthetic human look at the position of the real hand. Figure 8.8 shows the example where the movement of the hand correspondingly moves (turns) the head. There do not yet exist rules establishing the correspondence of a given gesture and expression. However, experimentation has led to some natural associations. For example, a gesture from

Figure 8.8. *Animation control with gesture.*

a closed fist to a completely open hand can indicate the total onset of an expression like ''surprise''. Similarly, bending the fingers may be attached to ''blinks'' or to ''head nods''. The advantage of the gesture recognition system is to have the flexibility of defining one's own gestures for a given expression. One of the main disadvantages of using gesture dialog as a means control for facial animation is the poor precision offered by the DataGlove. This prohibits the use of this device for fine-tuning.

8.6.4   Live Video Digitizer

As already discussed in Sections 2.4.2 and 7.5.5, another means of driving the facial animation is through tracking the motion of a real person. The motion of a real person may be captured by a Live Video Digitizer (LVD). The analysis of moving images provides the basic motion parameters to drive the synthetic facial animation. One of the objectives here is to be able to extract the basic motion parameters and apply them to the synthetic animation in real time. The approach (Magnenat Thalmann et al. 1993) consists of using deformable curves (snakes) (Terzopoulos and Waters 1991) together with simple image processing techniques. An elliptical snake is used around the mouth region. For eyes, pixel quantization is used to determine if eyes are closed or open. For some parts the motion extraction can be considered as template matching where some reference parameters (e.g., eyebrow height from nose tip) are compared with the respective reference parameters in the neutral face (Pandzic et al. 1994). Empirical rules are used to obtain the corresponding intensity for the associated motion parameter for the synthetic animation. The basic motion parameters as mentioned earlier are the MPAs in our case.

The advantage of such a mode of control is that it acts like a motion tracking process and does not require any abstraction levels for specification or synchronization of synthetic animation. Thus, it simplifies the job of the animator. On the other hand, it is constrained by the motion of the human performance and restricts the animator's innovation and creative imagination. Figure 8.9 shows motion mapping from the real face to the synthetic face.

8.7 Rendering of faces

The facial images arising from conventional types of rendering (e.g. continuous polygon shading) tend to look rather artificial and cartoon-like. This is particularly disconcerting for

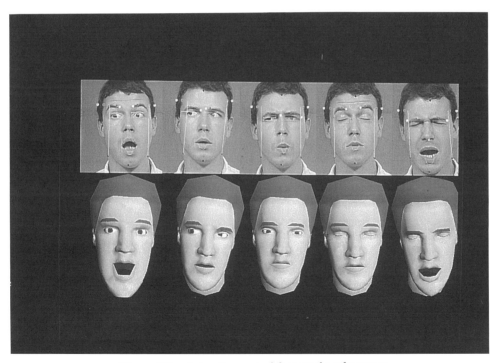

Figure 8.9. *Animation control from real performance.*

faces that are meant to be human in nature. All physical surfaces have a detailed structure visible to the human eye; this provides a tremendous amount of information about the nature of a substance. A means is required to communicate its color, reflectance and pigmentation, and whether skin is smooth or rough. This chapter describes a method by which realistic animated facial images can be generated. The approach that enables this to be achieved is texture-mapping a real photograph of a person onto the 3-D face model. Texture mapping is a relatively efficient way of creating the appearance of complex surface detail without going through the tedium of modeling and rendering every 3-D detail of a surface. The technique essentially involves projection of some pattern or image stored as a flat 2-D picture onto the surface of a 3-D object. Use of texture mapping for realism is not very recent (Blinn and Newell 1976, Heckbert 1986, Oka et al. 1987). However, most of the existing applications deal with mapping an image onto parametric surfaces and solid modeling primitives. Consequently, these techniques in general include mapping of a full image onto a surface. For facial image synthesis, merely projecting (mapping) a full image on the subject's face is not enough. There is a need to establish positional agreement between some parts of the model and the source image to be mapped. This is essential particularly when the 3-D face model is not constructed from the image(s).

Recently, efforts have been made to apply the texture-mapping technique to enhance the rendering of faces. Some of the techniques (Nahas et al. 1990) employ registered texture mapping which, although it gives realistic results, involves enormous data-handling. In addition, it requires special hardware for registering the data. Waters and Terzopoulos (1991) used an adaptive meshing technique which can be used to design coarser, non-uniform meshes capturing the essential structure of the high resolution facial maps from laser scanners. This technique, however, again needs special hardware and is time consuming. The method employed by Kurihara and Arai (1991) uses multiple photographs to reconstruct the 3-D model of a face using interpolation in 2-D cylindrical space. The photographs are composed into one picture using a weight function for each photograph in 2-D cylindrical space. In another approach by Yau and Duffy (1988) pre-stored sub-images are manipulated for animation, particularly for dynamic sequences of eyes and mouth. These sub-pictures can be recalled to incorporate discrete facial actions such as eye shifting, blinking and simple mouth movements; however the method is neither evident nor convenient. In addition, the facial model is like a mask grid and does not explicitly define features like eyes and lips.

In our multi-level system of facial animation we use rendering as an independent layer which does not get affected with changes at other levels. In addition, the process of texture-mapping is done only once using the neutral face and while animating the face, we do not manipulate the picture. An interactive tool is employed which facilitates matching the feature points of the 3-D model with the features of the 2-D picture. With the help of this tool we establish the positional certainty of the key points (Kalra and Magnenat Thalmann 1993). Our attempt here is not to focus on the computational concepts of texturing itself as we use standard rendering methods (e.g. rayshade). Instead we provide a means to obtain rather easily a geometric mapping (parameterization) for a highly irregular polygonal surface such as a human face.

8.7.1 Our approach

The approach used is in part similar to that proposed by Kurihara and Arai (1991). In their approach a 3-D model of the face is reconstructed using a set of photographs under orthographic view. Then texture mapping is used. In our case, the 3-D model and the picture to be mapped exist separately. Therefore, we are not restricted to using only a cylindrical projection for obtaining 2-D projected points. In addition, the viewing transformation does not have to be orthographic. The steps for our underlying approach are described as follows (Kalra and Magnenat Thalmann 1993).

Selection of 3-D feature points
For texture mapping, a face can be divided into groups. This division facilitates attaching each group to a portion of a picture or several pictures if needed. A group is basically a composition of polygons. Typically groups can be `front_face`, `left_side`, `right_side`, etc. The selection of polygons during group construction is made easy by providing collective and constrained polygon picking: e.g., selecting polygons of the same color, or polygons within a snapped region of the screen window, special routines for groups with closed boundaries. Once groups are selected, the user can mark some feature points for each of the groups. The features are meant to appropriately match similar features on the picture. These feature points include points for which positional certainty is necessary to establish, for example, extreme points of lips and eyes.

The system can automatically select the points on the boundary of the group chosen. These are marked as "boundary" points. These boundary points are used for binding two groups in the texture space, if necessary. Binding is necessary to ascertain the same texture coordinates for the same points in different groups but in the same picture.

2-D projection
In order to project the selected 3-D points we employ two techniques: a) interactive approximation for viewing transformation and b) cylindrical projection.

a. Interactive Viewing Transformation
Here, a particular view of the 3-D model is selected interactively. It is approximately similar to that of the 2-D picture. Once the appropriate view has been selected, the viewing transformation is applied to obtain the 2-D projection of all the points for that group. Algorithms (Kurihara and Arai 1991, Parke 1975) to derive the viewing transformation from a set of pictures can also be used. However, these algorithms are useful when a 3-D reconstruction is desired from the pictures. For our purposes, where the 3-D face model and

the picture to be mapped are independent, interactive adjustment of viewing transformation gives the desired results.

b. Cylindrical Projection

In cylindrical projection, the transformation function from 3-D model space to 2-D cylindrical space is defined as

$$C_S(\theta, h) = \tan^{-1}(z/x, y) \tag{8.7}$$

A similar transformation is used for the 2-D picture to be mapped.

Delaunay triangulation

We employ linear interpolation in a triangular domain to obtain the texture coordinates of the feature points and other points of the mesh acquired from the 3-D model. Delaunay triangulation (Sibson 1978, Moccozet and Magnenat Thalmann 1992) is used to triangulate the 2-D projected feature points for each group. Some other techniques for triangulation could also be used. Delaunay triangulation is locally equiangular, and its max-min angle property avoids formation of very thin triangles and provides more or less a regular triangulation. This is desirable in an interpolation method.

The texture coordinates for the feature points are directly derived from the texture-space. For the other interior points, barycentric coordinates are used to obtain the texture coordinates. A point P inside a triangle described by its vertices V_1, V_2, V_3 in the texture space has the following relationship (Farin 1990):

$$P = uV_1 + vV_2 + wV_3 \tag{8.8}$$

where u, v, w are the barycentric coordinates of the point P.

Feature matching

Feature matching pertains to matching the feature points of the 3-D model with the picture in hand. An interactive tool is provided to accomplish this task. Users can pick and move each point and place it on the picture appropriately. Some global operations such as mesh scaling, translation and rotation can also be performed. An option of `freeze` sets the texture coordinates of all the points of the group. The option `bind` binds the boundaries of two or more groups.

Picture composition

A single picture with one particular view may not be adequate for mapping onto the entire head. In the case of multiple photographs obtained with known angles, they can be composed into one by blending them all. However, the lighting conditions for the pictures when they are taken should be the same. Once each picture is expanded into 2-D cylindrical space, a bandwidth is selected and a blending function is used to compose the pictures. We use a linear blending function to obtain a smooth transition within the bandwidth; other suitable functions may also be used.

This composition method is very simple and yields desired results only when the luminance and chromatic characteristics of individual pictures match perfectly. Even slight differences in images across the boundary can make the boundary noticeable. We propose the use of a multi-resolution spline technique (Burt and Adelson 1983, LeMeur 1991) for combining two images into a larger image mosaic. In this technique, the images are first decomposed into a set of band-pass filtered component images. These component images are then assembled into a corresponding band-pass mosaic using a weighted average within a transition zone. Finally these band-pass mosaic images are summed to obtain the desired image. Use of pyramid algorithms offers easy and efficient filtering and splining operations. A one dimensional graphical representation of the iterative ''reduce'' (filtering) operation in the pyramid construction is shown in Figure 8.10(a). Each row of dots represents pixels of the filtered images. The lowest row, P_0, is the original image. The value of each next row P_1 is computed as a weighted average of 5×5 subarray of P_0 nodes. Nodes of P_2 are then computed similarly from P_1 using the same pattern of weights. Consequently, a pyramid structure is built. The sample density and resolution are decreased from level to level of the pyramid, hence, the operation is called ''reduce''. In order to obtain the band-pass images, each level of the pyramid is subtracted from the next lower level. Due to the difference in the sample density, the subtraction is preceded by an operation of ''expand'', opposite to ''reduce''. The band images are then summed to get the resulting image. The implementation of this algorithm is a direct descendent of LeMeur (1991). A resulting image composing the front and side views is shown in Figure 8.10(b).

Examples

Separating 3-D construction and modeling from rendering provides the flexibility to use different models with different pictures. When imitating a real character, one has to use a 3-D model that conforms closely to the morphological aspects of the character and a real 2-D photograph of the character for texture mapping. However, employing different 2-D photographs and keeping the same 3-D model gives a richer variety of human-like synthetic faces. Figure 8.11 (on page 195 and in the plate section between pages 152 and 153) shows faces with expressions rendered using texture mapping.

8.7.2 Vascular emotions

There can be two major reasons for change in color of a face: physical conditioning or emotional state. Physical conditioning refers to change in color: e.g., reddening when physical exercise or strain occurs. Emotional state can also influence the color attributes of the face. In either situation, change in color is due to the change in the blood circulation. Our primary interest is to incorporate the change in color due to an emotional state. In the next

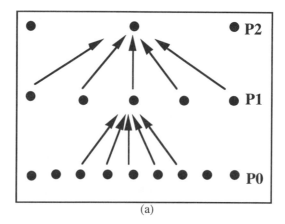

(a)

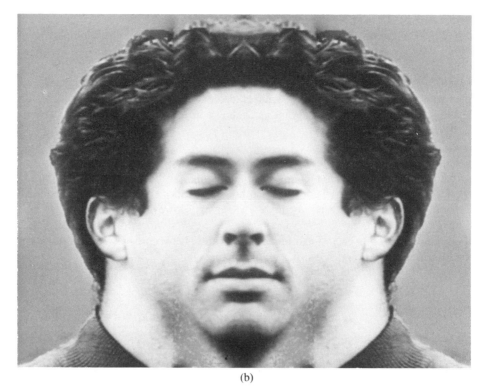

(b)

Figure 8.10. *Picture composition using multi-resolution spline technique.*

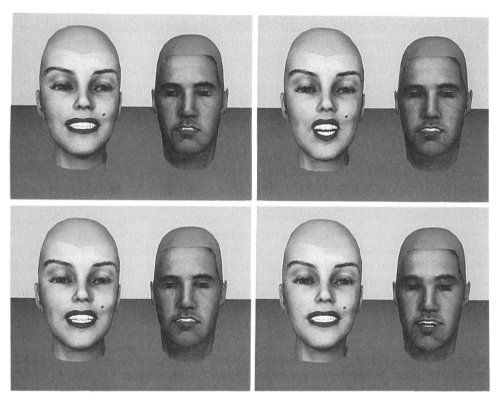

Figure 8.11. *Texture mapping of animated faces.*

section, we present our model of emotion which includes color variation during the execution of emotion (Kalra and Magnenat Thalmann 1994).

8.7.3 The model

One aspect of generating realistic faces is that skin color changes depending on the emotional state of an individual. The existing facility needs to be extended so that the color of selected portions of the face can be varied with time and allows us to provide emotional visual cues such as paleness due to fear, blushing due to embarrassment. Patel (1992) has included the skin toning effect as a change of color for all the polygons of face during an emotion. However, there does not exist as such a computational model of emotion which includes these visual characteristics during their execution.

The definition of emotion is in fact redefined as a function of two signals in time, one for its intensity and the other for the color. At any instance of time, state of emotion e_t can be defined as

$$e_t = k\, f_t(i, c) \tag{8.9}$$

where k is a constant, i is the parameter for intensity and c is the parameter for the color signal. Figure 8.12 illustrates an episode of a face with emotion over time having signals for its intensity and the color attributes. Emotions showing only spatial changes due to muscular activities, and the emotions showing only color changes due to the vascular activities can be considered as special cases of the above definition.

We have considered two emotional states where change of color is visible: blushing and pallor. These emotional states are relatively involuntary and uncontrollable and can be described as vascular phenomena.

Blushing: Blushing occurs when emotions are intense, often sending a surge of blood through the main artery. It may occur when a person is ashamed, wishes to flee, hide, conceal a previous act or confound someone's possible deprecating attribution (Zajonc 1985). It occurs when one least desires it to occur, it is not readily subject to voluntary control, and again it is vascular and not due to muscular expression (Shields et al. 1990).

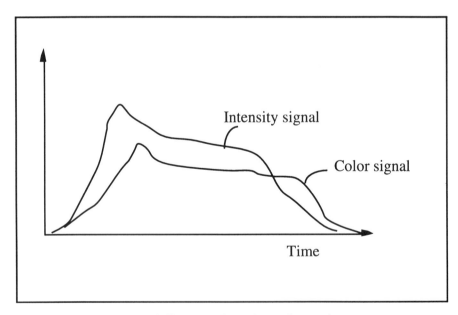

Figure 8.12.   *Muscular and vascular emotion.*

Pallor: Pallor occurs in temporary cerebral anemia and contraction of the facial capillaries remedies it by increasing cerebral blood flow. Pallor may occur due to shock, fear or pain. These actions diminish facial blood flow and redirect it to the brain to ease and recuperate.

For vascular expressions there does not exist a coding scheme yet which decomposes the expressions into some discrete actions, like FACS does for muscular expressions. We propose a similar approach to that adopted earlier for generating expressions due to muscle actions. That is, we define Minimum Perceptible Color Action (MPCA) analogous to the MPA which embodies the necessary parameters to change the color attributes due to blood circulation in blood vessels of different parts of the face. However, our intentions are not to provide a model for the flow of blood through the blood vessels. Instead we map parametrically the change of color to the vascular activity in that region. For the computational model, an image mask is considered to devise MPCAs. A shape inside the mask is defined which gives the region to be affected when the mask is applied onto the texture image. Each pixel inside this region of the mask may represent a percentage factor to be used for modifying the color attributes, such as saturation value, when applied to the texture image.

8.8 Discussion

Facial animation is a sub-module of the complete human animation system. The module of facial animation is integrated with other modules to enable full human body animation. This has been used as one of the work modules for the ESPRIT project HUMANOID: A Real-time and Parallel System for Simulation of Virtual Humans (Boulic et al. 1995). More details may be found in Chapter 11. The spatial integration is obtained at the level of skin envelope where the boundaries of the head and the neck are assembled. The skin deformations of the body are performed in another module. There does not exist automatic temporal synchronization of facial animation and the body-movement; however, the facial animation segment(s) can be inserted at the appropriate location while performing the movement of the entire body. The movements of the body are generated in the TRACK system (Boulic et al. 1995). Figure 8.13 shows the facial animation together with the body animation.

Facial animation is also integrated with rendering of hair. The hair rendering system to generate synthetic hair and fur consists of two independent modules for modeling and rendering hair (LeBlanc et al. 1991, Daldegan et al. 1993). The rendering module uses a modified version of *rayshade*, a raytracing program available in the public domain. More details may be found in Section 9.3. The current version of rayshade also incorporates primitives with texture mapping. Consequently, we can obtain a face with hair rendering, mustache, beard etc., and texture mapped skin. Figure 8.14 shows a sequence of images with texture mapped facial animation and hair rendering.

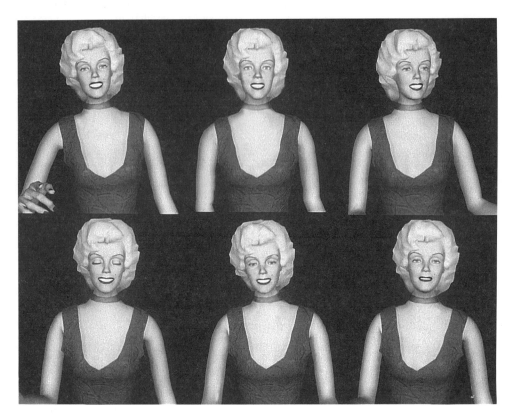

Figure 8.13.   *Example of facial animation with body animation.*

8.9   Conclusion and future work

Our prototype system for facial animation encapsulates different groups of activities of facial expressions and offers a better cross-sectional understanding of the complex problems involved in the computational model of facial animation. The system resolves the difficulty and complexity by providing a multi-level structure to the system where each level is independently controllable. Our particular interest has been to establish the relevant links and natural mappings from high level motion specification arising from emotions and speech to low level manipulation where distortion of the facial model occurs. The system is interactive aimed at rapid feedback to increase productivity. In addition to the spatial and temporal characteristics embedded in the system, we also incorporate visual or rendering characteristics such as skin texture and color. It is an open system where one can try several

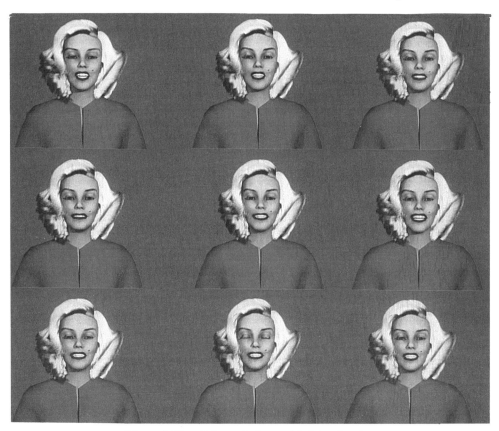

Figure 8.14. *Hair rendering and facial animation.*

possibilities and can experiment with different input accessories for specifying the animation.

Our comprehensive computational system for facial animation has several applications in different domains. The rudimentary facilities of the prototype system can be easily enhanced in order to accommodate particular application.

The developed system offers adequate facilities and desirable features – in particular, for modeling, animation and rendering of faces. Furthermore, it has provided insight to new exploratory avenues for further research. As follows, we identify some of the major areas for further research.

- *Construction and modeling corresponding to the actual anatomical structure*:
  Current modeling methods of representing a face as a surface are not adequate for constructing an anatomically true model of a human face. Moreover, an appropriate

approach to providing information about changes in the soft tissue – based on preservation of volume of soft tissue – and stress–strain tensorial relations is required. These necessities suggest solid design and construction of a human face based on actual medical data.

- *Muscle dynamics using finite element theory*:
  The muscle model used in the system does not provide a precise simulation of actual muscle and skin deformation. It cannot model furrows, bulges and wrinkles in the skin. In addition, as the model is based on surface deformations it does not take into account volumetric changes which occur in the muscle. Finite element theory widely used in engineering applications seems to be a promising approach for modeling the plastic and elastic deformations of objects like human flesh.

- *Wrinkles and aging*:
  The formation and appearance of wrinkles may be attributed primarily to two things: transitory wrinkles which appear as a part of expression when someone laughs, grimaces or frowns, and permanent wrinkles due to aging. The present system does not provide the facilities or means to generate wrinkles. However, the system is being extended to include these aspects using physically based methods for deformation simulation (Wu et al. 1994).

- *Behavior driven animation*:
  Behavior and story-driven animation offer a much higher level of animation development environment for the animator. Here, the animator would generate the actions in terms of high level behaviors, and these actions would be part of the system where a story is given to drive the animation.

- *Multimedia input components*:
  Facial animation inherently involves different media and sources of information to be processed. Our system provides a framework to include different media and a means to drive the animation. The system does not have audio/voice recognition support, the addition of which would make the system richer from a multimedia standpoint.

A widespread demonstration of interest in facial modeling and animation enabled for the first time a workshop forum, gathering researchers from animation, linguistics and psychology to present a global view on the actual state of the art in facial animation (Pelachaud et al. 1994). Among many other points, the main emphasis was given to produce a vocabulary list of signals that characterize faces and their motion, and the need for more precise details for lip movements and temporal data for muscle actions. Validation of models and controls was identified as necessary and useful.

8.10 Acknowledgments

This chapter contains primarily the condensed version of the thesis work of the author. The author would like to extend his thanks to his thesis supervisors Prof Nadia Magnenat

Thalmann and Prof Daniel Thalmann for their invaluable guidance and support. The collaboration of the team members from MIRAlab, University of Geneva and LIG, EPFL for the work is appreciated.

8.11 References

Balaguer J.F. and Gobbetti E. (1993) "Virtuality Builder II: On the Topic of 3D Interaction", in: Virtual Worlds and Multimedia (Eds. Magnenat Thalmann N. and Thalmann D.), pp. 99–110.

Benoit C., Adjoudani A., Angola O., Guiard-Marigny T. and Le Goff B. (1994) "Perception, Analysis and Synthesis of Talking Lips", in: Proc. IMAGINA '94, France, Feb 1994, pp. 142–163.

Bergeron P. and Lachapelle P. (1985) "Controlling Facial Expressions and Body Movements in the Computer Generated Animated Short 'Tony de Peltrie'", SIGGRAPH '85 Course Notes, Advanced Computer Animation Course.

Blinn J.F. and Newell M.E. (1976) "Texture and Reflection in Computer Generated Images", Comm. ACM, Vol. 19, No. 10, pp. 542–547.

Boulic R., Capin T., Huang Z., Kalra P., Lintermann B., Magnenat Thalmann N., Moccozet L., Molet T., Pandzic I.S., Saar K., Schmitt A., Shen J. and Thalmann D. (1995) "The HUMANOID Toolkit: An Environment for Real Time Animation of Multiple Deformable Human Characters", Proc. Eurographics '95, pp. 337–348.

Burt P.J. and Adelson E.H. (1983) "A Multiresolution Spline with Application to Image Mosaics", ACM Transaction on Graphics, Vol. 2, No. 4, pp. 217–236.

Chadwick J., Haumann D.R. and Parent R.E. (1989) "Layered Construction for Deformable Animated Characters", Proc. SIGGRAPH '89, Computer Graphics, Vol. 23, No. 3, pp. 243–252.

Cohen M.M. and Massaro D.W. (1990) "Synthesis of Visible Speech, Behavior Research Methods, Instruments, and Computers", Vol. 22, No. 2, pp. 260–263.

Cohen M.M. and Massaro D.W. (1993) "Modeling Coarticulation in Synthetic Visual Speech", Proc. Computer Animation '93, Geneva, Switzerland (Eds. Magnenat Thalmann N. and Thalmann D.), pp. 139–156.

Coquillart S. (1990) "Extended Free Form Deformation: A Sculpturing Tool for 3D Geometric Modeling", Proc. SIGGRAPH '90, Computer Graphics, Vol. 24, No. 4, pp. 187–196.

Coquillart S. and Jancene P. (1991) "Animated Free Form Deformation: An Interactive Animation Technique", Proc. SIGGRAPH '91, Computer Graphics, Vol. 25, No. 4, pp. 23–26.

Cybenko G. (1989) "Approximation by Superposition of a Signoidal Function", Math. Control Signals and Systems (2) pp. 303–314.

Daldegan A., Magnenat Thalmann N., Kurihara T. and Thalmann D. (1993) "An Integrated System for Modeling, Animating and Rendering Hair", Proc. Eurographics '93, Computer Graphics Forum, Vol. 12, No. 3, pp. 211–221.

deGraf B. (1989) in "State of the Art in Facial Animation", SIGGRAPH '89 Course Notes No. 26, pp. 10–20.

DiPaola S. (1990) "Implementation and Use of a 3D Parameterized Facial Modeling and Animation System", SIGGRAPH '90 Course Notes, pp. 62–73.

Ekman P. and Friesen W.V. (1969) "The Repertoire of Nonverbal Behavior: Categories, Origins, Usage, and Coding", Semiotica, Vol. 1.

Ekman P. and Friesen W.V. (1975) "Unmasking the Face: A Guide to Recognizing Emotions from Facial Clues", Englewood Cliffs: Prentice Hall.

Ekman P. and Friesen W.V. (1978) "Facial Action Coding System", Investigator's Guide Part 2, Consulting Psychologists Press Inc. Palo Alto.

Elson M. (1990) " 'Displacement' Facial Animation Techniques", SIGGRAPH '90 Course Notes, pp. 22–42.

Farin G. (1990) "Curves and Surfaces for Computer Aided Geometric Design, A Practical Guide", Second Edition, Boston: Academic Press.

Gobbetti E. (1993) ''An Object-Oriented Architecture Based on Constraint Imperative Programming for Building Interactive 3D Graphics Applications'', Ph.D. Thesis (in French) Department of Computer Science, Swiss Federal Institute of Technology, Switzerland.

Gross D. (1991) ''Merging Man and Machine'', Computer Graphics World, Vol. 14, No. 5, pp. 47–50.

Guenter B. (1989) ''A System for Simulating Human Facial Expression'', Proc. Computer Animation '89, Geneva, Switzerland, in State of the Art in Computer Animation (Eds. Magnenat Thalmann N. and Thalmann D.).

Heckbert P.S. (1986) ''Survey of Texture Mapping'', IEEE CG&A, Nov. 1986, pp. 56–67.

Hill D.R., Pearce A. and Wyvill B. (1988) ''Animating Speech: An Automated Approach Using Speech Synthesized by Rules'', The Visual Computer, Vol. 3, No. 5, pp. 277–289.

Jeffers J. and Barley M. (1971) ''Speechreading'' (Lipreading), CC Thomas.

Kalra P. (1993) ''An Interactive Multimodal Facial Animation System'', Ph.D. Thesis, Department of Computer Science, Swiss Federal Institute of Technology, Switzerland.

Kalra P. and Magnenat Thalmann N. (1993) ''Simulation of Facial Skin using Texture Mapping and Coloration'', Proc. ICCG '93, Bombay India, in Graphics, Design and Visualization (Eds. Mudur S.P. and Pattanaik S.N.), Amsterdam, pp. 363–74.

Kalra P. and Magnenat Thalmann N. (1994) ''Modelling of Vascular Expressions in Facial Animation'', Proc. Computer Animation '95, IEEE Computer Society, pp. 50–58.

Kalra P., Mangili A., Magnenat Thalmann N. and Thalmann D. (1991) ''SMILE: A Multilayered Facial Animation System'', Proc. IFIP WG 5.10, Tokyo, Japan (Ed Kunii Tosiyasu L.) pp. 189–198.

Kalra P., Mangili A., Magnenat Thalmann N. and Thalmann D. (1992) ''Simulation of Muscle Actions using Rational Free Form Deformations'', Proc. Eurographics '92, Computer Graphics Forum, Vol. 2, No. 3, pp. 59–69.

Kalra P., Gobbetti E., Magnenat Thalmann N. and Thalmann D. (1993) ''A Multimedia Testbed for Facial Animation Control'', International Conference of Multi-Media Modeling, MMM '93, Nov. 9–12, Singapore (Eds. Chua T.S. and Kunii T.L.), pp. 59–72.

Kaneko M., Koike A. and Hatori Y. (1992) ''Automatic Synthesis of Moving Facial Images with Expression and Mouth Shape Controlled by Text'', Proc. CGI '92, Tokyo (Ed. Kunii T.L.), pp. 57–75.

Kurihara T. and Arai K. (1991) ''A Transformation Method for Modeling and Animation of the Human Face from Photographs'', Proc. Computer Animation '91, Geneva, Switzerland (Eds. Magnenat Thalmann N. and Thalmann D.), pp. 45–57.

Larrabee W.F. (1986) ''A Finite Element Method of Skin Deformation: I Biomechanics of Skin and Soft Tissue: A Review; II An Experiment Model of Skin Deformation; III The Finite Element Model'', Laryngoscope, Vol. 96, pp. 399–405, 406–412, 413–419.

LeBlanc A., Turner R. and Thalmann D. (1991) ''Rendering Hair using Pixel Blending and Shadow Buffers'', Journal of Visualization and Computer Animation, Vol. 2, No. 3, pp. 92–97.

LeMeur P. (1991) ''Combinaison d'images multiresolution'', Diplome-Project, Swiss Federal Institute of Technology, Lausanne, Switzerland.

Lewis J.P. and Parke F.I. (1987) ''Automated Lipsynch and Speech Synthesis for Character Animation'', Proc. CHI '87 and Graphics Interface '87, Toronto, pp. 143–147.

Lewis J.P. (1991) ''Automated Lipsynch: Background and Techniques'', Journal of Visualization and Computer Animation, Vol. 2, No. 4, pp. 118–122.

Löfqvist A. (1990) ''Speech as Audible Gestures'', in Speech Production and Speech Modeling (Eds. Hardcastle W.J. and Marchal A.), Dordrecht: Kluwer Academic Publishers, 289–322.

Magnenat Thalmann N. and Kalra P. (1992) ''A Model for Creating and Visualizing Speech and Emotion, in Aspects of Automatic Natural Language Generation'' (Eds. Dale R., Hovy E., Räsner D., Stock O.), 6th International Workshop on National Language Generation, Trento, Italy, April 1992, pp. 1–12.

Magnenat Thalmann N. and Thalmann D. (1987) ''The Direction of Synthetic Actors in the film Rendez-vous à Montréal'', IEEE Computer Graphics and Applications, Vol. 7, No. 12, pp. 9–19.

Magnenat Thalmann N. and Thalmann D. (1991) ''Complex Models for Visualizing Synthetic Actors'', IEEE

Computer Graphics and Applications, Vol. 11, No. 5, pp. 32–44.

Magnenat Thalmann N., Primeau E. and Thalmann D. (1988) "Abstract Muscle Action Procedures for Human Face Animation", The Visual Computer, Vol. 3, No. 5, pp. 290–297.

Magnenat Thalmann N., Cazedevals A. and Thalmann D. (1993) "Modeling Facial Communication between an Animator and Synthetic Actor in Real Time", Proc. Modeling in Computer Graphics, Genova, Italy (Eds. Falcidieno B. and Kunii T.L.), pp. 387–396.

Mangili A. (1991) "SMILE: Manuel Utilisateur", LIG, EPFL.

Moccozet L. and Magnenat Thalmann N. (1992) "Controlling the Complexity of Objects Based on Polygonal Meshes", Proc. CG International '92, Tokyo, Japan, Springer-Verlag (Ed. Kunii T.L.), pp. 763–780.

Nahas M., Huitric H. and Saintourens M. (1988) "Animation of B-Spline Figure", The Visual Computer, No. 3, pp. 272–276.

Nahas M., Huitric H., Rijoux M. and Domey J. (1990) "Registered 3D Texture Imaging", Proc. Computer Animation '90, Geneva, Switzerland (Eds. Magnenat Thalmann N. and Thalmann D.), pp. 81–91.

Oka M., Tsutsui K. and Ohba A. (1987) "Real Time Manipulation of Texture Mapped Surfaces", Proc. SIGGRAPH '87, Computer Graphics, Vol. 21, No. 4, pp. 181–188.

Pandzic I.S., Kalra P., Magnenat Thalmann N. and Thalmann D. (1994) "Real Time Facial Interaction", Displays, Vol. 15, No. 3, pp. 157–163.

Parke F.I. (1972) "Computer Generated Animation of Faces", Proc. ACM National Conference, No. 1, pp. 451–457.

Parke F.I. (1974) "A Parametric Model for Human Faces", Ph.D. Dissertation, University of Utah.

Parke F.I. (1975) "A Model for Human Faces that Allows Speech Synchronized Animation", Computer and Graphics, Vol. 1, pp. 3–4.

Parke F.I. (1982) "Parametrized Models for Facial Animation", IEEE Computer Graphics and Applications, Vol. 2, No. 9, pp. 61–68.

Parke F.I. (1991) "Techniques for Facial Animation" in Magnenat Thalmann N. and Thalmann D. (eds) "New Trends in Animation and Visualization", John Wiley & Sons, Chichester, UK, pp. 229–241.

Patel M. (1992) "FACES", Technical Report 92-55 (Ph.D. thesis), University of Bath.

Patel M. and Willis P. (1991) "FACES: Facial Animation, Construction and Editing System", Proc. Eurographics '91, Vienna, Sept 1991, pp. 33–45.

Patterson E.C., Litwinowicz P.C., and Greene N. (1991) "Facial Animation by Spatial Mapping", Proc. Computer Animation '91, Geneva, Switzerland (Eds. Magnenat Thalmann N. and Thalmann D.), pp. 31–44, April.

Pearce A., Wyvill B. and Hill D.R. (1986) "Speech and Expression: A Computer Solution to Face Animation", Proc. Graphics Interface '86, Vision Interface '86, pp. 136–140.

Pelachaud C., Badler N.I. and Steadman M. (1991) "Linguistic Issues in Facial Animation", Proc. Computer Animation '91, Geneva, Switzerland (Eds. Magnenat Thalmann N. and Thalmann D.), pp. 15–30.

Pelachaud C., Badler N.I. and Viaud M.L. (Eds) (1994) "Final Report to NSF of the Standards for Facial Animation Workshop", University of Pennsylvania, Philadelphia, USA.

Pieper S. (1989) "More than Skin Deep: Physical Modeling of Facial Tissue", MS.c. Thesis, MIT Media Lab, Cambridge, MA.

Platt S. and Badler N.I. (1981) "Animating Facial Expressions", Proc. SIGGRAPH '81, Computer Graphics, Vol. 15, No. 3, pp. 245–252.

Reeves B. (1990) "Simple and Complex Facial Animation: Case Studies", SIGGRAPH '90 Tutorial Notes, pp. 90–106.

Rumelhart D.E., Hinton G.E. and Williams R.J. (1986) "Learning Internal Representations by Error Propagation", in: Rumelhart D.E., McClellend J.L. (eds.), Parallel Distributed Processing, Vol. 1, pp. 318–362.

Sederberg T.W. and Parry S.R. (1986) "Free Form Deformation of Solid Geometric Models", Proc. SIGGRAPH '86, Computer Graphics, Vol. 20, No. 4, pp. 151–160.

Shields S.A., Mallory M.E. and Simon A. (1990) "The Experience and Symptoms of Blushing as a Function of Age and Reported Frequency of Blushing", Journal of Nonverbal Behavior 14(3), Vol. 4, No. 3, pp. 171–187.

Sibson R. (1978) "Locally Equiangular Triangulations", The Computer Journal, Vol. 21, No. 3, pp. 243–245.

Terzopoulos D. and Waters K. (1990) "Physically-Based Facial Modeling, Analysis and Animation", Journal of Visualization and Computer Animation, Vol. 1, pp. 73–80.

Terzopoulos D. and Waters K. (1991) "Techniques for Realistic Facial Modeling and Animation", Proc. Computer Animation '91, Geneva, Switzerland, (Eds. Magnenat Thalmann N. and Thalmann D.), pp. 59–74.

Viaud M.L. and Yahia H. (1992) "Facial Animation with Wrinkles", 3rd Workshop on Animation, Eurographics '92, Cambridge.

Waite C.T. (1990) "The Facial Action Control Editor, Face: A Parametric Facial Expression Editor for Computer Generated Animation", Master's Thesis, Massachusetts Institute of Technology, Cambridge, Massachusetts.

Wang C.L.Y. (1993) "Langwidere: Hierarchical Spline Based Facial Animation System with Simulated Muscles", Master's Thesis, University of Calgary, Department of Computer Science, Calgary, Oct.

Waters K. (1987) "A Muscle Model for Animating Three Dimensional Facial Expression", Proc. SIGGRAPH '87, Computer Graphics, Vol. 21, No. 4, pp. 17–24.

Waters K. and Terzopoulos D. (1991) "Modeling and Animating Faces using Scanned Data", Journal of Visualization and Computer Animation, Vol. 2, No. 4, pp. 123–128.

Williams L. (1990) "Performance Driven Facial Animation", Proc SIGGRAPH '90, Computer Graphics, Vol. 24, No. 3, pp. 235–242.

Wu Y., Magnenat Thalmann N. and Thalmann D. (1994) "A Plastic-Visco-Elastic Model for Wrinkles in Facial Animation and Skin Aging", Proc. Pacific Graphics '94, Beijing, pp. 201–213.

Yau J.F.S. and Duffy N.D. (1988) "A Texture Mapping Approach to 3D Facial Image Synthesis", Computer Graphics Forum, Vol. 7, pp. 129–134.

Zajonc R.B. (1985) "Emotion and Facial Efference: A Theory Reclaimed", Science, Vol. 228, pp. 15–21.

Zeltzer D. (1982) "Motor Control Techniques for Figure Animation", IEEE Computer Graphics and Applications, Vol. 2, No. 9, pp. 53–59.

CHAPTER 9

Sculpting, Clothing and Hairdressing our Virtual Humans

Nadia Magnenat Thalmann and Pascal Volino
MIRALab, University of Geneva

Abstract
Scenes involving virtual humans imply many complex problems to manage. We slowly come to the point of simulating real-looking virtual humans, taking into account body, face and cloth deformations. In a short while, we will not be able to see any difference between a real person and a virtual one. However, the synthesis of realistic virtual humans leads to obtaining and including the specific features of the character of interest. For well-known personalities such as Marilyn, Humphrey or Elvis, there is less scope for mistakes as the deviations will be very easily detected by the spectator. In this chapter, we do not discuss the aspects of animating actors, which are covered in other chapters, we emphasize three different key issues in the creation of realistic virtual actors: the creation of their shape, the creation and animation of their clothes, and the creation and animation of their hair.

9.1 Sculpting the shape of a virtual actor

In order to create a well-known personality, it is essential to create an accurate three-dimensional face. Traditional methods based on real persons or reduced models (plaster models) are the following ones:

- **Three-dimensional reconstruction from two-dimensional photographs**
  Two or three projections (photos) are entered and the computer is used to derive the 3-D coordinates. Synthetic Marilyn and Bogey in the film *Rendez-vous in Montreal* (Magnenat Thalmann and Thalmann 1987) were created using this approach.

- **Reconstruction from cross sections**
  This popular method consists of reconstructing an object from a set of serial cross sections, like tracing the contours from a topographic map. This method (Magnenat Thalmann and Thalmann 1990) has been used to create *Eglantine*, a computerized mannequin, who never existed before.
- **Three-dimensional digitizing**
  The technique is simply to enter the 3-D coordinates using a 3-D digitizer. We used for example, the Polhemus 3-D-digitizer (based on magnetic fields) to create various objects. The method is less time-consuming than the two other methods, because no photos are needed. However, there are limitations in the shapes which can be digitized; cavities and small parts cannot be entered.

To construct this kind of shape, we proposed the use of an interactive sculpting approach (LeBlanc et al. 1991a). The surfaces of human face and body are irregular structures implemented as polygonal meshes. We have introduced a methodology (Paouri et al. 1991) for interactive sculpting using a six-degree-of-freedom interactive input device like the SpaceBall. When used in conjunction with a common 2-D mouse, full three dimensional user interaction is achieved, with the SpaceBall in one hand and the mouse in the other. The SpaceBall device is used to move around the object being sculpted in order to examine it from various points of view, while the mouse carries out the picking and deformation work onto a magnifying image in order to see every small detail in real time (e.g. vertex creation, primitive selection and local surface deformations). In this way, the user not only sees the object from every angle but he can also apply and correct deformations from every angle interactively.

Typically, the sculpting process may be initiated in two ways: by loading and altering an existing shape or by simply starting one from scratch. For example, we will use a sphere as a starting point for the head of a person and use cylinders for limbs. We will then add or remove polygons according to the details needed and apply local deformations to alter the shape. When starting from scratch points are placed in 3-D space and polygonized. However, it may be more tedious and time consuming.

With this type of 3-D interaction, the operations performed while sculpting an object closely resemble traditional sculpting. The major operations performed using this software include creation of primitives, selection, local surface deformations and global deformations.

To select parts of the objects, the mouse is used in conjunction with the SpaceBall to quickly mark out the desired primitives in and around the object. This amounts to pressing the mouse button and sweeping the mouse cursor on the screen while moving the object with the SpaceBall. All primitives (vertices, edges and polygons) can be selected. Mass picking may be done by moving the object away from the eye (assuming a perspective projection) and careful, minute picking may be done by bringing the object closer.

These tools make it possible to produce local elevations or depressions on the surface and to even out unwanted bumps once the work is nearing completion. Local deformations are applied while the SpaceBall device is used to move the object and examine the progression of the deformation from different angles. Mouse movements on the screen are used to produce vertex movements in 3-D space from the current viewpoint. The technique is intended to be a metaphor analogous to pinching, lifting and moving of a stretchable fabric material. Pushing the apex vertex inwards renders a believable effect of pressing a mould into clay. These tools also make it possible to produce global deformations on the whole object or some of the selected regions. For example, if the object has to grow in a certain direction, it can be obtained by scaling or shifting the object on the region of interest. Figure 9.1 shows examples of creation of faces using our sculpting approach.

9.2 Cloth modeling and animation

9.2.1 State-of-the-art in cloth modeling and animation

In most computer-generated films involving virtual humans, clothes are simulated as a part of the body with no autonomous motion. However, in recent years, software has been

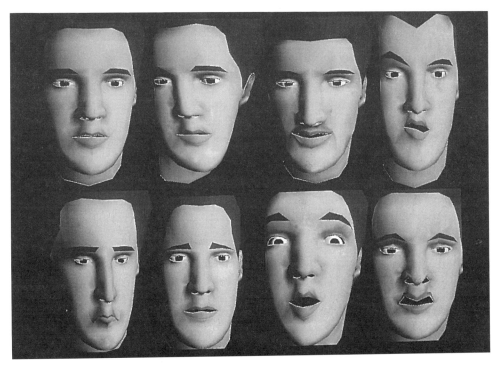

Figure 9.1. *Examples of faces created with the sculpting approach.*

developed and applied to the interactive design of 2-D garment panels and to optimizing the layout of garment panels on the fabric. In Hinds and McCartney's work (Hinds and McCartney 1990), a static trunk of a mannequin's body is represented by bicubic B-spline surfaces. Garment panels are considered to be surfaces of complex shapes in 3-D. The garment panels are designed around the static mannequin body, and then are reduced to 2-D cutting patterns. This approach is contrary to the traditional approach to garment design. The garment is modeled by geometric methods. To visualize the folds and drapes, harmonic functions and sinusoidal functions are superimposed on the garment panels. Mangen and Lasudry (1991) proposed an algorithm for finding the intersection polygon of any two polygons. This is applied to the automatic optimization of the layout of polygonal garment panels in 2-D rectangular fabrics. Both of these projects concern stages of garment design and manufacturing in real industrial contexts.

For modeling more realistic clothes, two separated problems have to be solved: the motion of the cloth without collision detection and the collision detection of the cloth with the body and with itself.

Previous works on deformable object animation using physically based models have permitted animation of cloth-like objects in many kinds of situations. Weil (1986) pioneered cloth animation using an approximated model based on relaxation of the surface. Haumann and Parent (1988) produced animations with flags or leaves moving in the wind, or curtains blowing in a breeze. Kunii and Godota (1990) used a hybrid model incorporating physical and geometrical techniques to model garment wrinkles. Aono (1990) simulated wrinkle propagation on a handkerchief using an elastic model. Terzopoulos et al. (1987) developed a general elastic model and applied it to a wide range of objects including cloth. Interaction of clothes with synthetic actors in motion (Lafleur et al. 1991; Carignan et al. 1992; Yang and Magnenat Thalmann 1993) marked the beginning of a new era in cloth animation in more complex situations (see Section 9.2.2 for more details). However, there were still a number of restrictions on the simulation conditions on the geometrical structure and the mechanical situations, imposed by the simulation model or the collision detection.

Deformable objects may be represented by different geometrical models. Triangular grids are most common, but polynomial surfaces (Witkin and Welch 1990; Baraff and Witkin 1992) and particle systems (Breen et al. 1994) are also used for solutions to specific mechanical simulations. Yielding nice and accurate deformations, they constrain both the initial shape and the allowed deformations. Each model requires different techniques for modeling complex objects such as panels-and-seaming for cloth objects (Yang and Magnenat Thalmann 1993). Furthermore, global mechanical models such as finite elements and finite difference are not suitable for situations involving constraints and nonlinearities as non-marginal situations all over the surfaces. These situations happen when modeling the highly nonlinear deformations required for wrinkles and crumples (Denby 1976), and when there are numerous collisions and much friction.

Collision detection and response has been used mainly for stopping cloth from penetrating the body and, more marginally, for preventing self-collisions between different parts of the cloth. The first time-consuming problem was to extract the possible colliding elements from the whole set of elements composing the cloth and the body surfaces. Many techniques have been developed, based on different ideas and adapted for various surface representations. For example, mathematical algorithms have been developed for situations where the surfaces are represented by curved patches or parametric surfaces, as described in Baraff (1990); Baraff and Witkin (1992); Von Herzen et al. (1990); Duff (1992) and Snyder et al. (1993). In the case of representing surfaces by a huge set of flat polygons, techniques based on rasterization (Shinya and Forgue 1991) or the tracking of the closest distance on the convex hull (Moore and Wilhelms 1988; Lin and Manocha 1993) have been developed. Unfortunately, these techniques are not well suited for efficient detection on deformable surface animations, as they require either expensive Z-buffer rendering or constructing the convex hull of the objects at each frame.

9.2.2 A physics-based approach

The Terzopoulos model
After some comparisons (Magnenat Thalmann and Yang 1991), Terzopoulos' elastic surface model (Terzopoulos et al. 1987) was chosen for our system with the damping term replaced by a more accurate term. The fundamental equation of motion corresponds to an equilibrium between internal forces (Newton term, resistance to stretching, dissipative force, resistance to bending) and external forces (collision forces, gravity, seaming and attaching forces, wind force):

$$\rho(a)\frac{\mathrm{d}^2 r}{\mathrm{d}t^2} + \frac{\delta}{\delta r}\int_\Omega \int \|E\|^2 \mathrm{d}a_1 \, \mathrm{d}a_2 + \frac{\delta}{\delta v}\int_\Omega \int \|\dot{E}\|^2 \mathrm{d}a_1 \, \mathrm{d}a_2$$
$$+ \frac{\delta}{\delta r}\int_\Omega \int \|B - B_0\|^2 \mathrm{d}a_1 \, \mathrm{d}a_2 = \sum F_{\mathrm{ex}} \tag{9.1}$$

$$\dot{E}_{ij}(r(a)) = \frac{\mathrm{d}}{\mathrm{d}t} E_{ij} = \frac{1}{2}\dot{G}_{ij} = \frac{\partial r}{\partial a_i} \cdot \frac{\partial v}{\partial a_j} + \frac{\partial r}{\partial a_j} \cdot \frac{\partial v}{\partial a_i} \tag{9.2}$$

We choose to replace the third term (dissipative force) because the one used in Terzopoulos et al. (1987) is scalar. So, no matter where energy comes from, it will be dissipated. For example, gravitational energy is dissipated, resulting in a surface which achieves a limiting speed and is not continually accelerated. In our case (Carignan et al. 1992), we use Raleigh's dissipative function (Eringen and Suhubi 1974) generalized for a continuum surface (Platt and Barr 1988). As E is the strain (a measure of the amount of deformation), $\mathrm{d}E/\mathrm{d}t$ is the "speed" at which the deformation occurs. This means that the surface integral may be considered a rate of energy dissipation due to internal friction. This implies that the variational derivative with respect to velocity of the surface integral will

minimize the "speed" of the deformation. With this approach, no dissipation occurs when the surface undergoes rigid body displacement like when falling in an air-free gravity field. This improves the realism of motion.

To apply the elastic deformable surface model, the polygonal panel should be discretized using the finite difference approximation method. We have proposed a new algorithm to calculate the elastic force on an arbitrary element. This algorithm is effective for discretizing not only an arbitrary polygonal panel (concave or convex), but also other kinds of polygonal panels with holes inside them.

The introduction of seaming and attaching forces
In the animation of deformable objects consisting of many surface panels, the constraints that join different panels together and attach them to other objects are very important. In our case, two kinds of dynamic constraints are used in two different stages. When deformable panels are separated, forces are applied to the elements in the panels to join them according to the seaming information. The same method is used to attach the elements of deformable objects to other rigid objects.

After the creation of deformable objects, another kind of dynamic constraint is used to guarantee seaming and attaching. For the attaching, the elements of the deformable objects are always kept on the rigid object, so they have the same position and velocity as the elements of the rigid object to which they are attached. For the seaming and joining of the panels themselves, two seamed elements move with the same velocity and position, but the velocity and position depend on those of the individual elements. According to the law of momentum conservation, total momentum of the elements before and after seaming should remain the same.

A more general collision algorithm
Basically, collisions are detected before a cloth's vertices come through the body's polygons and we have to find the position of the point of impact on the polygon, the velocity and the normal of that point. Moreover, all forces (including internal forces) acting on vertices should be computed.

We have also described a method of collision avoidance (Lafleur et al. 1991) that creates a very thin force field around the surface of the obstacle to be avoided. This force field acts like a shield rejecting the points. Although the method works for a simple case of a skirt, use of this type of force is somewhat artificial and cannot provide realistic simulation with complex clothes. In fact, the effect degrades when the force becomes very strong, looking like a "kick" given to the cloth. Figure 9.2 shows an example from the film *Flashback* (Magnenat Thalmann and Thalmann 1991).

To improve realism, we have proposed (Carignan et al. 1992) to use the law of conservation of momentum for perfectly inelastic bodies. This means we consider all energy to be lost within a collision.

Concerning our user interface (Werner et al. 1993), we work as a tailor does, designing

Figure 9.2. *Collision detection in the film* Flashback.

garments from individual two-dimensional panels seamed together. Figure 9.3 shows an example of a panel.

Figures 9.4 and 9.5 show examples of clothes.

9.2.3   Simulating autonomous clothes using physics-based models

Introduction

Until now, cloth simulation programs have tried to get realistic results for garments worn by an animated body. The garments were considered as a set of flat polygons made of a regular triangle mesh, and held together by seaming forces. For calculation speed, geometrical assumptions were made to reduce collision detection time according to the specific situation where an actor wears a garment. That situation is in fact a rather "simple" mechanical context with well-defined collision situations, and quite smooth deformation.

Our system (Volino et al. 1995) intends to get out of this specificity and to be able to simulate cloth in any situation that may be encountered in real life. This involves for example a cloth being put on a body, thrown away, folded, crumpled, ... Situations such as

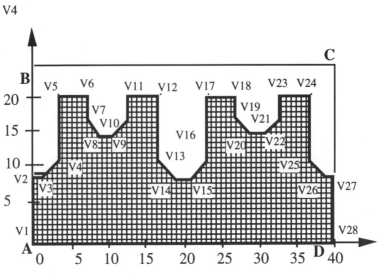

Figure 9.3.   *Panel.*

Figure 9.4.   *A synthetic actress with clothes.*

Figure 9.5. *A synthetic actress with clothes.*

crumpling involve very difficult geometrical and mechanical situations, such as numerous and interdependent collisions and very high deformations. Our system should be robust enough to cope with all situations that may occur.

Since it is more than just a simulation program that animates cloth worn by a moving body, our system can simulate a very wide range of deformable surfaces in whatever scene involving moving objects.

The main evolution has been the development of new techniques ensuring accurate and robust simulation in any of these situations.

Compared to earlier systems, we have put emphasis on the following points:

- **Versatility**
  Our system does not just animate cloth worn by a moving body like in the previous systems; it was designed to animate any kind of mechanical surface in any kind of environment, a cloth being a particular mechanical surface and a moving actor being a particular environment. For instance, we could imagine simulating the cloth motion in various situations, such as falling on the ground or crumpling in a dryer machine.

- **Non-regular discretization**
  Regular triangular discretizations are no longer required for the simulated surfaces. We do not need to have rectangular flat surfaces to be assembled for getting a cloth or whatever object. Any triangular mesh, regular or not, can be used as input for the definition of a deformable object (provided that the triangles are small enough for allowing acceptable curvature). The design process gets simplified and any kind of object shapes may be imported from various sources. If necessary, local rediscretization is made possible without constraints. Furthermore a cloth now can be handled as a single object rather than as a collection of panels kept seamed together during all the simulation process. As any object is now processed in the same way, the system is more flexible and easier to manipulate.
- **Robustness for the mechanical model**
  In some difficult situations involving for example crumpling of very deformable surfaces, the mechanical context becomes very difficult due to the nonlinearities caused by the complex and numerous collisions. Furthermore, the deformations may become high compared to the size of the discretization, bringing more problems that may cause the numerical simulation algorithms to "explode". Stability control has been implemented for preventing difficult situations from degenerating into instability. The deformation and kinetic energy is monitored within the structure and if their variation indicates possible instability, the energy is spread artificially to the neighboring elements, decreasing the perturbations. Instability has been practically removed from any "reasonable" situation that may occur during simulation. A very wide range of mechanical parameters can now be explored without fearing "explosions", and very difficult collision situations no longer crash the simulation.
- **Robustness for collision handling**
  Crumpling surfaces introduce very numerous and interdependent collisions. Evaluating them requires efficient geometrical algorithms. Quite often, the situation and the dependencies are too complex for evaluating precisely all the collisions and the corresponding response in a reasonable time. Furthermore, as we intend to deal with any kind of surface in any kind of geometrical situations, it is not possible to take advantage of any "in–out" orientation information for the colliding surfaces. Elements accidentally crossing a colliding surface may thus have disastrous and unrecoverable effects on the simulation. Our system handles collisions in a robust way. Algorithms have been designed for correcting any collision orientation inconsistency that may result from an approximate response in a complex collision situation. If ever a surface crossing is detected, consistency correction is performed within the group of colliding elements and the situation will recover correctly as the simulation goes on.

Description of the system

A cloth is represented by an assembly of fabric panels, like real-life garments. After 2-D design that may be based on real cloth models, these panels are seamed together using mechanical simulation. The panels are then assembled and the garment becomes a single-piece object, that can be manipulated in any way.

The cloth system is divided into two separate parts:

- The 2-D panel editor
- The 3-D simulation system

The design process goes through three steps:

1) Garment panel design

Using the 2-D panel editor, the panels composing a cloth are defined geometrically. The editor provides help for geometry and dimensioning with different tools, such as grid matching, duplication and symmetries.

Seaming lines are then defined between and within the panels. The designer specifies which border lines should be seamed together. The tool provides help for maintaining consistency between the different seamings.

The garment is then stored in a file containing panel and seaming definitions.

2) Garment assembly

Using the 3-D simulation system, the panels composing a garment are then seamed together for composing a cloth.

The user defines the context in which the garment has to be assembled. Either it may be assembled ''in the air'' or around a body with several other cloths for getting a dressed character.

The panels are interactively moved to an initial position that will ensure correct assembly.

Seamings are represented by ''elastics'' that will match the seaming lines together. Mechanical computation is performed using the forces exerted by the elastics. Once the seaming lines are brought together, the different panels are merged together and a single cloth object is obtained, which may be handled as any other object.

At this point, the resulting cloth object may be saved for future use, but the mechanical simulation may also proceed directly for computing the animation.

3) Garment animation

The garment is put into the animated environment, composed by the moving body or any other object composing the scene.

The mechanical calculation moves the deformable surface according to its mechanical parameters (elasticity, thickness, ...) and the external solicitations:

- Collision response (repulsion and friction) to itself (self-collision)
- Collision response to other animated or fixed objects (other cloth, the body, any other object)
- External force fields (gravity, wind, ...)
- Other solicitations (fixed elements, user defined ''elastics'', ...)

The user may interactively change mechanical settings, block some points of the deformable surfaces, or interactively add "elastics" between any object, modifying the animation.

The mechanical model

Models based on global minimization or Lagrangian dynamics formulations are not suited for highly nonlinear situations where discontinuities generated by collisions are numerous. The main idea of our model is to integrate Newton's motion equation $F = ma$ in a direct way to keep quickly evaluated time steps small. Thus, nonlinear behaviors and discontinuous responses such as collisions will be handled in an accurate way. Furthermore, this direct formulation allows us easy and precise inclusion of any nonlinear mechanical behavior. With such a model, we can also act directly on the position and speed of the elements, and thus avoid handling collisions through strong repulsion forces that perturbate the simulation.

The animated deformable object is represented as a particle system by sets of vertices forming heterogeneous triangles, thus allowing surfaces of any shape to be easily modeled and simulated.

The object is considered to be isotropic and of constant thickness. Elastic properties of the object are partially described by the standard parameters (Morton and Hearle 1962) that are:

E_0 the Young modulus
ν the Poisson coefficient
ρ the density
T the thickness

To avoid the textile behaving like a rubber sheet, nonlinearity is added to its response through Young's Modulus which will be represented locally as a function of the unit elongation (ε):

$$E(\varepsilon) = \begin{array}{ll} E_0(1 + A\varepsilon) & 0 < \varepsilon < \varepsilon_{max} \\ E_0(1 - B\varepsilon) & \varepsilon_{min} < \varepsilon < 0 \\ E_{max} & \varepsilon < \varepsilon_{min}, \ \varepsilon > \varepsilon_{max} \end{array} \tag{9.3}$$

A, B, E_{max} and E_0 are defined from discretization size and real textile rigidity. Since buckle formation requires a change of area that increases with the size of the discretized elements, the discretization size alters the textile's easiness to buckle into double curvature. E_0 is then settled slightly below the real textile's rigidity. Choosing $A > B$ will help compression during double curvature manifestation without losing too much textile stretching stiffness. E_{max} is used only to limit internal force since a textile would have to break before reaching such a value. It is difficult to find a function that rules those parameters; this has not been done yet, we only adjust the parameters to get visual realism. Further work would allow a more precise adjustment of these parameters to represent more accurately specific types of textile.

Using Newton's second law *F=ma*, the motion equation consists of a pair of coupled first-order differential equations, for position and velocity. The system of equations is resolved using the second order (midpoint method) of the Euler–Cromer method.

The constraints implied in deformable object motion are subdivided in two categories:

- Continuous constraints, including internal and some external ones, such as wind (represented as a force proportional to the relative velocity of a surface and a viscous fluid) and gravity. Additional external forces are also applied by elastics binding two vertices together. Such elastics allow seaming and interactive manipulation of the objects.
- Discontinuous constraints resulting from collisions with other objects. They induce instantaneous change in the state of the object.

Internal strains are either in-plane, from planar extension and shearing, or out-of-plane, from bending and twisting. In-plane and out-of-plane deformations are evaluated separately. Considering the irregularity of the triangle mesh, the force evaluation should be independent of the size and shape of the triangles.

Elastic and shearing strain

A triangle is considered as a thin plate object in a plane stress situation. Each edge of the triangle is taken as a strain gauge giving strain measurement on the cloth surface. A set of three measurements, called ''strain rosette'', is enough for completely evaluating the state of strain. The strains or unit elongation given by each edge at an angle θ_i are related using:

$$\varepsilon_{\theta_i} = \varepsilon_u \cos^2 \theta_i + \varepsilon_v \sin^2 \theta_i + 2\gamma_{uv} \sin \theta_i \cos \theta_i \tag{9.4}$$

With this, we can compute the unit elongation (ε_u, ε_v) and shear (γ_{uv}) in an arbitrary (u,v) coordinate system. If we settle the u axis parallel to one of the edges, the corresponding angle is null and one of the equations is automatically solved. It is possible to use a fixed (u,v) orientation to handle anisotropic objects.

Then, the Hook law for a uniform isotropic material gives directly the stress components:

$$\sigma_{u,v} = \frac{E}{1 - v^2}[\varepsilon_{u,v} + v\varepsilon_{v,u}] \qquad \tau_{uv} = G\gamma_{uv} = \frac{E}{2(1 + v)}\gamma_{uv} \tag{9.5}$$

The stress components on a triangle are converted into in-plane forces on the triangle's edges. The force applied on edge j of triangle i is:

$$F_i^j = TL_j\{[\mathbf{m}_j \cdot \mathbf{u}\sigma_u - \mathbf{m}_j \cdot \mathbf{v}\tau_{uv}]\mathbf{u} + [\mathbf{m}_j \cdot \mathbf{v}\sigma_v + \mathbf{m}_j \cdot \mathbf{u}\tau_{uv}]\mathbf{v}\} \tag{9.6}$$

where $\mathbf{m}_j$ is a unit vector perpendicular to the edge and in the triangle plane (Figure 9.6). This force is then equally distributed on the two edges' vertices.

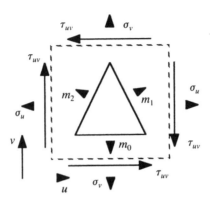

Figure 9.6. *Local constraints on a textile's surface are evaluated from the unit elongation of the triangle edges allowing the determination of the stress components in an arbitrary* (u, v) *orientation.*

Bending strain

The curvature force is very weak compared to in-plane forces, and tends to keep all the triangles in the same plane or initial curvature. The force evaluation must consider the possible case where the radius of curvature is lower than the size of the triangles.

The edge between two triangles is used as a hinge for curvature manifestation (Figure 9.7a) providing information on single curvature only. But it is known from the Mohr circle that it is always possible to decompose any twist strain into a combination of pure bending strains. Considering the arbitrary orientation of the edges, even if we have no control on it, twist strain is taken into account via the additive property of curvature.

Using the angle between the triangles normals (Figure 9.7), we look for the maximum curvature radius (R) for which the corresponding arc fits inside the triangles. Referring to Figure 9.7b, h is lower than or equal to the height of the triangles and L is greater than $h*a$, with $a < 1$. This adaptation will allow R to reach values smaller than the size of the triangles. The local curvature (K) is the inverse of R.

To prevent K and the bending force from reaching infinity, we limit K to a maximum. If the angle keeps on growing, a specific high bending constraint handling will be performed.

The associated momentum in width unit is:

$$M = DK = E\frac{T^3}{12(1 - v^2)}K \tag{9.7}$$

where D, the flexural rigidity, is taken as a reference since this parameter does not reflect the real behavior of a textile. The material is still isotropic. The force corresponding to M applied on vertices 2 and 3 is

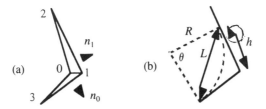

Figure 9.7. *(a) Basic form in which the curvature will appear with 4 vertices. (b) The angle of view is slightly different, θ is the angle between the normal, R the approximated radius of curvature and L and h are distances used to fit the arc inside the triangles.*

$$F_{2,3} = \frac{Mw}{h_{0,1}} h_{0,1} \qquad (9.8)$$

where w is the hinge's length, $h_{0,1}$ are the triangles' height. In respect to the equilibrium condition, the corresponding forces on vertices 1 and 2 will be

$$F_0 = F_1 = -\left(\frac{F_2}{2} + \frac{F_3}{2}\right) \qquad (9.9)$$

Collision detection and handling

For dealing with complex collision situations such as crumpling, we need efficient collision and self-collision detection, as well as a robust collision handling. Collision and particularly self-collision detection is often the bottleneck of simulation applications in terms of calculation time, because of the scene complexity that involves a huge number of geometrical tests for determining which elements are colliding.

In our case, the problem is complicated further because we are handling discretized surfaces that may contain thousands of polygons. We also are considering general situations where we cannot make any hypotheses about region proximities. Finally, we have to efficiently detect self-collisions within the surfaces. This prevents the use of standard bounding box algorithms because potentially colliding regions of a surface are always touching each other by adjacency.

A very efficient algorithm (Volino and Magnenat Thalmann 1994) for handling this situation has been implemented in the system. This algorithm is based on hierarchization and takes advantage of this adjacency which, combined with a surface curvature criterion, let us skip large regular regions from the self-collision detection. More precisely, the algorithm identifies regions on the surface hierarchy that do not verify any of the two conditions that can lead to self-collision within the region:

- The surface is curved enough for making a ''loop'' and hitting another part of the surface.

- The contour of the surface has such a shape that a minimal fold will bring superposition and collision of the surface.

This can be expressed in a more formal way like this:
* Let S be a continuous surface in the Euclidean space delimited by one contour C.

if: There exists a vector **V** for which at (almost) every point of S (**N** being the normal vector of the surface at the considered point)

and: The projection of C on a plane orthogonal to **V** along the direction of **V** has no self-intersections

then: There are no self-collisions on the surface S.

We then can skip spending time detecting collisions within an area or between two adjacent areas using the following statements:

I.   (a) If there can be found an area for which there exists a vector that has positive dot product with the normals of every triangle of the area and (b) if the 2-D projection of its contour along this direction does not intersect itself, then we need not look for self-intersections within that area.

II. If can be found two areas that are adjacent (connected by at least one vertex), then (a) if there exists a vector that has positive dot product with the normals of every triangles of both areas and (b) if the 2-D projection of their contours along this direction do not intersect each other, then we need not look for intersections between these two areas.

Once the possible colliding triangles of our surfaces are located, we extract different types of geometrical collisions:

- **Proximities**
  They are represented by couples of elements that are closer than a threshold distance. That may be triangle-to-vertex, edge-to-edge, and more marginally edge-to-vertex and vertex-to-vertex proximities. They illustrate collision interaction. They are used for computing collision response.
- **Interferences**
  They are represented by edge–triangle couples that are crossing each other. They illustrate situations where two surfaces are interpenetrating. They reveal inconsistent collision situations that have to be corrected.

Collision response implies the correction of position and velocity to prevent contact and crossing. However, this problem cannot be efficiently resolved in complicated situations such as interaction between multiple collisions. It may occasionally happen that some vertices move to ''the wrong side'' of a colliding surface, a situation with which the collision response must cope. Our contribution has been to create algorithms able to correctly orient the detected collisions so as to correct any wrong situation.

9.3 Hair modeling, animation and rendering

9.3.1 State-of-the-art in hair modeling, animation and rendering

In the field of human simulation, hair presents one of the most challenging problems. The difficulties of processing hair result from the large number and detailed geometries of the individual hairs, the complex interaction of light and shadow among the hairs, and the small scale of one hair's width in comparison to the rendered image. In fact, there are basically four problems to solve in order to produce realistic animated synthetic actors with hair: hair modeling and creation, hair motion, collision detection and hair rendering. In this section, we will first review the four problems and the various solutions proposed by researchers. Then, we will describe how we model and create hair and hairstyles. In the next section, we will explain a method to animate hair with collision detection. The fourth section surveys a rendering method and the last section presents a discussion and future developments.

The modeling problem is one of specification of hundreds of thousands of individual elements: their geometry, their distribution, their shape, their direction.

Hair animation should be based on physics models. However, the animation of individual strands is too time-consuming. Rosenblum et al. (1991) propose a technique to simulate human hair structure and dynamics. The hair structure is defined by connected straight cylindrical segments with a fixed width and it is modeled as a linear series of masses, springs and hinges. Hairs are rendered using Z-buffers and animated by a simple dynamic simulation with a physically-based approach. Anjyo et al. (1992) improved a physically-based modeling approach to compute the dynamic behavior of hair. For this purpose their hairstyle model consists of three basic steps: the definition of an ellipsoidal hull for the head model; the calculation of hair bending; finally, the adjustment of the hair style by cutting and modifying hair. This methodology offers satisfactory tools to make different hairstyles based on constraints like gravity and hair collision detection. As examples of design work they present some styles of straight hair. They have proposed methods using one-dimensional projective differential equations and pseudo-force fields. Both methods neglect the effect of collision between hairs for simplicity. Collisions of hair with other objects, such as the head, are simplified using a sphere or ellipsoid. The problem of self-collision of hair is very difficult. However, the collision between hair and other objects is required to generate natural movement of long hair.

The rendering of hair therefore constitutes a considerable anti-aliasing problem in which many individual hairs, reflecting light and casting shadows on each other, contribute to the shading of each pixel. Several researchers have published methods for rendering human hair, or the more limited problem of rendering fur. The problem itself falls into the category of

rendering naturalistic phenomena, and has much in common with the problem of rendering grass and trees, which has been addressed with much success.

Perlin and Hoffert (1989) employed volume densities, controlled with pseudo-random functions, to generate soft furlike objects. Perhaps the most impressive rendering of fur to date was achieved by Kajiya and Kay (1989) for a teddy bear using a generalization of 3-D texturing known as texels. Texels are a type of model intermediate between a texture and a geometry.

Csuri et al. (1979) were the first to render fur-like volumes. Each hair was modeled as a single triangle laid out on a surface and rendered using a Z-buffer algorithm for hidden surface removal. Better results were obtained by Gavin Miller (1988a,b) who rendered furry animals with images made of explicit hairs. Each hair was modeled with triangles to form a pyramid. Oversampling avoided aliasing. Although the number of hairs was relatively small and their thickness was large, these techniques were nonetheless rather computationally intense. Presumably, it would become impractical when scaled up to a full head of finer human hair. Watanabe and Suenaga (1989) modeled human hairs as connected segments of triangular prisms and were able to render a full head of straight human hair in a reasonably short time using a hardware Z-buffer renderer with Gouraud shading. Although the hair model had a realistic number of hairs (more than a million primitives), the illumination model was quite simplistic and apparently no attempt was made to deal with aliasing.

Perhaps the closest thing to a practical technique for rendering properly anti-aliased hair in the literature to date is the Reeves and Blau (1985) rendering of grass with particle systems. Since the original purpose of the technique (Reeves 1983) was to animate particles in motion, the points were displaced along their paths of motion during one frame to simulate motion blur, yielding three-dimensional line segments. Later, the same technique was used to represent static images with thin filaments, such as grass. As a result, the term ''particle'' often refers, in fact, to a filament which may have a considerable length, but is usually very thin.

9.3.2   Hair modeling

To create realistic images of hair styles and furry objects it is necessary to define an appropriate file of all individual hair curves, containing their hair segment geometry and material aspects. In the hair modeler program STYLER, the elaboration of such file characteristics follows two main steps:

- hair curve creation
- hair style definition

The hair segment database generated by these designing steps will be used in the rendering process.

To create images of human hair a complex modeler is needed, given the fact that human hair styles are much more complex than furry balls and require more modeling flexibility. The hair modeling program STYLER was originated from the SURFMAN surface generator (LeBlanc et al. 1991a). The STYLER program assigns to every polygon of the surface the information of the type of hair, the basic curve or hair segment, its orientation, and many stochastic parameters.

Each polygon has a curve identifier created by cylindrical straight segments joined by defining a sequence of points in the 3-D space. The three dimensional definition of the hair curve gives the designer more flexibility and control over the final configuration of the hair style.

The process of designing hair curves to create a style is:

- start the hair curve set by selecting ''new'' from the interface panel;
- create each curve by defining its number identifier and selecting the option ''add curve'';
- create straight segments, with the option ''insert point''.

The segments of these in-between points can be moved, split or deleted when a new hair segment or curve is created or modified. These facilities allow the creation of any kind of hair format.

Creating furry objects and human hair styles
The STYLER's modeling flexibility offers the designer the possibility to create a wide range of hair styles by assigning some specific information to the selected polygons (LeBlanc et al. 1991b). The hair curves are distributed on the surface's triangular mesh, conforming the hair style idealized by the designer. By *default*, the program assigns to each polygon of the mesh a regular hair configuration. The final hair style is reached by changing the *default* value of the following parameters for the selected polygons:

- material;
- jitter;
- hair orientation;
- scale value;

- density;
- angle variation;
- a seed for the random generator.

The material parameter is a color identifier for the hair set of each polygon. The jitter parameter defines a random base location for the hair on the polygon. Angle variation assigns a random angle applied to the tangent vector to the set of hair on the polygon. The scale value gives a random scale for each segment of hair in the selected set. The density value means the number of hairs per unit area; generally a human hair style has approximately 100,000 to 150,000 hairs.

The surface for hair modeling should only contain polygons where the hair will grow. The surface for the new hair file should be first prepared using the SURFMAN sculpting software. Once started, the surface cannot be modified or moved, otherwise the hairs may

not follow along as expected. It happens because each polygon of the SURFMAN surface has a database, as described above, that parameterizes hair growth, and a change in the number or orientation of the polygons will cause the drawing order to change and random values for each hair will differ.

To solve the problem of movement of the SURFMAN surface after the hair style is ready, we calculate the binormal vector equal to the cross vector of the new triangle normal and the old tangent vector, and calculate a new tangent vector as the cross vector of the normal and binormal. This method was used to solve the constraint of rendering more than one ready hair style placed differently.

To give the designer flexibility for modeling hair for any kind of object and in order to create different kinds of styles, all synthetic objects can be converted to the SURFMAN format and later used in STYLER for modeling the respective hair file segment.

The purpose of the hair modeler is to produce a hair segment file for the animation module. To create the hair style, the program offers some interactive facilities. First, the three-dimensional curved cylinder is composed of straight cylindrical segments connected by points. The "in-between" points can be moved in the space to be adjusted, modified, deleted or added. Just one type of individual hair can be assigned to each triangle in the scalp mesh. However the same hair can be assigned to various triangles. In order to adjust the hair orientation on the curved scalp surface, its direction can be modified by rotating the hair around the normal of its triangle. Details on the HairStyler interface may be found in Magnenat Thalmann and Daldegan (1993).

After defining each hair format and applying it to the respective triangle, the final style can be defined. The same hair style can have different lengths, by making it grow or shrink using a multiplication factor. A hair style generally has between 100,000 and 150,000 hairs, but this density can be regulated either for individual triangles or the entire scalp. Initially all the hairs placed in the triangle have the same length, orientation and symmetrical position. To make hair styles look more natural, all these parameters can be changed interactively. A random length, orientation and position can be assigned to each triangle hair set.

The STYLER was conceived based on polygonal mesh objects modeled by the SURFMAN sculpting software (LeBlanc et al. 1991a). In SURFMAN, synthetic objects in general are remodeled or sculpted from primitives such as spheres and cylinders or even from other complex objects like body parts, in order to generate new synthetic objects or human actors (Paouri et al. 1991).

STYLER maintains a database of information that parameterizes hair growth on each polygon. Each polygon has the following parameters:

- an identifier referring to a 3-D curve
- a material identifier for hairs on this polygon
- jitter for the base location of the curve
- orientation of the hairs, called a tangent vector in the world coordinates
- random angle variation applied to the tangent vector

- scaling value applied to the curve
- random value applied to the curve
- density (number of hairs per unit area)
- a seed for the random generator

Polygonal information is unique to a surface and, once created for that surface, cannot be used with a different surface. Furthermore, if the original surface is modified or deformed, the hairs may not follow along as expected. The reason for this is that if a triangle's shape is changed, the number of hairs within it will also change in proportion to the surface area, therefore hair drawing order will change and random values for each hair (jitter, scale, angle) will differ. Also if the shape of a triangle is changed, the tangent vector should be corrected. This can be done by calculating a binormal vector equal to the cross vector of the new triangle normal and the old tangent vector, and calculating a new tangent vector as the cross vector of the new normal and binormal.

Using the SURFMAN polygonal mesh objects as pattern surfaces for hair placement, different fur objects can be created using STYLER. A wide range of hair styles can be generated also from one single original set of few three-dimensional curved cylinder hairs, by varying the parameters of the STYLER options, mentioned above.

9.3.3   Hair animation

To generate natural hair animation, physical simulation must be applied. However, precise simulation including collision response is impractical because of the large number of individual hairs. Therefore, Anjyo et al. (1992) propose the use of simple differential equations of one-dimensional angular momenta. Simplified collision detection method using cylindrical representation has been described by Kurihara et al. (1993) and integrated into our system (Daldegan et al. 1993). We now summarize the approach.

The dynamic model of hair
A strand of hair (Anjyo et al. 1992) is modeled as a series of line segments (Figure 9.8). In this figure, s_i ($1 \leq i \leq k$) is a segment, P_i ($0 \leq i \leq k$) is a node, and k is the number of segments in each strand. We consider only the angles and the torques between the segments for simplicity.

Taking the polar coordinate system as shown in Figure 9.9, the variables $\theta_i(t)$ and $\phi_i(t)$ with time parameter t are governed by the ordinary differential equations:

$$I_i \frac{d^2\theta_i}{dt^2} + \gamma_i \frac{d\theta_i}{dt} = M_\theta$$

$$I_i \frac{d^2\phi_i}{dt^2} + \gamma_i \frac{d\phi_i}{dt} = M_\phi \tag{9.10}$$

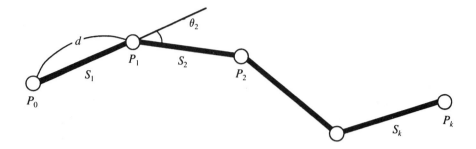

Figure 9.8. *Dynamic model of a single strand.*

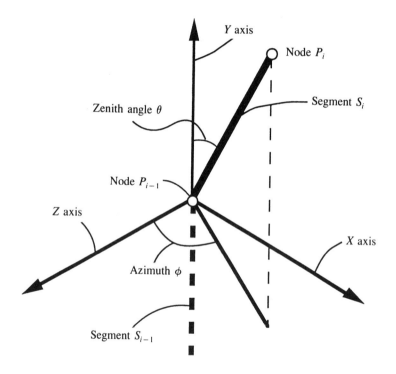

Figure 9.9. *The polar coordinate system for a hair segment.*

where I_i is the moment of inertia of the segment s_i, γ_i is the damping coefficient, and M_θ and M_ϕ are the torques according to θ and ϕ components respectively.

The torques M_θ and M_ϕ applied to the segment s_i are derived from the hinge effect $M_{\theta\text{spring}}$, $M_{\phi\text{spring}}$ between two segments, and external moment $M_{\theta\text{external}}$, $M_{\phi\text{external}}$:

$$M_\theta = M_{\theta\text{spring}} + M_{\theta\text{external}}$$
$$M_\phi = M_{\phi\text{spring}} + M_{\phi\text{external}} \tag{9.11}$$

$M_{\theta\text{spring}}$ and $M_{\phi\text{spring}}$ are defined as

$$M_{\theta\text{spring}} = -k_\theta(\theta - \theta_0)$$
$$M_{\phi\text{spring}} = -k_\phi(\phi - \phi_0) \tag{9.12}$$

where k_θ and k_ϕ are spring constants, and θ_0 and ϕ_0 are the initial angles.

External moments are derived from external forces, such as gravity, inertia and wind.

Collision detection

The collision detection method (Kurihara et al. 1993) is simple because the number of hairs is very large. This method uses a cylindrical representation of the human body which is divided into several parts including a head and trunk. Each part is described in a cylindrical coordinate system as (r, θ, y), where r is the radius, θ is the azimuth and y is the height. We create an array of radius on discretized azimuth $i\Delta\theta$ and height $J\Delta y (1 \le i \le m, 1 \le j \le n)$ by calculating the intersection between line and object. Along with the radius, we prepare the normal vector on each sample point for calculating collision response.

When a cylindrical table is created, collision is easily detected. First, we translate node point P into cylindrical coordinates as (r_p, θ_p, y_p). Second, we obtain the corresponding point Q of the object with the same azimuth θ_p and height y_p as point P. If we assume the object surface smoothness, radius r_q of Q can be approximated by linear interpolation using the prepared table. Collision detection is now reduced to comparing the radius part of point P and that of point Q. If r_q is greater than r_p then point P is inside the object. Otherwise point P is outside the object.

When point P is inside of the object, point T on the surface of the object that is nearest from P is calculated and required for collision response. This point T is approximated using linear interpolation.

If a hair strand is inside of the body, the reaction constraint method (Platt and Barr 1988) is applied to keep hair outside of the body. Let F_{input} be the applied force to node point P. Then unconstrained component of F_{input} is

$$F_{\text{unconstrained}} = F_{\text{input}} - (F_{\text{input}} \cdot N)N, \tag{9.13}$$

where N is the normal vector at point T. The constrained force to avoid the collision is

$$F_{\text{constrained}} = -(kPT + cV \cdot N)N, \tag{9.14}$$

where V is the velocity of point P, T is the nearest point on the surface from point P, k is the strength of the constraint and c is the damping coefficient.

The output force which is applied to point P is a summation of $F_{\text{unconstrained}}$ and $F_{\text{constrained}}$.

$$F_{\text{output}} = F_{\text{input}} - (F_{\text{input}} \cdot N)N - (kPT + cV \cdot N)N \qquad (9.15)$$

To simulate inelastic collision, we apply reaction constraint only if the input force is not lifting the point P away from the surface.

The wisp model

It is expensive to simulate all hundreds of thousands of strands of hair. When we observe real hairs, many neighboring strands move similarly. Thus, if we simulate the movement of a wisp of strands and not each strand, it reduces the computation time significantly. The wisp model of strands we have applied is very simple one. We simulate the movement of typical strands and generate other strands by adding random numbers to the origin of the typical strands. The hair styling program can change the density of strands. Thus, we can use low density to define typical strands.

Animation production process

The process of producing hair animation consists of the following steps.

- We translate hair segment data created by the HairStyler module into polar coordinates suited for numerical simulation. These angles are used as initial angles, θ_0 and ϕ_0 in equation (9.11). The number of strands is reduced by setting low density. Resulting strands are used as the typical strands in the wisp model.
- We create radius tables in cylindrical representation of the human body. These tables are used for efficient collision detection.
- We specify parameters for numerical simulation, such as moment of inertia, spring constant and external force. We also specify the head movement. Since trial and error is inevitable for generating animation, we start with a hair model with a small number (100) of strands and control parameters interactively. The movement of hair does not change according to the number of the strands because strand–strand interaction is not considered.
- We calculate motion of hair by numerical simulation.
- We generate a full hair model using wisp model from typical strands. We can use the preview program to generate rough shading display using graphics workstations. If the motion is satisfactory, we render using pixel blending and shadow buffer techniques.

Figure 9.10 shows an example of hair animation from the film *Fashion Show* (Magnenat Thalmann and Thalmann 1992).

9.3.4   Hair rendering

Rendering an image of hair with our system involves several steps:

- creating a database of hair segments

Figure 9.10.   *Hair animation.*

- creating shadow buffers from all lights
- rendering the hairless objects using all shadow buffers
- composing the hair on the hairless image

In our system, hair rendering is done by raytracing using a modified version of the public domain Rayshade program. An implementation module of the shadow buffer algorithm (Williams 1978; Reeves et al. 1987) has been added to the public domain Rayshade program, based on an earlier version of hair rendering based on pixel blending (LeBlanc et al. 1991b). It works fine for calculating shadows of normal objects and is also used to figure out the shadows cast by hair.

In the hair style rendering module, the process is step by step. First, the shadow of the scene is calculated for each light source i, as well as for the light sources for the hair shadows. The hair shadows are calculated for the object surface and individually for each hair. Finally the hair style is blended into the scene, using all shadow buffers. The result is an image with a three-dimensional realistic hair style rendering where complex shadow interaction and highlight effects can be seen and appreciated. In more detail, the full rendering pipeline may be summarized as follows:

Figure 9.11. *Synthetic actress with hairstyle.*

- We take the scene model description and project it onto each light source, creating one scene shadow buffer for each light source.
- We take the hair model and project it onto each light source, creating one hair shadow buffer for each light source. This is done by drawing each hair segment into a Z-buffer based frame buffer and extracting the resulting depth map.
- We compose the depth maps for the scene shadow buffer and the hair shadow buffer, resulting in a single composite shadow buffer for each light source.
- We generate the scene image and its Z-buffer, using the scene model description and the composite shadow buffers as input to the scene renderer, resulting in a fully rendered scene with hair shadows, but no hair.
- We blend the hair segments into the scene image, using the scene's Z-buffer to determine visibility and the composite shadow buffers to determine shadowing, yielding the final image with hair and full shadows. For this blending process, each strand of the hair model is breaking into straight 3-D line segments. The intensity H of each of the segment's endpoints is determined using the following hair intensity equation:

$$H = L_A K_A + \Sigma S_i L_i (KS \sin(\theta) + KS \cos^n(\phi + \theta - \pi)) \tag{9.16}$$

where L_i is the light intensity, K_A a is the ambient reflectance coefficient and L_A is the ambient light power incident per unit area. S_i is a shadowing coefficient, obtained by filtering the pixel at the hair strand's depth value against the shadow buffer for the i-th light source.

The raytracer basically has two roles in the hair rendering pipeline. The first is to construct shadow buffers from light sources, and the second is to render hairless objects with full shadowing (coming from the hair and the hairless objects).

There are in fact two ways of creating shadow buffers. The first is by rendering objects with the graphics hardware and reading the contents of the Z-buffer. The second is by using the raytracer and rendering the scene from the position of the light, asking it to reduce a Z-buffer image of the scene. After the shadow buffers have been created, the hairless objects have been rendered with full shadowing, and a Z-buffer from the camera position has been calculated, the hairs may be added to the scene.

Figure 9.11 (on page 230 and in the plate section between pages 152 and 153) shows an example of a synthetic actress with a hairstyle. Figure 9.12 (below and in the plate section between pages 152 and 153) show a variety of mustaches and beards designed using our STYLER program. These different combinations were generated by changing the scalar bias, the density, the angular bias and the jittering factor.

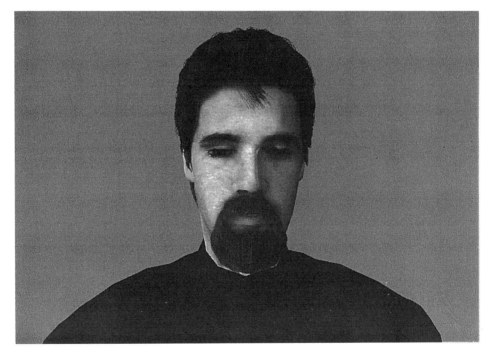

Figure 9.12. *Beards and mustaches.*

For rendering fur objects, another important and difficult feature to be achieved in computer graphics, we require a three-dimensional texture. In STYLER, depending on the density and hair length chosen, the fur rendered object is in fact a three-dimensional texture surface made by concentrated segments of lines, reflecting rays of light in different orientations, and shadows and highlight effects.

9.4 Acknowledgment

The research was sponsored by the "Fonds National pour la Recherche Scientifique". The authors are grateful to the people who contributed to this work, in particular Martin Courchesne, Agnes Daldegan, Tsuneya Kurihara, Arghyro Paouri and Ying Yang.

9.5 References

Anjyo K., Usami Y. and Kurihara T. (1992) "A Simple Method for Extracting the Natural Beauty of Hair", Computer Graphics, Vol. 26, No. 2, pp. 111–120.

Aono M. (1990) "A Wrinkle Propagation Model for Cloth", Proc. Computer Graphics International, Springer-Verlag, Tokyo, pp. 96–115.

Baraff D. (1990) "Curved Surfaces and Coherence for Non-Penetrating Rigid Body Simulation", Computer Graphics, Proc. SIGGRAPH '90), Vol. 24, No. 4, pp. 19–28.

Baraff D. and Witkin A. (1992) "Dynamic Simulation of Non-Penetrating Flexible Bodies", Proc. SIGGRAPH '92, Computer Graphics, Vol. 26, No. 2, pp. 303–308.

Breen D.E., House D.H. and Wozny M.J. (1994) "Predicting the Drape of Woven Cloth using Interacting Particles", Proc. SIGGRAPH '94, Computer Graphics, Vol. 28, No. 4, pp. 365–372.

Carignan M., Yang Y., Magnenat Thalmann N. and Thalmann D. (1992) "Dressing Animated Synthetic Actors with Complex Deformable Clothes", Proc. SIGGRAPH '92, Computer Graphics, Vol. 26, Vol. 2, pp. 99–104.

Csuri C., Hakathorn R., Parent R., Carlson W. and Howard M. (1979) "Towards an Interactive High Visual Complexity Animation System," Computer Graphics, Vol. 13, No. 2, pp. 289–299.

Daldegan A., Magnenat Thalmann N., Kurihara T. and Thalmann D. (1993) "An Integrated System for Modeling, Animating and Rendering Hair", Proc. Eurographics '93, Computer Graphics Forum, Vol. 12, No. 3, pp. 211–221.

Denby E.F. (1976) "The Deformation of Fabrics during Wrinkling — A Theoretical Approach", Textile Research Journal, Vol. 46, pp. 667–670.

Duff T. (1992) "Interval Arithmetic and Recursive Subdivision for Implicit Functions and Constructive Solid Geometry", Proc. SIGGRAPH '92, Computer Graphics, Vol. 26, No. 2, pp. 131–138.

Eringen A.C. and Suhubi, E.S. (1974) "Elastodynamics", Vol. 1, Academic Press, NY.

Haumann D.R. and Parent R.E. (1988) "The Behavioral Test-Bed: Obtaining Complex Behavior With Simple Rules", The Visual Computer, Vol. 4, pp. 332–347.

Hinds B.K. and McCartney J. (1990) "Interactive garment design", The Visual Computer, Vol. 6, pp. 53–61.

Kajiya J.T. and Kay T.L. (1989) "Rendering Fur with Three Dimensional Textures", Computer Graphics Vol. 23, No. 3, pp. 271–280.

Kunii T.L. and Gotoda H. (1990) "Modeling and Animation of Garment Wrinkle Formation processes", Proc. Computer Animation '90, Springer-Verlag, Tokyo, pp. 131–146.

Kurihara T., Anjyo K. and Thalmann D. (1993) "Hair Animation with Collision Detection", in: Models and Techniques in Computer Animation, Springer-Verlag, Tokyo, pp. 128–138.

Lafleur B., Magnenat Thalmann N. and Thalmann D. (1991) "Cloth Animation with Self-Collision Detection", Proc. IFIP Conference on Modeling in Computer Graphics, Springer, Tokyo, pp. 179–187.

LeBlanc A., Kalra P., Magnenat Thalmann N. and Thalmann D. (1991) "Sculpting With the Ball & Mouse Metaphor", Proc. Graphics Interface '91, Calgary, Canada.

LeBlanc A., Turner R. and Thalmann D. (1991b) "Rendering Hair using Pixel Blending and Shadow Buffers", Journal of Visualization and Computer Animation, Vol. 2, No. 3, pp. 92–97.

Lin M.C. and Manocha D. (1993) "Interference Detection between Curved Objects for Computer Animation", Proc. Computer Animation '93, Springer-Verlag, Tokyo, pp. 43–55.

Magnenat Thalmann N. and Daldegan A. (1993) "Creating Virtual Fur and Hair Styles For Synthetic Actors", in: Communicating with Virtual Worlds, Springer-Verlag, Tokyo, pp. 358–370.

Magnenat Thalmann N. and Thalmann D. (1987) "The direction of synthetic actors in the film Rendez-vous à Montréal", IEEE Computer Graphics and Applications, Vol. 7, No. 12, pp. 9–19.

Magnenat Thalmann N. and Thalmann D. (1990) "Synthetic Actors in Computer-Generated 3D Films", Springer-Verlag, Heidelberg.

Magnenat Thalmann N. and Thalmann D. (1991) "Flashback", video, 1 min., SIGGRAPH Video Review.

Magnenat Thalmann N. and Thalmann D. (1992) "Fashion Show", video, 1 min.

Magnenat Thalmann N. and Yang Y. (1991) "Techniques for Cloth Animation", in: New Trends in Animation and Visualization, edited by N. Thalmann and D. Thalmann, John Wiley & Sons Ltd., Chichester, pp. 243–256.

Mangen A. and Lasudry N.(1991) "Search for the Intersection Polygon of any Two Polygons: Application to the Garment Industry" Computer Graphics Forum, Vol. 10, pp. 19–208.

Miller G.S.P. (1988a) "From Wire-Frame to Furry Animals", Proc. Graphics Interface, pp. 138–146.

Miller G.S.P. (1988b) "The Motion Dynamics of Snakes and Worms", Computer Graphics, Vol. 22, No. 4, pp. 169–178.

Moore M. and Wilhelms J. (1988) "Collision Detection and Response for Computer Animation", Proc. SIGGRAPH '88, Computer Graphics, Vol. 22, No. 4, pp. 289–298.

Morton W.E. and Hearle J.W.S. (1962) "Physical properties of textile fibers", The textile institute, Butterworths, Manchester and London.

Paouri A., Magnenat Thalmann N. and Thalmann D. (1991) "Creating Realistic Three-Dimensional Human Shape Characters for Computer-Generated Films", Proc. Computer Animation '91, Geneva, Springer-Verlag, Tokyo.

Perlin K. and Hoffert E.M. (1989) "Hypertexture", Computer Graphics, Vol. 23, No. 3, pp. 253–262.

Platt J.C. and Barr A.H. (1988) "Constraint Methods for Flexible Models", Computer Graphics, Vol. 22, No. 4, pp. 279–288.

Reeves W.T. (1983) "Particle Systems — A Technique for Modeling a Class of Fuzzy Objects", Computer Graphics Vol. 17, No. 3, pp. 359–376.

Reeves W.T. and Blau R. (1985) "Approximate and Probabilistic Algorithm for Shading and Rendering Structured Particle Systems", Computer Graphics, Vol. 19, No. 3, pp. 313–322.

Reeves W.T., Salesin D.H. and Cook R.L. (1987) "Rendering Antialiased Shadows with Depth Maps", Computer Graphics, Vol. 21, No. 4, pp. 283–291.

Rosenblum R.E., Carlson W.E. and Tripp III E. (1991) "Simulating the Structure and Dynamics of Human Hair: Modelling, Rendering and Animation", Journal of Visualization and Computer Animation, Vol. 2, No. 4, pp. 141–148.

Shinya M. and Forgue M.C. (1991) "Interference Detection through Rasterisation", Journal of Visualisation and Computer Animation, Vol. 4, No. 2, pp. 132–134.

Snyder J.M., Woodbury A.R., Fleisher K., Currin B. and Barr A.H. (1993) "Interval Methods for Multi-Point Collisions between Time-Dependant Curved Surfaces", Computer Graphics annual series, pp. 321–334.

Terzopoulos D., Platt J.C. and Barr A.H. (1987) "Elastically Deformable Models", Proc. SIGGRAPH '87, Computer Graphics, Vol. 21, pp. 205–214.

Volino P., Courchesne M. and Magnenat Thalmann N. (1995) "Versatile and Efficient Techniques for Simulating Cloth and Other Deformable Objects", Proc. SIGGRAPH '95, pp. 137–144.

Volino P. and Magnenat Thalmann N. (1994) "Efficient Self-Collision Detection on Smoothly Discretised Surface Animations using Geometrical Shape Regularity", Proc. Eurographics '94, Computer Graphics Forum, Vol. 13, No. 3, pp. 155–166.

Von Herzen B., Barr A.H. and Zatz H.R. (1990) "Geometric Collisions for Time-Dependent Parametric Surfaces", Proc. SIGGRAPH '90, Computer Graphics, Vol. 24, No. 4, pp. 39–48.

Watanabe Y. and Suenaga Y. (1989) "Drawing Human Hair Using Wisp Model", Proc. Computer Graphics International '89, pp. 691–700.

Weil J. (1986) "The synthesis of Cloth Objects", Proc. SIGGRAPH '86, Computer Graphics, Vol. 4, pp. 49–54.

Werner H.M., Magnenat Thalmann N. and Thalmann D. (1993) "User Interface for Fashion Design", Graphics Design and Visualisation, IFIP Trans. Amsterdam, pp. 197–204.

Williams L. (1978) "Casting Curved Shadows on Curved Surfaces", Computer Graphics, Vol. 12, No. 3, pp. 270–274.

Witkin A. and Welch W. (1990) "Fast Animation and Control of Non-Rigid Structures", Proc. SIGGRAPH '90, Computer Graphics, Vol. 24, pp. 243–252.

Yang Y. and Magnenat Thalmann N. (1993) "An Improved Algorithm for Collision Detection in Cloth Animation with Human Body", Proc. Pacific Graphics '93, Computer Graphics and Applications, World Scientific Publishing, Singapore, Vol. 1, pp. 237–251.

CHAPTER 10

Planning for Animation

Norman I. Badler, Bonnie L. Webber, Welton Becket,
Christopher Geib, Michael Moore, Catherine Pelachaud, Barry
D. Reich and Matthew Stone
Department of Computer Science, University of Pennsylvania

Abstract

Under certain conditions, a synthetic agent must be made to sense its environment and respond to it in terms of reflexes, higher level intentions, expectations, and available skills. This chapter presents an effective way of doing this through the integration of a rich collection of interacting techniques, organized in a principled, structured representation. These techniques include planners and parallel transition networks to aid in overall task control, and goal-based sensing, response, and physics-based, kinematic or inverse kinematic behaviors to achieve environmentally-appropriate movements. After setting out a framework of definitions and describing the representational structures used in our approach, we will illustrate how they are embodied in four different systems.

10.1 Introduction

If there is any one truth of computer animation that has emerged from numerous efforts in recent years, it is that simple procedural techniques cannot capture the complexity of human motion, interaction, and communication. As one technique improves the veracity of one aspect of a movement simulation, other aspects become distorted or suppressed, and new problems appear. This is because human movement is the product of so many factors: physics, capabilities, emotion, experience, context, and interactions with other physical objects and agents. We should expect the world to require highly interconnected processes to improve simulation quality while retaining acceptable levels of specification burden and computational resources: it is rather unlikely that a complete behavioral simulation at the

235

sensory-motor level would be feasible. Nor should we expect it to be provided by an expert animator. Indeed, the latter has spawned the quest for more automated animation techniques (Badler et al. 1991; Badler et al. 1993b; Cohen 1992; Liu et al. 1994; Ngo and Marks 1993; van de Panne and Fiume 1993; Sims 1994; Tu and Terzopoulos 1994; Witkin and Kass 1988). While such techniques can potentially change the field in major ways, their modest results to date have led the community to turn increasingly to "performance based" animation – i.e., directly sensed motion of actors – as a viable method to produce realistic-quality human motion at low (programming or expert skill) cost (Badler et al. 1993a; Robertson 1994; Williams 1990).

"Performance based" animation (see Chapter 2), however, does not solve the problem of generating realistic and appropriate human movements in any of the following situations:

- Highly-variable situations, where one cannot a priori acquire the range of movements that people will make. Such situations can arise in real-time simulation activities, where the situation and actions of other agents cannot be predicted ahead of time.
- Dangerous situations, where one cannot involve a human actor.
- Time-critical situations, where the amount of time needed to program behaviors excludes programming as an option.

Such situations require immediate, situationally appropriate (reactive) behavior on the part of a synthetic agent.

Under such conditions, a synthetic agent must be made to sense its environment and respond to it in terms of reflexes, higher level intentions, expectations, and available skills. In this chapter, we argue that an effective way of doing this is through the integration of a rich collection of interacting techniques, organized in a principled, structured representation. These techniques include planners and parallel transition networks (Section 10.3.2) to aid in overall task control, and goal-based sensing, response, and (as necessary) physics-based, kinematic or inverse kinematic behaviors to achieve environmentally-appropriate movements. Together they simplify:

- the expression of local environmental influences without complicating their expression at the higher levels and
- the expression of situational awareness and influences at a higher level without the added complexity of managing all potential lower level variability,

while admitting:

- the aggregation of the intentions and expectations associated with individual tasks;
- the interaction of multiple agents, wherein agents can sense and react to the behavior and perceived intentions of other agents, as well as to the environment;
- the distinction between expected alternatives in the way a situation may develop and seizure of opportunity or total surprise at the circumstances;

- the independent but coordinated control of a human agent's locomotion, upper body motions, visual attention, and communication systems (speech and facial expression);
- the embedding of persistent data structures for cognitive knowledge or spatial maps as needed to remember or mark as known visible parts or characteristics of the environment;
- the emergence of human-like qualities as a consequence of executing the agent's representational models.

After setting out a framework of definitions and describing the representational structures used in our approach, we will illustrate how they are embodied in three different systems. Not only have these systems evolved in parallel with the approach we advocate, but they embody it to an ever-increasing degree: "Stepper" (Section 10.4), "Hide and Seek" (Section 10.5), and "Gesture Jack" (Section 10.6).

10.2 Definitions

There are essentially several interrelated concepts – those of agent, activity, goal, role, and context – that underlie our approach to automating the animation of environmentally-appropriate and task-appropriate agent behavior. Understanding these concepts should set the stage for understanding "Hide and Seek" and "Gesture Jack".

10.2.1 Agents

An agent is an object that is able to take action by virtue of having a sense–control–action (SCA) loop to produce locally-adaptive behavior (Section 10.3.1). An agent with only SCA loops determining its behavior is considered a purely "reactive" agent. Deliberative agents (such as human agents) also have higher-level control structures that affect more global, planned, or cognitive aspects of behavior, which in turn can affect the immediate formulation and parameters of an SCA loop (Section 10.3.2). (An object which causes events through purely physical forces is not considered an agent.) Because our interest is in behavioral realism rather than visual realism, we focus on human agents, whose behaviors we have the greatest familiarity with and expectations about, thus providing a grounding for judging realistic behavior. The definition, however, allows for other agents acting under non-human drives and motivations. Agents can, of course, sense and respond to the presence and actions of other agents.

10.2.2 Activities, goals, and behaviors

Simply stated, activities are anything one would describe an agent as doing. What is more important to the automated production of animated simulations is how activities are

specified. In a Natural Language (NL) like English, activities are specified as verbs ("walk"), verb phrases ("walk to the store"), and even whole paragraphs (e.g., "Walk to the store. Make sure you take your raincoat, and avoid taking Main Street because there's a parade today."). In our approach, activities are specified through the Parallel Transition Networks (PaT-Nets) described in Section 10.3.2. The important things to note about activity specifications in both NL and PaT-Nets are that:

- activities can be specified at many levels of abstraction, from look for a hider to move FINGER;
- activities can be specified either individually or as structures of more basic activities;
- activities are essentially processes that are terminated when one or another condition holds. Activity specifications can embody termination conditions intrinsically (e.g., "play the Moonlight Sonata" is intrinsically terminated when the player reaches the end of the sonata), or the termination conditions can be specified explicitly (e.g., "play poker for an hour or until you lose your shirt").

Crucial to the successful animation of human agents is the notion that activities have executable implementations. Appropriate structures for activities will assist construction of their computational analogues.

GOALS What an agent tries to achieve through its activities. Like activities, goals can be specified at different levels of abstraction – e.g., from learning to bluff at poker to getting to a particular location.

TASKS Usually a combination of one or more goals and, optionally, the activities that contribute to achieving them. At a high level, instructions can specify the task(s) an agent should carry out or goal(s) it should achieve. At a low level, instructions can specify activities.

SCHEMAS The "program" an agent follows while executing tasks. Parallel transition networks (PaT-Nets) are the schema "programming language". The task(s) may be produced by an explicit scripted procedure written as a PaT-Net schema, or the schema may itself be generated or modified by the actions of a planner or other decision-making system. The "outputs" of the schema are local variable or memory changes at the PaT-Net level, a set of behavioral instantiations to be executed at the SCA level, and any necessary communication links between the two.

BEHAVIORS In general, behaviors are considered "low level" capabilities of an agent, such as locomoting [to], reaching [for], looking [at], speaking [to], listening [to], etc.

10.2.3 Roles

An agent can adopt roles, each of which results in a set of tasks (a "working set") becoming relevant. The tasks associated with a role need not be instantiated immediately upon its adoption: for example, in the context of Hide and Seek, the role of hider is associated with a set of tasks including hiding, watching for the seeker, stealing home, and running from the seeker. The activities a hider is actually engaged in depends on the phase of the game and the seeker's (perceived) activity: s/he hides during the counting phase of the game, s/he watches for the seeker during the seeking phase of the game (and may also steal home during that phase), and s/he runs from the seeker during the pursue-and-tag phase of the game.

The working set concept, though primarily designed for computational efficiency, actually leads to the reasonable notion of deliberate ''context-switching'' when external events or internal desires force adoption of new roles. Thus if the dinner call is heard, the hider can drop one set of activities for another without waiting for current activities to be completed. The agent's organization into schemas and an SCA loop means that the abandoned activity's behavior set will be replaced by the ''go to one's house'' activity's behavior set: the transition will be seamless and natural. The agent will not continue to look for hiding places on the way home.

There are many circumstances in which multiple tasks may be active, and the agent must adopt behaviors which are selections or combinations of those possible. For example, it is not difficult to execute both locomotion and arm motions simultaneously, but the agent needs to decide whether to grasp for a new object while engaged in holding another. Some of these decisions can be made at the schema level (essentially by allocating and locking resources), while others are managed at the SCA level (such as walking and talking at the same time).

10.2.4   Contexts

A context may be the result of natural or other outside forces or the result of multiple agents agreeing that the context will hold until some later point. In the latter case, each agent initially adopts a mutually-accepted role in the context (e.g., speaker and listeners in the context of a conversation, seeker and hiders in the context of hide-and-seek, etc.), as well as accepting the rules and/or conventions for exchanging roles within that context and any mutually-accepted conditions under which the context will be dropped.

Contexts are not necessarily mutually-exclusive, so an agent may easily be in several contexts and therefore in several roles simultaneously. The activities the agent is engaged in at any one time may come from any of these activities, which may or may not be affected by the other contexts simultaneously at play. For example, two agents, both in the role of hiders in a game of Hide and Seek, may decide to engage in conversation, thereby adopting additional roles of speaker and hearer. Because, as hiders, they are trying to avoid detection, their conversation may be whispered or carried out through gesture or sign language. As another example, an agent in the role of hider in the context of Hide and Seek is also usually in the context of self-preservation. Therefore, s/he will avoid hitting obstacles as s/he moves to a hiding place, tries to steal home, or runs away from the seeker.

10.3   An intelligent agent architecture

An intelligent agent must interleave sensing, planning, decision-making, and acting. Accordingly, it is desirable to create an architecture that permits specification and exploration of each of these processes. Planning and decision-making can be accommodated through incremental, symbolic-level reasoning. When the agent decides to act, the symbolic actions must be instantiated in executable behaviors. Most behavioral systems use either state controllers or numerical feedback streams, but not both. By using both it is possible to obtain maximum flexibility and maintain appropriate levels of specification (Badler et al. 1993b; Becket and Badler, 1993).

We can characterize these two control levels as PaT-Nets and SCA loops.

- PaT-Nets are parallel state-machines that are easy for humans and automatic planning systems to manipulate. They are also good at sequencing actions based on the current state of the environment or of the system itself. They characterize the tasks in progress, conditions to be monitored, resources used, and any temporal synchronization.
- The SCA loop performs low-level, highly reactive control involving sensor feedback and motor control.

In this paradigm, the agent can instantiate explicit PaT-Nets to accomplish certain goals (e.g., go to the supply depot and pick up a new motor), while low-level control can be mediated through direct sensing and action couplings in the SCA loop (e.g., controlling where the agent's feet step and making sure that s/he does not run into or trip over any obstacles). Since the sensors can establish what the agent can perceive, the agent is able to react through the SCA loop, and if desired, use this information to confirm, adopt, or select higher-level (cognitive) actions: for example, if an obstacle cannot be surmounted, the current PaT-Net might need to be reconsidered. Since PaT-Net state transitions are explicitly represented, statistical distributions of alternative behaviors may be easily embedded.

PaT-Nets may instantiate themselves when certain events or conditions occur (Firby 1992; Georgeff and Lansky 1990), or they may be invoked or invented by high-level planning processes (Webber et al. 1995). They depend on the required action or mission, the agent's immediate intentions, and overall behavioral doctrine. For example, a PaT-Net to traverse a partly wooded area to achieve a target location safely may be based on a "locomote to target via suggested route" plan, but mediated through an SCA loop that uses sensor readings on the terrain type (do not walk through trees or into holes), and global policies (try not to place yourself in the view of any known hostile agents). With each step, the agent's action is affected by all these conditions.

The rest of this discussion is organized into a more comprehensive description of SCA loops and PaT-Nets. We will then have enough tools in place to illustrate the interactions between planning, PaT-Nets, and SCA behaviors in three domains: "Stepper", "Hide and Seek", and "Gesture Jack".

10.3.1 Low-level control: Sense–control–action loops

The SCA or behavioral loop is a continuous stream of floating point numbers from the simulated environment, through simulated sensors providing the abstract results of perception, through control decisions independently attempting to solve a minimization problem, out to simulated effectors or motor actions (walking, e.g.), which enact changes on the agent or the world. This loop continuously operates, connecting sensors to effectors through a network of nodes which for descriptive convenience are divided into sense (S), control (C), and action (A) phases.

The behavioral loop is modeled as a network of interacting SCA processes connected by arcs across which only floating point messages travel. An individual, conceptual path from sensors to effectors is referred to as a behavioral net. It is analogous to a complete behavior in an ''emergent behavior'' architecture such as Brooks' subsumption architecture (Brooks 1986), except that nodes may be shared between behaviors, and arbitration (competition for effector resources) may occur throughout the behavioral path and not just at the end-effector level. The behavioral loop is modeled as a network with floating point connections in order to allow the application of low-level, unsupervised, reinforcement learning in the behavioral design process. (This is being developed in Becket 1995.) Since our main use of SCA loops to date has been in locomotion reasoning, the remaining discussion will be in these terms.

Sensory nodes
Sensory nodes model or approximate the abstract, geometric results of object perception. They continuously generate signals describing the polar coordinate position (relative to the agent) of a particular object or of all objects of a certain type within a specified distance and field of view. A few of the sensors used are:

object sensors: These provide the current distance from the agent and angle relative to the forward axis of the agent of a particular object in the environment. While we find it sufficient for a sensor to abstract over object recognition, a more sophisticated approach would simulate the high-level results of vision of the agent using Z-buffering hardware to create a depth map of what the agent can see (Renault et al. 1990; Reynolds 1988).
range sensors: A range sensor collects all objects of a certain type within a given range and field of view, and performs a weighted average into signals giving the distance and angle of a single abstract object representing all detected objects. Signals into the sensor define the range, field of view, and weighting parameters (defining relative weights of distance and angle) and may be altered continuously in order to focus the sensor.
terrain mapper: This sensor perceives an internal map of the terrain as if it were an external entity. This is discussed in detail in Section 10.4.
human sensor: If an object is a human, that information is detected by this sensor.

Other sensors can be developed and embedded in the architecture as needs arise. More sophisticated virtual or synthetic sensors may be found in Chapter 11.

Control nodes

For locomotion reasoning we use two simple control nodes loosely based on Braitenberg's love and hate behaviors (Braitenberg 1984), but formulated as explicit minimizations using outputs to drive inputs to a desired value (similar to Wilhelms' (Wilhelms and Skinner 1990) use of Braitenberg's behaviors). Control nodes typically receive input signals directly from sensory nodes, and send outputs directly to action nodes, though they could be used in more abstract control situations. Our two control behaviors are:

attract: Create an output signal in the direction of the input signal, but magnified according to distance and angle scalar multipliers and exponents. This node works only when input signals exceed a threshold distance or angle.

avoid: Create an output signal in the opposite direction of the input, magnified according to scalar multipliers and exponents, whenever inputs fall below a threshold distance or angle.

These nodes incorporate both scalar multipliers and exponents, to allow modeling the non-linearities typically observed in animal responses to perceived inputs (Reynolds 1987).

Action nodes

Action nodes connect to the underlying human body model and directly execute routines defined on the model (such as walking, balance, hand position, and torso orientation) and arbitrate among inputs, either by selecting one set of incoming signals or averaging all incoming signals. An example is the walk controller, which decides where to place the agent's next footstep and then connects to the locomotion generator (Badler et al. 1993b) to achieve the step.

10.3.2   High-level control: PaT-Net schemas

Low-level control is designed to connect to a general symbolic reasoning process, including a model of parallel automata called Parallel Transition Nets (PaT-Nets) (Becket 1994) and various planners. A sample PaT-Net is shown conceptually in Figure 10.1. Each net description is a class in the object-oriented sense and contains a number of nodes connected by arcs. Nodes contain arbitrary Lisp expressions to execute as an action whenever the node is entered. A transition is made to a new node by selecting the first arc with a true condition (defined as a Lisp expression). Nodes may also support probabilistic transitions where the probability of a transition along an arc is defined rather than a condition. Monitors are supported that, regardless of which state the net is in, will execute an action if a general condition evaluates to true.

A running network is created by making an instance of the PaT-Net class. Because a running net is actually an encapsulated, persistent object, it may have local state variables available to all actions and conditions, and may also take parameters on instantiation. The running PaT-Net instances are embedded in a Lisp operating system that time-slices them into

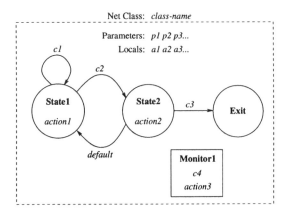

Net Class: *class-name*

Parameters: *p1 p2 p3...*
Locals: *a1 a2 a3...*

Figure 10.1. *A sample PaT-Net shown graphically.*

the overall simulation. This operating system allows PaT-Nets to spawn new nets, kill other running nets, communicate through semaphores and priority queues and wait (sleep) until a condition is met (such as waiting for another net to exit, for specific time in the simulation, or for a resource to be free). Running nets can, for example, spawn new nets and then wait for them to exit (effectively a subroutine call), or run in parallel with the new net, communicating if necessary through semaphores. Because PaT-Nets are embedded in an object-oriented structure, new nets can be defined that override, blend, or extend the functionality of existing nets. Several different PaT-Nets will be illustrated in the remaining sections.

10.4   Stepper

Stepper is an instance of the two-level (PaT-Net and SCA loop) architecture providing locomotion reasoning and control for simulated human agents in simulated environments (Reich et al. 1994). Locomotion reasoning determines the characteristics of an agent's locomotion: i.e., what types of attractions, avoidances, and posture changes will achieve the goal (Figure 10.2).

At the low level, Stepper uses an SCA loop to generate human locomotion. A set of influences (combinations of simulated sensors and attraction or avoidance) determine an agent's behavior. At the high level, a set of PaT-Nets schedule and control these influences.

10.4.1   The sense–control–action loop for human locomotion

Stepper makes use of Jack's framework for general object locomotion, which in turn makes use of an SCA loop that performs "anticipatory sensing". That is, in the sense phase,

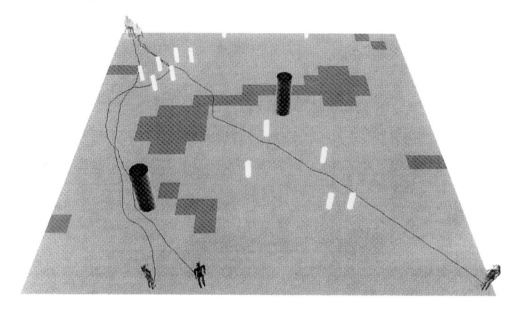

Figure 10.2. *Attraction, avoidance, and terrain awareness.*

sensors "anticipate" the environment at each potential next foot position, in order to determine in the control phase where the agent should step. The agent takes the chosen step in the action phase. A human steps at discrete positions in a continuous space, and cannot change the targeted step location while a step is in progress. The advantage of anticipatory sensing over some kind of averaging is described in Section 10.4.3.

Individual influences bound to the agent affect anticipatory sensing. An influence captures both what aspects of the environment are relevant to monitor and the degree to which they should attract or repel the agent from a particular position. An agent can be influenced by natural features of the terrain (e.g., muddy ground, bodies of water), man-made features of the environment (e.g., sidewalks), locations for which it is headed, etc.

An influence determines how an agent acts. In our system, the combination of a sensor and a control behavior (attraction or avoidance) is an influence (Figure 10.3). An influence maps a foot position to the stress of stepping there. From among the possible choices, the control phase of the SCA loop leads the agent to take the least stressful step.

An influence activates when "bound" to an agent. While active, its output contributes to the stress calculations. Influences may be bound or unbound at any time during a simulation, and hence activated or deactivated. Locomotion is performed by binding influences to humans. The SCA loop, constantly monitoring the environment, immediately initiates the appropriate locomotion.

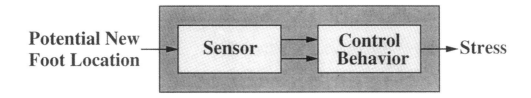

Figure 10.3. *An influence.*

10.4.2 Architectural overview

Each iteration of the SCA loop includes sensing, control, and action. Three phases compose sensing: (1) generation of possible steps, (2) polling of active influences, and (3) calculation of overall stress. The first phase determines a set of points to which the agent can next step. Then, in the second phase, polling of active influences determines stress values for each point; stress is proportional to an agent's desire not to step at a given point. Finally, the sum of the stress values for each point determines the overall stress for that point, given the active influences.

The control step selects the least stressful potential point and directs the action step to execute the locomotion.

Generation of new foot positions: The first part of sensing generates candidate foot positions. Three parameters determine the set of possible positions:

- Minimum Step Length
- Maximum Step Length
- Maximum Turning Angle (θ)

Given the agent's position and orientation, these parameters define a fan-shaped region in space (Figure 10.4). The agent can step anywhere within this region. The set of states, P, that the agent can be in next corresponds to the set of points to which the agent can step next. The set of points is the intersections of concentric arcs and uniformly spaced radii. The user determines the number of arcs and radii. The user may also add the agent's current location to the set of points being considered. If this point is selected as the point to which to step, then the agent does not move. Care must be taken when choosing this option to avoid situations where the agent may get stuck in a local minimum.

Polling influences: For each state $p2\ P$, the system simulates p and then polls the influences. Each influence returns a stress value. The higher the stress value, the less desirable the state. The stress value is multiplied by a user-defined scalar and raised to a user-defined power. This gives the user control over the relative contributions of the influences.

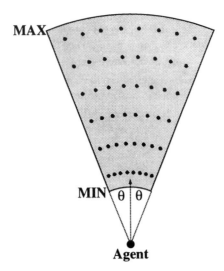

Figure 10.4.   *Calculating the next foot position.*

Influences have access to the entire environmental database and are effectively omniscient. The designer of the influence is responsible for limiting the amount or type of knowledge extracted. Sometimes an influence computes two stress values: one based on the agent's position and one based on its orientation. In this case, two sets of user-defined constants are needed.

Calculation of overall stress: The overall stress of a particular state is the sum of the weighted stresses output by each active influence. An influence is active if bound to the agent; influences may be bound and unbound at any time during a simulation.

Stepping: Once each state's overall stress has been computed, the system selects the state with the lowest overall stress. Invocation of the locomotion system causes the agent to step to the appropriate point. When the step is completed, the agent enters a new state and the SCA loop continues.

10.4.3 Advantages of anticipatory sensing

In calculating the stress values of all possible next foot positions, the system looks one step into the future. As an alternative to this anticipatory sensing approach, a velocity vector resulting from the blended output of all active influences could be used to determine the next footstep. However, this would result in severe instability around threshold boundaries. This occurs because we allow thresholds in our sensor and control behaviors and as a result the potential field space is discontinuous. Taking a discrete step based on instantaneous information may step across a discontinuity in field space. Consider the situation in Figure 10.5 where a goal on the opposite side of the wall attracts the agent, who avoids the wall up to some threshold distance. If the first step is scheduled at position $p1$, the agent will choose to step directly toward the goal and will end up at $p2$. Now within the threshold distance for walls, the agent will step away from the wall and end up at $p3$, outside the threshold. This process then repeats until the agent clears the wall, producing an extremely unrealistic sawtooth path about the true gradient in the potential field. Anticipatory sensing, by considering and choosing among all possible next steps, avoids this problem.

Currently, anticipatory sensing only looks one step into the future and calculates the resulting stress, based on the present environment. One extension under development moves beyond this simplification by projecting moving objects (including humans) into the future. Instead of avoiding an object based on its present location, an object will be avoided based on where it is likely to be after the current step. Probabilistic methods will be used to determine the likely location of the object.

A second extension under development projects the agent and objects several steps into the future. The contribution of a step to the stress calculations will be greatest for the first step and decrease for each additional step. This should produce paths that better reflect human patterns of locomotion.

10.4.4 PaT-Nets for human locomotion

PaT-Nets introduce decision-making into the agent architecture. They monitor the SCA loop (which may be thought of as modeling instinctive or reflexive behavior) and make decisions in special circumstances. For example, the observed behavior resulting from the combined use of different influences can sometimes break down. The agent may get caught in a dead-

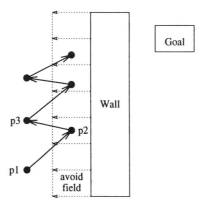

Figure 10.5. *Sawtooth path due to potential field discontinuities.*

end or other local minimum. Actions sometimes fail and unexpected events sometimes occur. PaT-Nets can recognize these situations, modify the agent's behavior by binding and unbinding influences, and then return to a monitoring state. During a simulation, PaT-Nets bind and unbind influences in Stepper, thereby altering agent behavior.

Consider an example with Tom chasing Jerry. The ChaseNet shown in Figure 10.6 begins in state 1.

An attraction to Jerry binds to Tom. As Tom begins to run toward Jerry the net passes to state 2; the ChaseNet enters the monitoring state. When Jerry ceases to be visible to Tom (Jerry may have run around a corner or behind an object), the net enters state 3. An attraction to the location where Jerry is most likely to be found, generally Jerry's last known location, binds to Tom. Tom begins to run toward this location as the ChaseNet transitions to state 4. If Tom arrives at this location and does not see Jerry, the ChaseNet transitions to state 5 and Tom searches in the direction Jerry was last known to be heading.

Clearly, chasing requires reasoning and decision-making beyond the scope of the SCA loop alone. PaT-Nets provide this reasoning, and schedule and control the low-level influences to direct the agent to act in the desired manner.

10.5 Hide and Seek

In Moore et al. (1995) we describe a planning system for players in a game of "Hide and Seek" and its vertical integration into a system called ZAROFF that selects reactive behaviors

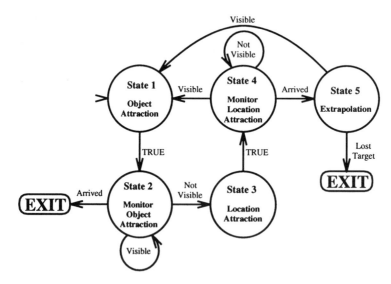

Figure 10.6. *ChaseNet state diagram.*

to execute in an animated simulation. By interleaving planning and acting, the players dynamically react to changes in the environment and changes in information about where the other players may be hiding. Adaptation is also supported through least-commitment planning, as the planner only looks ahead one action at each level of its abstraction hierarchy. The implementation follows the two-level agent architecture: the Intentional Planning System (ITPLANS) (Geib 1995) interacts with a Search Planner (Moore 1993) to perform the "high-level" reasoning for the system, and these two components in turn interact with a set of "low-level" SCA nodes based on Stepper (Figures 10.7 and 10.8).

10.5.1   System architecture

Our division of the control of a player between a planning component and a reactive behavior component reflects a distinction between deliberative actions (ones requiring non-local reasoning about the past, the present, and possible futures) and non-deliberative actions. In this sense, keeping track of where you are located in a complex environment and what hiding places have been checked requires deliberate effort, while walking from one place to another generally does not. Together, these two components create realistic animations of human decision-making and locomotion while playing hide and seek.

Figure 10.9 depicts information flow in ZAROFF. To control the player in the role of seeker, the system starts by initializing the plan with the input goal (finding a hiding human), populating the database with the initial locations of all the objects and human figures in the simulation, and creating a partial map from what the player can see around him. ITPLANS

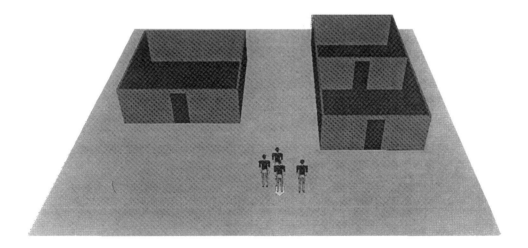

Figure 10.7.   *The start of a game of Hide and Seek.*

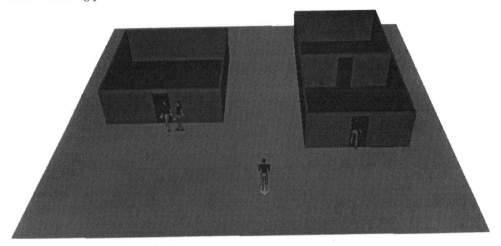

Figure 10.8.   *Hiders hiding – seeker counting.*

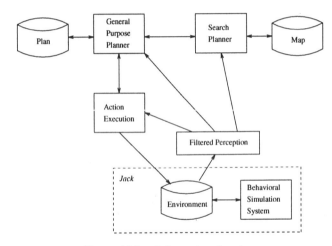

Figure 10.9.   *Information flow in* ZAROFF.

and the SCA loop start processing simultaneously. The planner queries the state of the database through the Filtered Perception module to decide how to elaborate the plan and select an action. If necessary, the Search Planner is consulted to assist in planning how to find things. When ITPLANS decides on an action, it instructs Action Execution to carry it out. Further planning is suspended until the action has terminated (successfully or unsuccessfully).

In making decisions about what to do next, each component makes use of its own internal simulation, which differs from the graphical animation of the environment. ITPLANS uses abstract descriptions of the effects of each action to choose one which will move closer to the specified goal. The Search Planner simulates the movements of an agent on its internal map of the environment. Stepper simulates taking the next step in several alternate locations. At each level of decision-making, an internal simulation is used at an appropriate granularity.

10.5.2   Planning in ZAROFF

ITPLANS (Geib 1992) is a hierarchical planner, in which hierarchical expansion only takes place to the degree necessary to determine the next action to be carried out. It consists of an incremental expansion of the frontier of the plan structure to successively lower levels of abstraction. The incremental nature of the plan allows the system to make commitments at the appropriate level of detail for action while not committing the system to future actions that might be obviated by changes in the world. The close coupling of ITPLANS with the environment manifests itself in two ways.

First, the traversal and pruning process the planner follows at each interval relies on being able to determine the actual state of the world and compare that with its goals. During the expansion process ITPLANS examines the state of the world and its memory to determine if any of the goals within its plan have been satisfied. When a goal has been satisfied serendipitously, it can be pruned out of the plan structure, and the system can move on to consider its next goal.

Second, ITPLANS "leans on the world" (Agre 1988) when predicting the results of its actions. Rather than maintaining a complete model of the world and the state that results from executing the action, ITPLANS uses a simpler method based on associating conditional add and delete lists with each action. ITPLANS assumes that a given proposition is true in the state that results from the action if (1) the proposition is explicitly added by the add list or (2) the proposition is true now in the world and it is not contained on the delete list. By this method, ITPLANS can make predictions about the results of executing an action without modeling the entire world state.

10.5.3   Search planning

A consequence of limited perception is the occasional need to find objects. Our approach is to isolate this reasoning in a specialized module, a Search Planner that translates information acquisition goals to high-level physical goals to explore parts of the environment. Searches are planned by first identifying known regions where an object may be located and then systematically exploring this space. A plan is developed for exploring each region in turn.

After such an exploration plan is executed, the environment is observed to determine whether the agent can see an object with the desired properties. During this observation phase, new potential regions may be seen by the agent. These new regions are considered for future exploration as needed.

10.5.4 Distinctions between the upper and lower levels

ZAROFF's stratification into higher-level and lower-level components is a reflection of differences in informational needs. For example, one common low-level behavior is responsible for causing a figure to locomote from one position to another. Locomotion decisions require very detailed information – e.g., foot positions, distances, and angles.

In contrast, ITPLANS is responsible for sequencing locomotion actions with actions to open doors in order to explore various hiding places within the game field. The information needed to build plans at this level is at a different level of abstraction. ITPLANS needs to know "Is the door open?", "Am I at the door?", etc. While such information can be derived from lower-level information, neither of the modules has need of the information that the other uses.

Differences in information needs provide one reason to separate higher-level and lower-level components, but there are other differences as well. One is level of commitment to future action. In locomotion, while each foot step brings the agent close to its current goal, no commitment is made to steps that it has yet to take. In contrast, ITPLANS makes commitments to act in specified ways in the future. For example, when the agent decides to walk to the door, it has already committed to opening the door once it has gotten there. While such commitments are tempered by possible changes in the environment, as long as a commitment remains active, it can affect the agent's decision-making and behavior.

While both the higher-level and lower-level components of ZAROFF are environmentally responsive, another difference motivating the separation of these two levels is the "granularity" of their reactivity, in both the form and time-scale of the environmental feedback they depend on. On the one hand, lower-level behaviors are locked into an SCA loop and are thus tightly coupled to the environment. On the other hand, the higher-level system only receives feedback from the world "between actions", when the lower-level system chooses to relinquish control. Thus, ITPLANS only receives feedback whenever there is no low-level behavior executing. This means that the time intervals over which the two different components receive feedback differ in magnitude. This discussion has noted a number of differences between the high level components of the ZAROFF system and the lower level control system. We now argue why they are valuable within the system architecture.

Separating low-level motor control from high-level planning decisions is valid: a symbolic planner is inappropriate for making decisions about foot placement, and likewise local potential field calculations are inappropriate for making long-range plans. While the benefits of adding a reactive controller to a planner are well known, the relationship between these two components is symbiotic. While the reactive controller adds flexibility and an ability to handle local disturbances to the plan, if properly constructed the high-level planning can result in the reduction of the complexity of the problem that the controller must solve.

Our solution to the problem of path planning illustrates this: path planning is done by navigating from one "landmark" to another. That is the search planner breaks any extended locomotion task into a series of smaller locomotion tasks. These "way points" are then passed one at a time to the locomotion controller to move the system to the desired location. Thus by performing symbolic path planning in the form of identifying waypoints for the trip, each of the individual problems that the lower-level system must solve are reduced in size.

10.6 Gesture Jack

"Gesture Jack" is a demonstration system that consists of two embodied agents holding a conversation where one agent has a specific goal and the other tries to help achieve it (Cassell et al. 1994). All parts of the conversation have been automatically synthesized and animated: intonation, gesture, head and lip movements, and their inter-synchronization. Gesture Jack combines a dialogue planner (which moderates the communicative acts between the agents) with PaT-Nets (which control the speaker/listener roles and various non-verbal aspects of the intercourse). Motor actions drive the face, head, lips, and eyes. PaT-Net schemas control head and eye movements, as these relate directly to the agent's role in the conversation. The face and lips are controlled directly from behavior inputs to the SCA loop, but the absence of direct sensory inputs means that the SCA loop is much simplified in comparison to ZAROFF.

The test scenario consists of two agents: Gilbert, a bank teller, and George, a patron who asks Gilbert for help in obtaining $50. The dialogue is unnaturally repetitive and explicit in its goals because the dialogue generation planner lacks the conversational inferences that allow human conversationalists to follow leaps of reasoning. Therefore, the two agents have to specify in advance each of the goals they are working towards and steps they are following (see Section 10.6.2).

Gilbert: Do you have a blank check?
George: Yes, I have a blank check.
Gilbert: Do you have an account for the check?
George: Yes, I have an account for the check.
Gilbert: Does the account contain at least fifty dollars?
George: Yes, the account contains eighty dollars.
Gilbert: Get the check made out to you for fifty dollars and then I can withdraw fifty dollars for you.
George: All right, let's get the check made out to me for fifty dollars.

When Gilbert asks a question, his voice rises. When George replies to a question, his voice falls. When Gilbert asks George whether he has a blank check, he stresses the word ''check''. When he asks George whether he has an account for the check, he stresses the word ''account''.

Every time Gilbert replies affirmatively (''yes''), or turns the floor over to Gilbert (''all right''), he nods his head, and raises his eyebrows. George and Gilbert look at each other when Gilbert asks a question, but at the end of each question, Gilbert looks up slightly. During the brief pause at the end of affirmative statements (always George here) the speaker blinks. To mark the end of a question, Gilbert raises his eyebrows.

In saying the word ''check'', Gilbert sketches the outlines of a check in the air between him and his listener. In saying ''account'', Gilbert forms a kind of box in front of him with his hands: a metaphorical representation of a bank account in which one keeps money. When he says the phrase ''withdraw fifty dollars'', Gilbert withdraws his hand towards his chest.

10.6.1   Gesture Jack structure

In the Gesture Jack system, we have attempted to adhere to a model of face-to-face interaction suggested by the results of empirical research (Scherer 1980). In particular, each conversational agent is implemented as an autonomous construct that maintains its own representations of the state of the world and the conversation, and whose behavior is determined by these representations. (For now, the two agents run copies of the same program, initialized with different goals and world knowledge.) The agents communicate with one another only by the symbolic messages whose content is displayed in the resulting animation. (If their SCA loops were fully modeled, they would actually be able to interpret the speech and gestures of the other agent.) The architecture of a conversational agent is shown in Figure 10.10.

In this section, we provide an outline of how each agent decides what to say, determines the contribution of this content to the conversation, and uses the resulting representations to accompany speech with contextually appropriate intonation, gesture, facial expression, and gaze.

10.6.2   Dialogue planner

The selection of content for the dialogue by an agent is performed by two cascaded planners. The first is the domain planner, which manages the plans governing the concrete actions which an agent will execute; the second is the discourse planner, which manages the communicative actions an agent must take in order to agree on a domain plan and in order to remain synchronized while executing a domain plan.

The input to the domain planner is a database of facts describing the way the world works, the goals of an agent, and the beliefs of the agent about the world, including the beliefs of

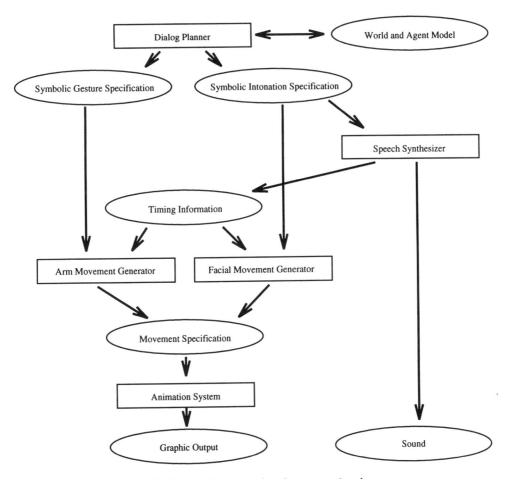

Figure 10.10. *Architecture of each conversational agent.*

the agent about the other agent in the conversation. The domain planner executes by decomposing an agent's current goals into a series of more specific goals according to the hierarchical relationship between actions specified in the agent's beliefs about the world. Once decomposition resolves a plan into a sequence of actions to be performed, the domain planner causes an agent to execute those actions in sequence. As these goal expansions and action executions take place, the domain planner also dictates discourse goals that an agent must adopt in order to maintain and exploit cooperation with their conversational partner.

The domain planner transmits its instructions to take communicative actions to the discourse planner by suspending operation when such instructions are generated and

relinquishing control to the discourse planner. Several stages of processing and conversational interaction may occur before these discourse goals are achieved. The discourse planner must identify how the goal submitted by the domain planner relates to other discourse goals that may still be in progress. Then content for a particular utterance is selected on the basis of how the discourse goal is decomposed into sequences of actions that might achieve it.

When the dialogue is generated, the following information is saved automatically: (1) the timing of the phonemes and pauses, (2) the type and place of the accents, (3) the type and place of the gestures (Cassell et al. 1994; Prevost and Steedman 1993; Steedman 1991). This speech and timing information is critical for synchronizing the facial and gestural animation.

10.6.3   Symbolic gaze specification

In the current version of the program, head and eye behaviors are not differentiated, and follow the same movement pattern. Gesture Jack uses four types of gaze (defined in terms of head motion), related to dialogic function (Argyle and Cook 1976; Collier 1985) (Figure 10.11).

planning: corresponds to the first phase of a turn when a speaker organizes her thoughts. A speaker tends to look away at this point. Then, during the ''<pause> You can write the check'' execution phase, a speaker looks more at a listener. For a short turn (duration less than 1.5 sec.), speaker and listener establish eye contact (mutual gaze) (Argyle and Cook 1976).

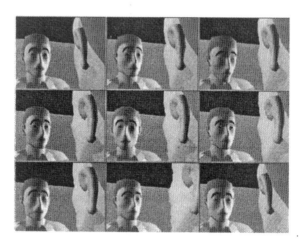

Figure 10.11.   *Facial expressions and gaze behavior corresponding to: ''All right. <pause> You can write the check''.*

comment: accompanies and comments speech, by occurring in parallel with accent and emphasis. Accented or emphasized items are punctuated by head nods; the speaker looks toward the listener. A speaker also gazes at a listener more when asking a question, looking up at its end.

control: controls the communication channel and functions as a synchronization signal: responses may be demanded or suppressed by looking at the listener. When a speaker wants to relinquish her turn, she gazes at the listener at the end of the utterance. When a listener asks for the turn, she looks up at the speaker.

feedback: is used to collect and seek feedback. A listener can emit different reaction signals to the speaker's speech. The speaker looks toward the listener during grammatical pauses to obtain feedback on how utterances are being received. This is frequently followed by the listener looking at the speaker and nodding. In turn, if the speaker wants to keep her turn, she looks away from the listener. In this and other ways, listener and speaker react to each other's behavior.

10.6.4   Using PaT-Nets in Gesture Jack

Interaction between agents and synchronization of gaze and hand movements to the dialogue for each agent are accomplished using PaT-Nets, which allow coordination rules to be encoded as simultaneously executing schemas. Each agent has its own PaT-Net: probabilities and other parameters appropriate for an agent are set for the PaT-Net, given its current role as listener or speaker. Then as agents' PaT-Nets synchronize the agents with the dialogue and interact with the unfolding simulation, they schedule activity that achieves a complex observed interaction behavior.

The PaT-Net input file is a list of lists of the form:

(Speaker Listener Utterance Start-time)

The PaT-Net parses each "utterance-input" and schedules actions when conditions are true. It stops when no phonemes remain in the utterance. At this point, the agents' Gesture and Gaze PaT-Nets send information about timing and type of action to the animation system. The animation itself is carried out by Jack.

The Gaze and Gesture PaT-Net schedule motions as necessary, given the current context, in semi-real time. Animation is performed as the input utterances are scanned, which allows for interactive control and system extensibility.

10.6.5   Gaze PaT-Net

Each of the four dialogic functions (planning, comment, control, and feedback) appears as a sub-network in the PaT-Net, represented by a set of nodes, a list of conditions and their

associated actions. Each node has an associated probability, based on an analysis of two-person conversations, noting where and when a person is gazing, smiling and/or nodding. Each of these signals is binary-valued, i.e., gaze is equal to 1 when a person is looking at the other person, 0 when looking away. The conversation is annotated every tenth of a second. Six turn-states are considered, three per agent. When an agent holds the floor she can be speaking while the other agent is pausing (normal turn) or speaking (overlapping talk or a backchannel signal), or they can be pausing simultaneously. For each of these turn-states, we compute the co-occurrence of signals (nod, smile, and gaze) and their probability. Separate PaT-Net nodes correspond to each different turn-state and signal occurrence; for example, the occurrence of a "within-turn signal" corresponds to the action: agent1 looks at agent2 while having the floor and pausing.

Figure 10.12 shows the Gaze PaT-Net (node names in bold, actions in italic, and conditions specified on the arcs) and two sub-PaT-Nets: Head-Start and Gaze-Start. The latter support independent control of head and gaze (e.g. gazing at or away from the other agent, and other head movement such as nodding, shaking, etc). Each dialogic function is associated with a set of nodes. A node is entered only if the input condition is true, with its action(s) occurring probabilistically. For example, the dialogic function planning is defined by the following nodes and conditions: if a short turn is detected, the node G-Short-Turn is entered, with probability P of the speaker and listener looking at each other. The other node corresponds to begin-turn (comprising all phonemes between the first one and the first accented segment), where the speaker looks away.

10.6.6   Gaze animation

For each phoneme, the Gaze PaT-Net is entered and a decision made regarding head movement. If no action is performed on a phoneme, the PaT-Net waits for the next available phoneme.

Some actions performed by an agent influence the behavior of the other agent. In the case of the feedback node, different branching is possible depending on whether the speaker performs a "looking at the listener" action. The probability of a back-channel occurring ("listener looking at speaker") is smaller if the speaker does not look at the listener and greater otherwise.

Head motions are performed by tracking an invisible object in the current environment. All swing, nod, and turn movements are obtained by giving new coordinates to the object. A head movement is performed by giving the new position of the object, the starting time and duration of the movement. The head velocity has a smooth easy-in/easy-out pattern, that is it accelerates at the beginning and decelerates before stopping. A nod is simulated by moving the invisible object in the vertical plane, while swing and turn are executed by moving it in the horizontal plane. Each of these displacements takes as parameters the number of times to perform the move (simulation of multiple nods or swings), and distance (execution of large

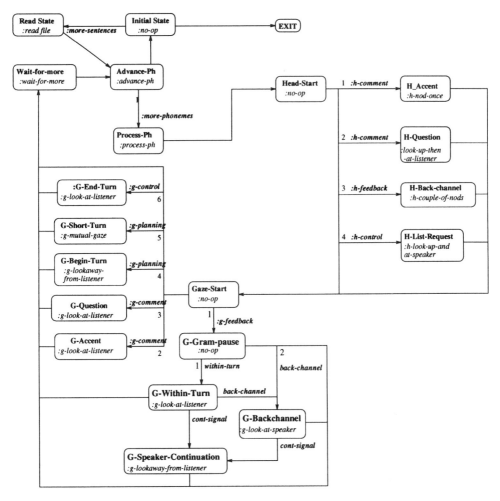

Figure 10.12. *Gaze PaT-Net.*

or small head nods). Varying these parameters allows one to use the same function for different conditions. For example, when punctuating an accent, the speaker's head nod will be of larger amplitude than the feedback head nods emitted by the listener. A gaze direction is sustained until a change is made by another action.

We illustrate a PaT-Net execution with the following example:

Gilbert: Get the chEck made OUt to you for fifty dollars <pause>
And thEn <pause> I can withdrAw fifty dollars for you.

- planning: This is a long utterance, so the node short-turn is not entered. For the first few phonemes (''Get the ch''), the node beginning-turn is entered, but the low-probability action speaker gazes away does not occur. Therefore the speaker (Gilbert) keeps his current gaze direction (looking at George).
- comment: On accented items (''chEck'', ''thEn'' and ''withdrAw''), the node accent of the function comment is reached. In the first two cases the probability allows the actions speaker gazes at the listener to be performed by Gilbert, while nod-once by Gilbert results on ''withdraw''.
- control: At the end of the utterance (i.e., the phonemes between the last accented segment and the last phonemes – here, ''fifty dollars for you''), speaker and listener perform an action: speaker gazes at listener from the node end of turn and listener gazes at the speaker and up from the node turn request.
- feedback: The two intonational phrases of our example (get the check made out to you for fifty dollars and then) are separated by a pause; this corresponds to a within-turn situation. The node G-feedback is entered. If the probability allows it, the action speaker gazes at the listener is performed. If not, the arc going to the node back-channel is immediately traversed without waiting for the next phonemic segment. After a program-specified delay (0.2 sec.) the probabilities associated with the actions are checked once more. If allowed the node back-channel is reached and the action can happen: listener gazes at the speaker. In either case, the final step corresponds to the reaching of the node speaker-continuation after some delay. The action speaker gazes away from the listener is then performed.

10.7 Conclusion

We have demonstrated through these three systems that the combination of high-level control through planners and PaT-Nets with low-level SCA loops yields interesting, human-like, ''intelligent'' behaviors. Removing any one of these three components would incapacitate performance in notable and indeed crippling ways.

For example, if the planners were removed from Hide and Seek, then all decision-making and actions would need to be encoded in PaT-Nets, including the opportunistic generation of new goals (go to a found hider rather than the location the seeker was heading toward) and a hider's choice of where to hide and a seeker's choice of where to seek next. In the case of the dialogue planner in Gesture Jack, its symbolic reasoning (such as backward chaining or question generation) to determine a series of intermediate steps toward an overall goal would have to be encoded in PaT-Nets. Overloading PaT-Nets with these sorts of reasoning and planning would require a full programming language capability to specify arc transitions and a loss of locality that would be an end to any perspicuity. Indeed, the burden would once again be returned to the animator who would need to virtually ''program'' the entire agent to select actions and anticipate any contingencies based on whatever features the immediate environment presented.

If the PaT-Net schemas were omitted, the planners would be forced to do too much work to see that sequential or coordinated tasks were carried out. Rather than making the planner disambiguate overlapping or interleaved activities, the schemas can manage resource allocation and coordinated activities. Thus the PaT-Nets in Gesture Jack can manipulate the head nods and eye movements needed for speaker/listener turn-taking without imposing a load on the actual dialog content planner.

If the SCA loop were omitted, the burden of managing all the environmental complexity must be foisted off onto some higher-level (symbolic reasoning) controller. It appears unrealistic to expect that a symbolic planner worry about where to place a foot during locomotion (Stepper). Likewise, a PaT-Net should not be used to explicitly manage the sensory feedback and decision-making that can check for and avoid hazardous terrain features or other obstacles. The low-level SCA loop provides a kind of ''reflex'' action which can adapt to situations without requiring cognitive overhead.

We believe that ongoing research into embodied human-like simulated agents will find, as we have, that this architecture of high-level schemas and planners combined with low-level SCA loops will achieve increasing success in producing intelligent and realistic behavior.

10.8 Acknowledgments

This research is partially supported by ARO DAAL03-89-C-0031 including U.S. Army Research Laboratory; ARPA AASERT DAAH04-94-G-0362; DMSO DAAH04-94-G-0402; ARPA DAMD17-94-J-4486; U.S. Air Force DEPTH through Hughes Missile Systems F33615-91-C-0001; DMSO through the University of Iowa; and NSF CISE CDA88-22719.

10.9 References

Agre P. (1988) ''The Dynamic Structure of Everyday Life''. Technical Report 1085, MIT Artificial Intelligence Laboratory.

Argyle M. and Cook M. (1976) Gaze and Mutual Gaze. Cambridge University Press, Cambridge.

Badler N.I., Barsky, B.A. and Zeltzer D. (editors) (1991) Making Them Move: Mechanics, Control, and Animation of Articulated Figures. Morgan-Kaufmann, San Mateo, CA.

Badler N.I., Hollick M.J. and Granieri J. (1993a) ''Real-Time Control of a Virtual Human using Minimal Sensors''. Presence 2(1), pp. 82–86.

Badler N.I., Phillips C.B. and Webber B.L. (1993b) Simulating Humans: Computer Graphics Animation and Control. Oxford University Press, New York.

Becket W. and Badler N.I. (1993) ''Integrated Behavioral Agent Architecture''. In The Third Conference on Computer Generated Forces and Behavior Representation, Orlando, FL.

Becket W.M. (1995) Reinforcement Learning for Reactive Navigation of Simulated Autonomous Bipeds. PhD thesis, University of Pennsylvania.

Becket W.M. (1994) The Jack Lisp API. Technical Report MS-CIS-94-01, University of Pennsylvania.

Braitenberg V. (1984) Vehicles: Experiments in Synthetic Psychology. MIT Press, Cambridge, MA.

Brooks R.A. (1986) "A Robust Layered Control System for a MobileRobot". IEEE Journal of Robotics and Automation, Vol. 2, No. 1, pp. 14–23.

Cassell J., Pelachaud C., Badler N., Steedman M., Achorn B., Becket W., Douville B., Prevost S. and Stone M. (1994) "Animated Conversation: Rule-Based Generation of Facial Expression, Gesture and Spoken Intonation for Multiple Conversational Agents". Computer Graphics, Annual Conference Series, pp. 413–420.

Cohen M.F. (1992) "Interactive Spacetime Control for Animation". Computer Graphics, 26(2), pp. 293–302.

Collier G. (1985) Emotional Expression. Lawrence Erlbaum Associates, New York.

Firby R.J. (1992) "Building Symbolic Primitives with Continuous Control Routines". Proc. First Int'l Conference on Artificial Intelligence Planning Systems, Morgan Kaufman Publishing, San Mateo, CA, pp. 62–69.

Geib C.W. (1992) Intentions in means-end planning. Technical Report MS-CIS-92-73, Department of Computer and Information Science, University of Pennsylvania.

Geib C.W. (1995) The Intentional Planning System: ITPLANS. PhD thesis, University of Pennsylvania.

Georgeff M.P. and Lansky A.L. (1990) "Reactive Reasoning and Planning". In Readings in Planning, J. Allen, J. Hendler, and A. Tate (editors), Morgan Kaufmann, San Mateo, CA, pp. 729–734.

Liu D., Gortler S.J. and Cohen M.F. (1994) "Hierarchical Spacetime Control". Computer Graphics, Annual Conference Series, pp. 35–42.

Moore M.B. (1993) Search plans. Technical Report MS-CIS-93-56, Department of Computer and Information Science, University of Pennsylvania.

Moore M.B., Geib C.W. and Reich B.D. (1995) "Planning and Terrain Reasoning". In AAAI Spring Symposium on Integrated Planning Applications (also, Technical Report MS-CIS-94-63, Computer and Information Science, University of Pennsylvania).

Ngo J.T. and Marks J. (1993) "Spacetime Constraints Revisited". Computer Graphics, Annual Conference Series, pp. 343–350.

van de Panne M. and Fiume E. (1993) "Sensor–Actuator Networks". Computer Graphics, Annual Conference Series, pp. 335–342.

Prevost S. and Steedman M. (1993) "Generating Contextually Appropriate Intonation". Proc. 6th Conf. of the European Chapter of the Assoc. for Computational Linguistics, Utrecht, pp. 332–340.

Reich B.D., Ko H., Becket W. and Badler N.I. (1994) "Terrain Reasoning for Human Locomotion". In Proceedings of Computer Animation '94, Geneva. IEEE Computer Society Press, Los Alamitos, pp. 996–1005.

Renault O., Magnenat-Thalmann N. and Thalmann D. (1990) "A Vision-Based Approach to Behavioral Animation". The Journal of Visualization and Computer Animation, 1(1), pp. 18–.

Reynolds C.W. (1987) "Flocks, Herds, and Schools: A Distributed Behavioral Model" Computer Graphics, 21(4), pp. 25–34.

Reynolds C.W. (1988) "Not Bumping into Things". SIGGRAPH Course 27 Notes: Developments in Physically-Based Modeling, pp. G1–G13.

Robertson B. (1994) "Caught in the Act". Computer Graphics World 17(9), pp. 23–28.

Scherer K.R. (1980) "The Functions of Nonverbal Signs in Conversation". In The Social and Physiological Contexts of Language, H. Giles and R. St. Clair (editors), Lawrence Erlbaum, New York, pp. 225–243.

Sims K. (1994) "Evolving Virtual Creatures". Computer Graphics, Annual Con. Series, pp. 15–22.

Steedman M. (1991) "Structure and Intonation". Language 67, pp. 260–296.

Tu X. and Terzopoulos D. (1994) "Artificial Fishes: Physics, Locomotion, Perception, and Behavior". Computer Graphics, Annual Conference Series, pp. 43–50.

Webber B., Badler N., Di Eugenio B., Geib C., Levison L. and Moore M. (1995) "Instructions, Intentions and Expectations". Artificial Intelligence Journal, 1995, 73, pp. 253–269.

Wilhelms J. and Robert Skinner R. (1990) "A 'Notion' for Interactive Behavioral Animation Control". IEEE Computer Graphics and Applications, 10(3), pp. 14–22.

Williams L. (1990) "Performance-Driven Animation". Computer Graphics, 24(4), pp. 235–242.

Witkin A. and Kass M. (1988) "Spacetime Constraints". Computer Graphics, 22(4), pp. 159–168.

CHAPTER 11

How to Create a Virtual Life?

Daniel Thalmann, Hansrudi Noser and Zhiyong Huang
Computer Graphics Lab, Swiss Federal Institute of Technology

Abstract

Virtual Life is a new area dedicated to the simulation of life in virtual worlds, human–virtual interaction and immersion inside virtual worlds. Virtual Life cannot exist without the growing development of Computer Animation techniques and corresponds to the most advanced concepts and techniques of it. In this chapter, we present current research developments in the Virtual Life of autonomous synthetic actors. After a brief description of the perception action principles with a few simple examples, we emphasize the concept of virtual sensors for virtual humans. In particular, we describe in detail our experiences in implementing virtual vision, tactility and audition. We then describe perception-based locomotion, a multisensor-based method of automatic grasping and vision-based ball games. We also discuss problems of integrating autonomous humans into virtual environments.

11.1 Introduction

As a virtual world is completely generated by computer, it expresses itself visually, with sounds and feelings. Virtual worlds deal with all the models describing physical laws of the real world as well as the physical, biological and psychological laws of life. Virtual Life is linked to problems in artificial life but differs in the sense that these problems are specific to virtual worlds. It does not deal with physical or biological objects in real life but only with the simulation of biological virtual creatures. Virtual Life is at the intersection of Virtual Reality and Artificial Life (Magnenat Thalmann and Thalmann 1994), it is an interdisciplinary area strongly based on concepts of real-time computer animation, autonomous agents and mobile

263

robotics. Virtual Life cannot exist without the growing development of Computer Animation techniques and corresponds to the most advanced concepts and techniques of it.

In this chapter, we first review the state-of-the-art in this emerging field of Virtual Life, then we emphasize the aspect of Virtual Life of Synthetic Actors, relating the topics to the previous chapters. The objective is to provide autonomous virtual humans with the skills necessary to perform stand-alone roles in films, games (Bates et al. 1992) and interactive television (Magnenat Thalmann and Thalmann 1995). By autonomous we mean that the actor does not require the continual intervention of a user. Our autonomous actors should react to their environment and make decisions based on perception, memory and reasoning. With such an approach, we should be able to create simulations of situations such as virtual humans moving in a complex environment they may know and recognize, or playing ball games based on their visual and tactile perception. We also describe techniques to interact with these virtual people in Virtual Environments.

11.1.1   State-of-the-art in virtual life

This kind of research is strongly related to the research efforts in behavioral animation as introduced by Reynolds (1987) to study the problem of group trajectories: flocks of birds, herds of land animals and fish schools. This kind of animation using a traditional approach (keyframe or procedural laws) is almost impossible. In the Reynolds approach, each bird of the flock decides its own trajectory without animator intervention. Reynolds introduces a distributed behavioral model to simulate flocks. The simulated flock is an elaboration of a particle system with the simulated birds being the particles. A flock is assumed to be the result of the interaction between the behaviors of individual birds. Working independently, the birds try both to stick together and to avoid collisions with one another and with other objects in their environment. In a module of behavioral animation, positions, velocities and orientations of the actors are known from the system at any time. The animator may control several global parameters: e.g. weight of the obstacle avoidance component, weight of the convergence to the goal, weight of the centering of the group, maximum velocity, maximum acceleration, minimum distance between actors. The animator provides data about the leader trajectory and the behavior of other birds relatively to the leader. A computer-generated film has been produced using this distributed behavioral model: *Stanley and Stella*.

Haumann and Parent (1988) describe behavioral simulation as a means to obtain global motion by simulating simple rules of behavior between locally related actors. Lethebridge and Ware (1989) propose a simple heuristically-based method for expressive stimulus–response animation. Wilhelms (1990) proposes a system based on a network of sensors and effectors. Ridsdale (1990) proposes a method that guides lower-level motor skills from a connectionist model of skill memory, implemented as collections of trained neural networks.

We should also mention the huge literature about autonomous agents (Maes 1991a) which represents a background theory for behavioral animation. More recently, genetic algorithms were also proposed by Sims (1994) to automatically generate morphologies for artificial creatures and the neural systems for controlling their muscle forces. Tu and Terzopoulos (1994a) described a world inhabited by artificial fishes.

11.1.2 Principle of behavioral animation

A simulation is produced in a synchronous way by a behavioral loop such as:

```
t_global = 0.0
    code to initialize the animation environment
while (t_global < t_final) {
    code to update the scene
    for each actor
        code to realize the perception of the environment
        code to select actions based on sensorial input, actual state and specific behavior
    for each actor
    code executing the above selected actions
    t_global + = t_interval}
```

The global time t_global serves as a synchronization parameter for the different actions and events. Each iteration represents a small time step. The action to be performed by each actor is selected by its behavioral model for each time step. The action selection takes place in three phases. First, the actor perceives the objects and the other actors in the environment, which provides information on their nature and position. This information is used by the behavioral model to decide the action to take, which results in a motion procedure with its parameters: e.g. grasp an object or walk with a new speed and a new direction. Finally, the actor performs the motion.

The control of the motion is based on stimulations from the environment. A stimulation consists of information about the nature of the stimulation source and its position. The stimulation source can be an actor, an object or a position to reach. A transfer function, applied on the stimulation, computes an acceleration which is used to control the motion (Braitenberg 1984, Wilhelms 1990). For example, the transfer function of a collision avoidance behavior increases the intensity of the acceleration and modifies the direction as a function of the distance in order to avoid the obstacle.

A complex behavior generally emerges from the interaction of simpler behaviors. A set of behaviors can be sorted in a precedence order (Maes 1991b). The behavior of a walking human in a crowded street results from the interaction between a forward walking behavior, and a collision avoidance behavior with other humans. The second behavior will take precedence over the first when there is a risk of collision. A behavior can also be described with a sequence of simpler behaviors. Therefore, the behavioral model is based on a hierarchical decomposition in two layers (Hügli et al. 1994, Tyrell 1993). The first layer

decomposes a behavior in behavioral units and the second layer decomposes a behavioral unit to elementary behaviors.

An elementary behavior is stimulated by a specific category of actors or objects and applies a transfer function on the perceived stimulation to control a walking action. A road crossing behavior can be stimulated by incoming cars and the transfer function computes a positive acceleration in direction of the other side of the road only when there are no incoming cars.

A behavioral unit is a part of a complex behavior and is composed of one or several elementary behaviors performed in sequence. A finite-state machine is used to represent this sequence. Every state of the machine is linked with an elementary behavior and has a boolean transition function. Only one state of the machine is active at a time and this state is the elementary behavior currently performed. The boolean transition function evaluates if the elementary behavior is finished and when it is the case the transition to the next state is achieved. The transition condition can carry on the intensity of the stimulation or a maximum delay for performing the action linked to the behavior. An active behavioral unit can also inhibit another unit if its behavior takes precedence over the other unit's behavior. For this purpose, a unit has a degree of activation and a degree of inhibition. The degree of activation is determined by the intensity of the stimulation perceived by the active elementary behavior of the unit and the degree of inhibition is modified by another preceding unit. The behavioral unit with the highest degree of activation and the lowest degree of inhibition is selected as the active behavior and the motion is produced by its current elementary behavior.

We implemented simple behaviors using this approach. Figure 11.1 shows actors following a leader. Figure 11.2 shows actors in a virtual office with a distinct queue for each counter.

11.2 Virtual sensors

11.2.1 Perception through virtual sensors

The problem of simulating the behavior of a synthetic actor in an environment may be divided into two parts: 1) to provide to the actor a knowledge of his environment, and 2) to make him react to this environment.

The first problem consists of creating an information flow from the environment to the actor. This synthetic environment is made of 3-D geometric shapes.

One solution is to give the actor access to the exact position of each object in the complete environment database corresponding to the synthetic world. This solution could work for a very "small world", but it becomes impracticable when the number of objects increases. Moreover, this approach does not correspond to reality where people do not have knowledge about the complete environment.

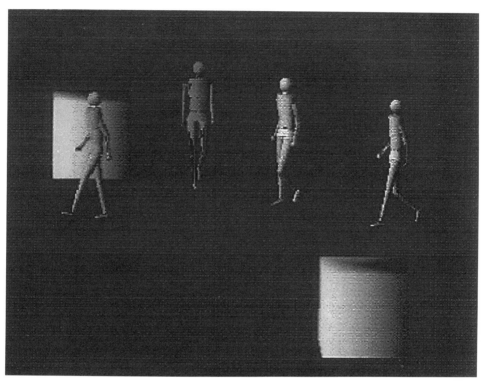

Figure 11.1. *Virtual actors following a leader.*

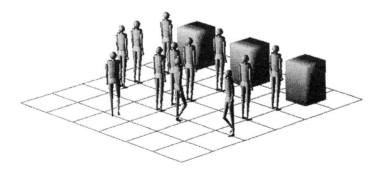

Figure 11.2. *Virtual actors in a virtual office with a distinct queue for each counter.*

Another approach has been proposed by Reynolds (1987): the synthetic actor has knowledge about the environment located in a sphere centered on him. Moreover, the accuracy of the knowledge about the objects of the environment decreases with the distance. This is of course a more realistic approach, but as mentioned by Reynolds, an animal or a human being has always around him areas where his sensitivity is more important. Consider, for example, the vision of birds (birds have been simulated by Reynolds): they have a view angle of 300° and a stereoscopic view of only 15°. The sphere model does not correspond to the sensitivity area of the vision. Reynolds goes one step further and states that if actors can see their environment, they will improve their trajectory planning.

This means that the vision is a realistic information flow. Unfortunately, what is realistic for a human being walking in a corridor seems unrealistic for a computer. However, using hardware developments like the **graphic engine** (Clark 1982), it is possible to give a geometric description of 3-D objects together with the viewpoint and the interest point of a synthetic actor in order to get the vision on the screen. This vision may then be interpreted like the synthetic actor vision. This is our approach as described in this chapter. More generally, in order to implement perception, virtual humans should be equipped with visual, tactile and auditory sensors. These sensors should be used as a basis for implementing everyday human behavior such as visually directed locomotion, handling objects and responding to sounds and utterances. For synthetic audition, in a first step, we model a sound environment where the synthetic actor can directly access positional and semantic sound source information of an audible sound event. Simulating the haptic system corresponds roughly to a collision detection process. But the most important perceptual subsystem is the vision system. A vision-based approach for virtual humans is a very important perceptual subsystem and is for example essential for navigation in virtual worlds. It is an ideal approach for modeling a behavioral animation and offers a universal approach to pass the necessary information from the environment to the virtual human in the problems of path searching, obstacle avoidance and internal knowledge representation with learning and forgetting. In the next sections, we describe our approach for the three types of virtual sensors: vision, audition and haptic.

11.2.2　Virtual vision

Although the use of vision to give behavior to synthetic actors seems similar to the use of vision for intelligent mobile robots (Horswill 1993, Tsuji and Li 1993), it is quite different. This is because the vision of the synthetic actor is itself a synthetic vision. Using a synthetic vision allows us to skip all the problems of pattern recognition and distance detection, problems which still are the most difficult parts in robotics vision. However some interesting work has been done in the topic of intelligent mobile robots, especially for action-perception coordination problems. For example, Crowley (1987), working with surveillance robots states that ''most low level perception and navigation tasks are algorithmic in nature; at the highest levels, decisions regarding which actions to perform are based on knowledge relevant to each situation''. This remark gives us the hypothesis on which our vision-based model of behavioral animation is built.

We first introduced (Renault et al. 1990) the concept of synthetic vision as a main information channel between the environment and the virtual actor. Reynolds (1993, 1994) more recently described an evolved, vision-based behavioral model of coordinated group motion, and also showed how obstacle avoidance behavior can emerge from evolution under selection pressure from an appropriate measure using a simple computational model of visual perception and locomotion. Genetic Programming is used to model evolution. Tu and Terzopoulos (1994a, b) also use a kind of synthetic vision for their artificial fishes.

In Renault et al. (1990), each pixel of the vision input has the semantic information giving the object projected on this pixel, and numerical information giving the distance to this object. So, it is easy to know, for example, that there is a table just in front at 3 meters. With this information, we can directly deal with the problematic question: "what do I do with such information in a navigation system?" The synthetic actor perceives his environment from a small window of typically 30×30 pixels in which the environment is rendered from his point of view. As he can access Z-buffer values of the pixels, the color of the pixels and his own position he can locate visible objects in his 3-D environment. This information is sufficient for some local navigation.

We can model a certain type of virtual world representation where the actor maintains a low-level fast synthetic vision system but where he can access some important information directly from the environment without having to extract it from the vision image. In vision-based grasping for example, an actor can recognize in the image the object to grasp. From the environment he can get the exact position, type and size of the object which allows him to walk to the correct position where he can start the grasping procedure of the object based on geometrical data of the object representation in the world. This mix of vision-based recognition and world representation access will make him fast enough to react in real time. The role of synthetic vision can even be reduced to a visibility test and the semantic information recognition in the image can be done by simple color coding and non-shading rendering techniques. Thus, position and semantic information of an object can be obtained directly from the environment world after being filtered. Figure 11.3 shows an example of local navigation using synthetic vision.

11.2.3 Virtual audition

In real life, the behavior of persons or animals is very often influenced by sounds. For this reason, we developed a framework for modeling a 3-D acoustic environment with sound sources and microphones. Now, our virtual actors are able to hear (Noser and Thalmann 1995). Any sound source (synthetic or real) should be converted to the AIFF format and processed by the sound renderer. The sound renderer takes into account the real time

Figure 11.3.   *Vision-based local navigation.*

constraints. So it is capable to render each time increment for each microphone in "real time" by taking into account the final propagation speed of sound and the moving sound sources and microphones. So, the Doppler effect, for example, is audible.

In sound event generation, we integrated in our L-system-based software (Noser et al. 1992, Noser and Thalmann 1993) a peak detector of a force field which allows us to detect collision between physical objects. These collisions can be coupled to sound emission events. For example, tennis playing with sound effects (ball–floor and ball–racket collisions) has been realized.

The acoustic environment is composed of sound sources and a propagation medium. The sound sources can produce sound events composed of a position in the world, a type of sound, and a start and an end time of the sound. The propagation medium corresponds to the sound event handler which controls the sound events and transmits the sounds to the ears of the actors and/or to a user and/or a soundtrack file. We suppose an infinite sound propagation speed of the sound without weakening of the signal. The sound sources are all omnidirectional, and the environment is non-reverberant.

11.2.4   Virtual tactility

One of our aims is to build a behavioral model based on tactile sensory input received at the level of skin from the environment. This sensory information can be used in tasks as touching objects, pressing buttons or kicking objects. For example at basic level, humans should sense physical objects if any part of the body touches them and gather sensory information. This sensory information is made use of in such tasks as reaching out for an object, navigation etc. For example if a human is standing, the feet are in constant contact with the supporting floor. But during walking motion each foot alternately experiences the loss of this contact. Traditionally these motions are simulated using dynamic and kinematic constraints on human joints. But there are cases where information from external environment is needed. For example when a human descends a staircase, the motion should change from walk to descent based on achieving contact with the steps of the stairway. Thus the environment imposes constraints on the human locomotion. We propose to encapsulate these constraints using tactile sensors to guide the human figure in various complex situations other than the normal walking.

As already mentioned, simulating the haptic system corresponds roughly to a collision detection process. In order to simulate sensorial tactile events, a module has been designed to define a set of solid objects and a set of sensor points attached to an actor. The sensor points can move around in space and collide with the above mentioned solid objects. Collisions with other objects out of this set are not detected. The only objective of collision detection is to inform the actor that there is a contact detected with an object and which object it is. Standard collision detection tests rely on bounding boxes or bounding spheres for efficient simulation of object interactions. But when highly irregular objects are present, such tests are bound to be ineffective. We need much "tighter" bounding space than a box or a sphere could provide. We make use (Bandi and Thalmann 1995) of a variant of a digital line drawing technique called DDA (Fujimoto et al. 1986) to digitize the surface of such objects to get very tight fitting bounds that can be used in preliminary collision detection. The digitization of these objects can be stored in octree structures which permits optimum use of memory space. When we deal with "static" objects, the digitized objects can be permanently stored in memory for the duration of simulation, thus avoiding the trouble of digitizing them at every simulation step.

11.3   Perception-based actions

11.3.1 Action level

Synthetic vision, audition and tactility allow the actor to perceive the environment. Based on this information, his behavioral mechanism will determine the actions he will perform. Actions may be at several degrees of complexity. An actor may simply evolve in his

environment or he may interact with this environment or even communicate with other actors. We will emphasize three types of actions: navigation and locomotion, grasping and ball games.

Actions are performed using the common architecture for motion control developed in the European projects HUMANOID (Boulic et al. 1995) and HUMANOID-2. HUMANOID has led to the development of a complete system for animating virtual actors (see Figure 11.4) for film production. HUMANOID-2 currently extends the project for real-time applications and behavioral aspects as described in this chapter. The heart of the HUMANOID software is the motion control part which includes 5 generators: keyframing, inverse kinematics, dynamics (see Figure 11.5), walking and grasping, and high-level tools to combine and blend them. An interactive application TRACK (Boulic et al. 1994a) has also been developed to create films and sequences to be played in real-time playback for multimedia applications.

11.3.2   Perception-based navigation and locomotion

When the actor evolves in his environment, a simple walking model is not sufficient, the actor has to adapt his trajectory based on the variations of terrain by bypassing, jumping or

Figure 11.4.   *Synthetic actors.*

Figure 11.5. *Dynamics-based motion.*

climbing the obstacles he meets. The bypassing of obstacles consists of changing the direction and velocity of the walking of the actor. Jumping and climbing correspond to more complex motion. These actions should generate parameterized motion depending on the height and the length of the obstacle for a jump and the height and location of the feet for climbing the obstacle. These characteristics are determined by the actor from his perception.

The actor can be directed by giving his linear speed and his angular speed or by giving a position to reach. In the first case, the actor makes no perception (virtual vision). He just walks at the given linear speed and turns at the given angular speed. In the second case, the actor makes use of virtual vision enabling him to avoid obstacles. The vision-based navigation can be local or global. With a local navigation, the agent goes straight on to his goal and it is possible that he cannot reach it. With a global navigation, the actor first tries to find a path to his goal and if the path exists, the actor follows it until he reaches the goal position or until he detects a collision by his vision. During global navigation the actor memorizes his perceived environment by voxelizing it (as explained in Section 11.3.3), based on his synthetic vision. The next section will give more details on local and global navigation.

We developed a special automata for walking in complex environments with local vision-based path optimization. So an actor continues walking even if he detects a future collision in front of him. By dynamically figuring out a new path during walking he can avoid the collision without halting. We also proposed a system for the automatic derivation of a human curved walking trajectory (Boulic et al. 1994b) from the analysis provided by its synthetic vision module. A general methodology associates the two low-level modules of vision and walking with a planning module which establishes the middle term path from the knowledge of the visualized environment. The planning is made under the constraint of minimizing the distance, the speed variation and the curvature cost. Moreover, the planning may trigger the alternate walking motion whenever the decreasing in curvature cost is higher than the associated increasing in speed variation cost due to the corresponding halt and restart. The analysis of walking trajectories on a discrete environment with sparse foothold locations has also been completed (Boulic et al. 1993) regarding the vision-based recognition of footholds, the local path planning, the next step selection and the curved body trajectory. The walking model used is based on biomechanical studies of specific motion pattern (Boulic et al. 1990). Figure 11.6 (below and in the plate section between pages 152 and 153) shows an example of walking from the film *Still Walking* (Magnenat Thalmann and Thalmann 1991).

Figure 11.6. *Biomechanical model for walking from the film* Still Walking.

11.3.3   Global and local navigation

The task of a navigation system is to plan a path to a specified goal and to execute this plan, modifying it as necessary to avoid unexpected obstacles (Crowley 1987). This task can be decomposed into global navigation and local navigation. The global navigation uses a prelearned model of the domain which may be a somewhat simplified description of the synthetic world and might not reflect recent changes in the environment. This prelearned model, or map, is used to perform a path planning algorithm.

The local navigation algorithm uses the direct input information from the environment to reach goals and sub-goals given by the global navigation and to avoid unexpected obstacles. The local navigation algorithm has no model of the environment, and does not know the position of the actor in the world.

Once again to make a comparison with a human being, close your eyes, try to see the corridor near your room, and how to follow it. No problem, you were using your ''visual memory'', which corresponds to the global navigation in our system. Now stand up and go to the corridor near your room, then close your eyes and try to cross the corridor ... There the problems begin (you know that there is a skateboard in front of your boss's door but ...). This is an empirical demonstration of the functionalities of the local navigation as we define it in our system.

The global navigation needs a model of the environment to perform path planning. This model is constructed with the information coming from the sensory system. Most navigation systems developed in robotics for intelligent mobile robots are based on the accumulation of accurate geometrical descriptions of the environment. Kuipers and Byun (1988) give a nearly exhaustive list of such methods using quantitative world modeling. In robotics, due to low mechanical accuracy and sensory errors, these methods have failed in large scale areas. We do not have this problem in Computer Graphics because we have access to the world coordinates of the actor, and because the synthetic vision or other simulations of perception systems are more accurate. We develop a 3-D geometric model, based on a grid, implemented as an octree. Elfes (1990) proposed a 2-D geometric model based on a grid but using a Bayesian probabilistic approach to filter non-accurate information coming from various sensor positions. Roth-Tabak (1989) proposed a 3-D geometric model based on a grid but for a static world.

In the last few years, research in robot navigation has tended towards a more qualitative approach to world modeling, first to overcome the fragility of purely metrical methods, but especially, because humans do not make spatial reasoning on a continuous map, but rather on a discrete map (Sowa 1964). Kuipers and Byun (1988) present a topological model as the basic element of the cognitive map. This model consists of a set of nodes and arcs, where nodes represent distinctively recognizable places in the environment, and arcs represent travel edges connecting them. Travel edges corresponding to arcs are defined by local navigation strategies which describe how a robot can follow the link connecting two distinct places. These local navigation strategies correspond to the Displacement Local Automata

(DLAs) implemented in the local navigation part of our system. These DLAs work as a black box which has the knowledge to create goals and sub-goals in a specific local environment. They can be thought of as low-level navigation reflexes which use vision, reflexes which are automatically performed by the adults.

The octree as visual memory representation

Noser et al. (1995) use an octree as the internal representation of the environment seen by an actor because it offers several interesting features. With an octree we can easily construct enclosing objects by choosing the maximum depth level of the subdivision of space. Detailed objects like flowers and trees do not need to be represented in complete detail in the problem of path searching. It is sufficient to represent them by some enclosing cubes corresponding to the occupied voxels of the octree. The octree adapts itself to the complexity of the 3-D environment, as it is a dynamic data structure making a recursive subdivision of space. Intersection tests are easy. To decide whether a voxel is occupied or not, we only have to go to the maximum depth (5–10) of the octree by some elementary addressing operations. The examination of the neighborhood of a voxel is immediate, too.

Another interesting property of the octree is the fact that it represents a graph of a 3-D environment. We may consider, for example, all the empty voxels as nodes of a graph, where the neighbors are connected by edges. We can apply all the algorithms of graph theory directly on the octree and it is not necessary to change the representation.

Perhaps the most interesting property of the octree is the simple and fast transition from the 2-D image to the 3-D representation. All we have to do is take each pixel with its depth information (given by the Z-buffer value) and calculate its 3-D position in the octree space. Then, we insert it in the octree with a maximum recursion depth level. The corresponding voxel will be marked as occupied with possible additional information depending on the current application.

The octree has to represent the visual memory of an actor in a 3-D environment with static and dynamic objects. Objects in this environment can grow, shrink, move or disappear. In a static environment (growing objects are still allowed) an *insert* operation for the octree is sufficient to get an approximate representation of the world. If there are moving or disappearing objects like cars, other actors, or opening and closing doors, we also need a *delete* operation for the octree. The *insert* operation is simple enough. The *delete* operation, however, is more complicated. Our approach follows.

At a given instant, each pixel is inserted into the octree and the corresponding voxel is marked with the actual time stamp. After the insertion of all image pixels, all the voxels in the vision volume are tested whether they have disappeared or not. The principle of such a test is shown in Figure 11.7.

An occupied voxel has to be deleted only if there is no real object either at its position or in front of it. This condition is expressed by equation (11.1).

$$d_{scene} > d_{octree} \text{ (distances from the observer)} \tag{11.1}$$

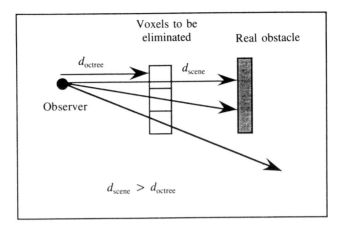

Figure 11.7. *Object removal in the octree.*

The distance of the voxel of the octree from the observer has to be smaller than the distance of a real object or the background. To get the distance of the voxel from the observer you have to transform the observer into the octree coordinate system and apply the corresponding modeling and perspective transformation to the voxel. Doing this with all voxels in the vision volume, we get the image of the memory in normalized coordinates and can compare it directly with the Z-buffer values of the 2-D synthetic world image.

The algorithm of path finding is based on path searching in a graph. Each free voxel not occupied by an obstacle is interpreted as a node of the graph. All the neighbor voxels are considered to be connected by an edge. So, the octree represents a graph with nodes and edges. The algorithm of path searching uses the principle of backtracking and memorizes all tested nodes in a sorted list. With this list of already tested nodes, circuits can be avoided, and situations without a path from a given source to a given destination can be detected. In a first approach, a path is represented by a sequence of free nodes. To avoid a combinatorial explosion of possibilities in graph searching, we use a heuristic depth first search. The first type of heuristic is characterized by the choice of the neighbors of the current voxel. For example, if we know that the search is done in a plane (2-D), we will only examine the neighbors in that plane. So, we can reduce the numbers of new voxels to be tested from 26 to 8. The second type of heuristic is determined by the order of the new neighbors to be tested. If we are searching a path from the current position to an aim, we will sort the list of the new neighbors according to their distance from the aim and we will continue the depth first search with the nearest neighbor to the aim. The third type of heuristic is determined by some additional conditions on the new neighboring voxels to be examined. If we want, for example, the actor to be bound to the ground (if he/she cannot fly) in a 3-D environment with stairs, ramps, bridges, holes, etc., we can use only neighbors which have an occupied

voxel beneath themselves. With these simple conditions, our actor is now able to avoid holes, use bridges, and mount or descend stairs and ramps.

The path finding procedure is a mental process of the actor, which is based on the contents of his visual memory (octree). This means that during his reasoning on a possible path, he does not move. Very often, though, he is placed in an unknown environment, which he has still not seen and memorized. In this case, he cannot find a path using, for example, some conditional heuristic. So, he is forced to explore his environment guided by his vision and a heuristic. This exploring is an active process and the actor has to walk and memorize what he sees. In this case, a heuristic depth first search step can be used to guide the actor to guarantee that he finds a way if one exists.

If the actor, for example, is enclosed in a house, there will be no path to a destination outside the house. In this case, he will explore the parts of the interior accessible to him according to the heuristic. He will finish his search by having memorized the interior of the house and the conclusion that he is enclosed. He should avoid turning infinitely in a loop and he can recognize that he has checked all possibilities to find an exit.

To illustrate the capabilities of the synthetic vision system, we have developed several examples. First, an actor is placed inside a maze with an impasse, a circuit and some animated flowers. The actor's first goal is a point outside the maze. After some time, based on 2-D heuristic, the actor succeeds in finding his goal. When he had completely memorized the impasse and the circuit, he avoided them. After reaching his first goal, he had nearly complete visual octree representation of his environment and he could find again his way without any problem by a simple reasoning process. We have also implemented a more complex environment with flowers and butterflies; the complex flowers were represented in the octree memory by enclosing cubes.

Local navigation system

The local navigation system can be decomposed into three modules. The *vision* module, conceptually the perception system, draws a perspective view of the world in the vision window, constructs the vision array and can perform some low level operation on the vision array. The *controller* module, corresponding to the decision system, contains the main loop for the navigation system, and decides on the creation of the goals and administrates the DLAs. The *performer*, corresponding to the task execution system, contains all the DLAs.

- **The Vision module**

  We use the hardware facilities of the Silicon Graphics workstation to create the synthetic vision; more precisely we use the flat shading and Z-buffer drawing capabilities of the graphic engine. The vision module has a modified version of the drawing routine traveling the world; instead of giving the real color of the object to the graphic engine, this routine gives a code, called the *vision_id*, which is unique for each object and actor in the world. This code allows the image recognition and interpretation. Once the drawing is done, the window buffer is copied into a 2-D array. This array contains the vision_id and the Z-buffer depth for each pixel. This array is referred to as the *view*.

- **The Controller module**

  In local navigation there are two goals. These two goals are geometrical goals, and are defined in the local 2-D coordinate system of the actor. The actor himself is the center of this coordinate system, one axis is defined by the direction ''in front'', the other axis is defined by the ''side'' direction. The global goal, or final goal, is the goal the actor must reach. The local goal, or temporary goal, is the goal the actor creates to avoid the obstacles encountered in the path towards the global goal. These goals are created by the DLA, or given by the animator or by the global navigation system. The main task of the controller is to create these goals and to make the actor reach them.

  Goal creation and actor displacement are performed by the DLAs. The controller selects the appropriate DLA either by knowing some internal set-up of the actor, or by visually analyzing the environment. For example, if the actor has a guide, the controller will choose the DLA *follow_the_guide*. Otherwise, from a 360 look-around, the controller will determine the visible objects and then determine the DLA corresponding to these objects. No real interpretation of the topology of the environment (as in Kuipers and Byun 1988) has yet been implemented. The choice of the DLA is hardcoded by the presence of some particular objects, given by their *vision_id*.

  The actor has an internal clock administrated by the controller. This clock is used by the controller to refresh the global and local goal at regular intervals. The interval is given by the *attention_rate*, a variable set-up for each actor that can be changed by the user or by the controller. This variable is an essential parameter of the system: with a too high attention rate the actor spends most of his time analyzing the environment and real-time motion is impossible; with a too low attention rate, the actor starts to act blindly, going through objects. A compromise must be found between these two extremes.

- **The Performer module**

  This module contains the DLAs. There are three families of DLA: the DLAs creating the global goal (follow_the_corridor, follow_the_wall, follow_the_visual_guide), the DLAs creating the local goal (avoid_obstacle, closest_to_goal), and the DLAs effectively moving the actor (go_to_global_goal). The DLAs creating goals only use the vision as input. All these DLAs have access to a library of routines performing high level operations on the vision. A detailed algorithm of the use of vision to find the avoidance goal is described by Renault et al. (1990).

11.3.4 Perception-based grasping

With the advent of virtual actors in computer animation, research in human grasping has become a key issue in this field. Magnenat Thalmann et al. (1988) proposed a semi-

automatic way of grasping for a virtual actor interacting with the environment. A knowledge-based approach is suitable for simulating human grasping, and an expert system can be used for this purpose (Rijpkema and Girard 1991). Kunii et al. (1993) have also presented a model of hands and arms based on manifold mapping.

Our approach is based on three steps:

- **Inverse kinematics** to find the final arm posture.
- **Heuristic grasping decision**. Based on a grasp taxonomy, Mas and Thalmann (1994) proposed a completely automatic grasping system for synthetic actors. In particular,

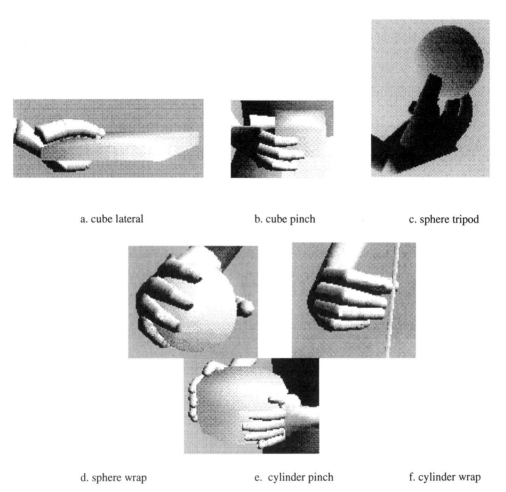

a. cube lateral   b. cube pinch   c. sphere tripod

d. sphere wrap   e. cylinder pinch   f. cylinder wrap

Figure 11.8.   *The different grasping ways for different objects.*

the system can decide to use a pinch when the object is too small to be grasped by more than two fingers or to use a two-handed grasp when the object is too large. Figure 11.8 shows several examples.

- **Multi-sensor hand**. Our approach (Huang et al. 1995) is adapted from the use of proximity sensors in Robotics (Espiau and Boulic 1985), the sensor–actuator networks (van de Panne and Fiume 1993) and recent work on human grasping (Mas and Thalmann 1994). In our work, the sphere multi-sensors have both tactile and length sensor properties, and have been found very efficient for synthetic actor grasping problem. Multi-sensors are considered as a group of objects attached to the articulated figure. A sensor is activated for any collision with other objects or sensors. Here we select sphere sensors for their efficiency in collision detection (Figure 11.9).

Each sphere sensor is fitted to its associated joint shape with different radii. This configuration is important in our method because when a sensor is activated in a finger, only the articulations above it stop moving, while others can still move. By doing it this way, all the fingers are finally positioned naturally around the object, as shown in Figure 11.10.

To summarize: after the hand center frame is aligned with the object frame, the fingers are closed according to the different strategies, e.g. pinch, wrap, lateral, etc., while sensor–object and sensor–sensor collisions are detected. When one sensor is activated, all articulations above it are blocked. The grasping is completed when the remaining sensors are activated or the joints reach their limit.

All the grasping functions mentioned above have been implemented and integrated into the TRACK system (Boulic et al. 1994a). The examples shown in this section were performed on

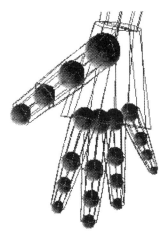

Figure 11.9. *The hand with sphere sensors at each joint.*

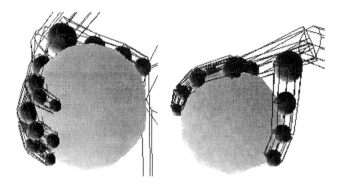

Figure 11.10.   *One example showing sensors in grasping.*

SGI Indigo 2 in real time. The first example shows an actor using two hands for grasping a cube and a cylinder. The strategies are different according to the types of the objects (Figure 11.11). The second example (Figure 11.12) shows two actors grasping a frustum. The first actor uses two hands to grasp the thick part, while the second only uses one hand. In Figure 11.13, we extend the grasping method to interactions between two actors.

11.3.5   Vision-based tennis playing

Tennis playing is a human activity which is severely based on the vision of the players. In our model, we use the vision system to recognize the flying ball, to estimate its trajectory and to localize the partner for game strategy planning. The geometric characteristics of the

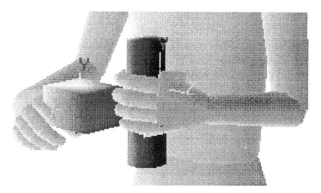

Figure 11.11.   *Grasp different objects with two hands.*

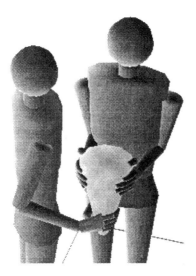

Figure 11.12.   *Two actors grasp a frustum at different positions in different ways.*

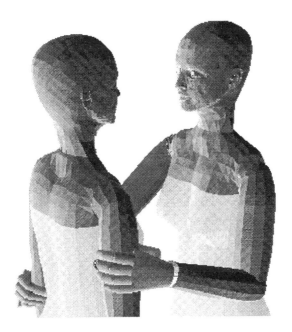

Figure 11.13.   *Interaction between two actors modeled by triangle meshes.*

tennis court, however, make part of the player's knowledge. For the dynamics simulation of the ball, gravity, net, ground and the racket we use the force field approach developed for the L-system animation system. The tracking of the ball by the vision system is controlled by a special automaton. A prototype of this automaton is already able to track the ball, to estimate the collision time and collision point of ball and racket and to perform successfully a hit with given force and a given resulting ball direction. In a first step, we have a prototype where only two rackets with synthetic vision can play against each other, in order to develop, test and improve game strategy and the physical modeling. Figure 11.14 shows the prototype system. The integration of the corresponding locomotor system of a sophisticated actor is under development as seen in Figure 11.15.

In the navigation problem each colored pixel is interpreted as an obstacle. No semantic information is necessary. In tennis playing, however, the actor has to distinguish between the partner, the ball and the rest of the environment. The ball has to be recognized, its trajectory has to be estimated and it has to be followed by the vision system. At the beginning of a ball

Figure 11.14.   *Vision-based tennis players.*

Figure 11.15.   *Marilyn playing tennis.*

exchange, the actor has to verify that his partner is ready. During the game the actor needs also his partner's position for his play strategy.

To recognize objects in the image we use color coding. The actor knows that a certain object is made of a specific material. When it scans the image it looks for the corresponding pixels and calculates its average position and its approximate size. Thus each actor can extract some limited semantic information from the image.

Once the actor has recognized the ball, he follows it with his vision system and adjusts at each frame his field of view. To play tennis each partner has to estimate the future racket–ball collision position and time and to move as fast as possible to this point. At each frame (1/25 sec) the actor memorizes the ball position. So, every n-th frame the actor can derive the current velocity of the ball. From this current velocity and the current position of the ball he can calculate the future impact point and impact time. We suppose that the actor wants to hit the ball at a certain height h.

In the next phase the actor has to play the ball. Now he has to determine the racket speed and its orientation to play the ball to a given place. Before playing the ball the actor has to decide where to play. In our simulation approach he looks where his partner is placed and then he plays the ball in the most distant corner of the court.

All the above features are coordinated by a specialized "tennis play" automaton. First an actor goes to his start position. There he waits until his partner is ready. Then he looks for the ball, which is thrown into the game. Once the vision system has found the ball, he always follows it by adjusting the field of view angle. If the ball is flying towards the actor, he starts estimating the impact point. Once the ball has passed the net, the actor localizes his partner with his vision system during one frame. This information is used for the game strategy. After playing the ball, the actor goes back to his start point and waits until the ball comes back to play it again.

11.4   Virtual Environments

11.4.1   Presence and immersion

Presence is the fact or condition of being present and it is something (as a spirit) felt or believed to be present. This spirit is essential in Virtual Reality (VR). As stated by Slater and Usoh (1994), immersion may lead to a sense of presence. This is an emergent psychological property of an immersive system, and refers to the participant's sense of "being there" in the world created by the Virtual Environment system. Astheimer et al. (1994) define an immersive system as follows: if the user cannot tell which reality is "real", and which one is "virtual", then the computer-generated one is immersive.

We are currently creating interactive and immersive real-time simulations of our smart virtual actors. These actors will be able:

- to move from one place to another by walking, bypassing, jumping or climbing obstacles.
- to move objects in the Virtual Space.

The simulation will be performed in Virtual Environments allowing the participant (real human) to move the objects in the Virtual Space using VR-devices.

In the next section, we analyze the problems of processing virtual sensors in the case of Virtual Environments.

11.4.2   Virtual sensors in Virtual Environments

We have seen that virtual vision can be a powerful tool in modeling virtual autonomous actors in virtual worlds. Such actors in virtual worlds can have different degrees of autonomy and different sensing channels to the environment where they behave in a certain manner. In robotics for example, the agent (the robot) only gets information of the world by his sensors. If he has a vision sensor, he has to extract all the semantic information of the world from an image. This is a very difficult task and thus, according to the actual state of knowledge, his intelligence is very restricted and his behavior is limited to some navigational tasks by avoiding collisions.

In virtual worlds the situation is different as we can provide some extra information to the actor making them more intelligent and faster. Until now, we tried to make the actors completely independent of the virtual worlds' internal representation and they only got the vision image and their position as sensory information. Thus, vision-based navigation, collision avoidance, visual memory and tennis playing could be successfully modeled. We now integrate actors in VR where real-time constraints demand fast and intelligent reactions of actors with a set of elementary actions like grasping objects, sitting on chairs, jumping over obstacles, pressing buttons, running, ... To reach this goal we model a certain type of virtual world representation where the actor maintains a low-level fast synthetic vision system but where he can access some important information directly from the environment without having to extract it from the vision image.

A human being can participate in VR by the head-mounted display and the earphones. He cannot get any internal VR information. His only source of knowledge from the VR is communicated by the vision and the sound (and perhaps some tactile sensory information). His behavior is strongly influenced by this sensory input and his proper intelligence. In order to process the virtual actor vision in a similar way to the vision of the participant, we need to have a different model. In this case, the only information obtained by the virtual actor will be the vision image with the Z-buffer values and the shaded and colored pixels (he may also get the sound signal and some tactile sensor information). Such a virtual actor would be independent of each VR representation (as a human too) and he could in the same manner communicate with human participants and other virtual actors.

For virtual audition, we encounter the same problem as in synthetic vision. The real-time constraints in VR demand fast reaction to sound signals and fast recognition of the semantic it carries. Thus, we plan in a first step to model a sound environment where the synthetic actor can directly access positional and semantic sound source information of an audible sound event. This allows him to localize and recognize one or more sound sources in a reliable way and to react immediately. In Section 7.5, Pentland et al. describe an experience in this area using the ALIVE system.

This access to the sound environment representation, however, makes him dependent on it and lets the communication problem with human participants in VR remain unresolved. That is why, we try to realize a really independent actor as already mentioned above. This type of actor will get the same sound signal (digitized) as any other human participant in VR through his earphones. From these sound signals (stereo) the actor can estimate the position of a sound source and with an added speech recognition module he should be capable to extract some semantic information of some spoken language. Thus the synthetic actor should be able to understand and speak a reduced set of vocabulary allowing him also to communicate with human participants in VR.

Concerning virtual haptic sense, we have already implemented a case of 3-D interaction with VR technology. The participant may place an object into the Virtual Space using the

CyberGlove and the virtual actor will try to grasp it and put it on a virtual table for example. The actor interacts with the environment by grasping the object and moving it. At the beginning of interactive grasping, only the hand center sensor is active. The six palm values from CyberGlove are used to move it toward the object. Inverse kinematics is used to update the arm postures from hand center movement. After the sensor is activated, the hand is close enough to the object final frame. The hand center sensor is deactivated and multi-sensors on the hand are now used to detect sensor–object collision. The following process is similar to the multi-sensor method discussed in Section 11.3.4. The major difference is that the grasping strategy is defined interactively. One example is shown in Figure 11.16.

11.5 Conclusion

In this chapter, we have presented a new approach to implement autonomous virtual actors in virtual worlds based on perception and virtual sensors. We believe this is an ideal approach for modeling a behavioral animation and that it offers a universal approach to pass the necessary information from the environment to an actor in the problems of path searching, obstacle avoidance, game playing and internal knowledge representation with learning and forgetting characteristics. We also think that this new way of defining animation is a convenient and universal high-level approach to simulate the behavior of

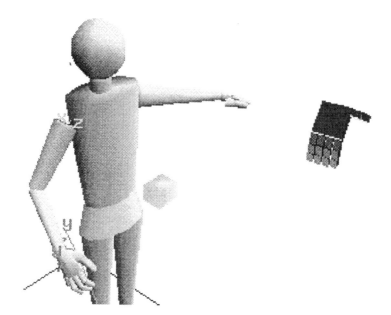

Figure 11.16.   *3D interactive grasping with CyberGlove.*

intelligent human actors in dynamic and complex environments including virtual environments.

11.6 Acknowledgments

The authors are grateful to the people who contributed to this work, in particular Srikhan Bandi, Pascal Bécheiraz, Ronan Boulic and Serge Rezzonico. The research was supported by the Swiss National Science Research Foundation, the Federal Office for Education and Science, and is part of the Esprit Project HUMANOID and HUMANOID-2.

11.7 References

Astheimer P., Dai, Gobel M. Kruse R., Müller S. and Zachmann G. (1994) "Realism in Virtual Reality", in: Magnenat Thalmann and Thalmann (eds), Artificial Life and Virtual Reality, John Wiley & Sons, Chichester, pp. 189–208.

Bandi S. and Thalmann D. (1995) "An Adaptive Spatial Subdivision of the Object Space for Fast Collision Detection of Animated Rigid Bodies", Proc. Eurographics '95. Computer Graphics Forum, Vol. 14, No. 3, Blackwell Publishing, Oxford, pp. 259–270.

Bates J., Loyall A.B. and Reilly W.S. (1992) "An Architecture for Action, Emotion, and Social Behavior", Proc. Fourth Europeans Workshop on Modeling Autonomous Agents in a Multi Agents World, S. Martino al Cimino, Italy.

Boulic R., Thalmann D. and Magnenat Thalmann N. (1990) "A Global Human Walking Model with Real Time Kinematic Personification", The Visual Computer, Vol. 6, No. 6.

Boulic R., Noser H. and Thalmann D. (1993) "Vision-Based Human Free-Walking on Sparse Foothold Locations", Fourth Eurographics Workshop on Animation and Simulation, Barcelona, Spain, Eurographics, pp. 173–191.

Boulic R., Huang Z., Magnenat Thalmann N. and Thalmann D. (1994a) "Goal-Oriented Design and Correction of Articulated Figure Motion with the TRACK System", Comput. & Graphics, Vol. 18, No. 4, pp. 443–452.

Boulic R., Noser H. and Thalmann D. (1994b) "Automatic Derivation of Curved Human Walking Trajectories from Synthetic Vision", Computer Animation '94, Geneva, IEEE Computer Society Press, Los Alamitos, pp. 93–103.

Boulic R., Capin T., Kalra P., Lintermann B., Moccozet L., Molet T., Huang Z., Magnenat Thalmann N., Saar K., Schmitt A., Shen J. and Thalmann D. (1995) "A System for the Parallel Integrated Motion of Multiple Deformable Human Characters with Collision Detection", EUROGRAPHICS '95, Maastricht.

Braitenberg V. (1984) "Vehicles, Experiments in Synthetic Psychology", The MIT Press, Cambridge, USA.

Clark J.H. (1982) "The Geometric Engine: A VLSI Geometry System for Graphics", Proc. SIGGRAPH '82, Computer Graphics, Vol. 10, No. 3, pp. 127–133.

Crowley J.L. (1987) "Navigation for an Intelligent Mobile Robot", IEEE Journal of Robotics and Automation, Vol. RA-1, No. 1, pp. 31–41.

Elfes A. (1990) "Occupancy Grid: A Stochastic Spatial Representation for Active Robot Perception", Proc. Sixth Conference on Uncertainty in AI.

Espiau B. and Boulic R. (1985) "Collision Avoidance for Redundants Robots with Proximity Sensors", Proc. of Third International Symposium of Robotics Research, Gouvieux, October.

Fujimoto A., Tanaka T. and Iwata K. (1986) "ARTS: Accelerated Ray-Tracing System", IEEE CG&A, Vol. 6, No. 4, pp. 16–26.

Haumann D.R. and Parent R.E. (1988) "The Behavioral Test-bed: Obtaining Complex Behavior from Simple

Rules'', The Visual Computer, Vol. 4, No. 6, pp. 332–347.

Horswill I. (1993) "A Simple, Cheap, and Robust Visual Navigation System", in: From Animals to Animats 2, Proc. 2nd Intern. Conf. on Simulation of Adaptive Behavior, MIT Press, Cambridge, USA, pp. 129–136.

Huang Z., Boulic R., Magnenat Thalmann N. and Thalmann D. (1995) "A Multi-sensor Approach for Grasping and 3D Interaction", Proc. CGI '95, Computer Graphics, Earnshaw R.A. and Vince J. (eds) Academic Press, London, pp. 235–253.

Hü H., Facchinetti C., Tiéche F., Müller J.P., Rodriguez M. and Gat Y. (1994) "Architecture Of An Autonomous System: Application to Mobile Robot Navigation", in Proceedings of Symposium on Artificial Intelligence and Robotics, pp. 97–110.

Kuipers B. and Byun Y.T. (1988) "A Robust Qualitative Approach to a Spatial Learning Mobile Robot", SPIE Sensor Fusion: Spatial Reaoning and Scene Interpretation, Vol. 1003.

Kunii T.L., Tsuchida Y., Matsuda H., Shirahama M. and Miura S. (1993) "A Model of Hands and Arms Based on Manifold Mappings", Proceedings of CGI '93, pp. 381–398.

Lethebridge T.C. and Ware C. (1989) "A Simple Heuristically-based Method for Expressive Stimulus-Response Animation", Comput. & Graphics, Vol. 13, No. 3, pp. 297–303.

Maes P. (ed.) (1991a) "Designing Autonomous Agents", Bradford MIT Press, Cambridge, USA.

Maes P. (1991b) "Bottom-Up Mechanism for Behavior Selection in an Artificial Creature", Proc. First International Conference on Simulation of Adaptive Behavior.

Magnenat Thalmann N. and Thalmann D. (1991) "Still Walking", video, 1 min.

Magnenat Thalmann N. and Thalmann D. (1994) "Creating Artificial Life in Virtual Reality" in: Magnenat Thalmann and Thalmann (eds), Artificial Life and Virtual Reality, John Wiley, Chichester, pp. 1–10.

Magnenat Thalmann N. and Thalmann D. (1995) "Digital Actors for Interactive Television", Proc. IEEE, July.

Magnenat Thalmann N., Laperrière R. and Thalmann D. (1988) "Joint-Dependent Local Deformations for Hand Animation and Object Grasping", Proceedings of Graphics Interface '88, pp. 26–33.

Mas S.R. and Thalmann D. (1994) "A Hand Control and Automatic Grasping System for Synthetic Actors", Proceedings of Eurographic '94, pp. 167–178.

Noser H. and Thalmann D. (1993) "L-System-Based Behavioral Animation", Proc. Pacific Graphics '93, pp. 133–146.

Noser H. and Thalmann D. (1995) "Synthetic Vision and Audition for Digital Actors", Proc. Eurographics '95.

Noser H., Thalmann D. and Turner R. (1992) "Animation Based on the Interaction of L-Systems with Vector Force Fields", Proc. Computer Graphics International, in: Kunii T.L. (ed), Visual Computing, Springer, Tokyo, pp. 747–761.

Noser H., Renault O., Thalmann D. and Magnenat Thalmann N. (1995) "Navigation for Digital Actors based on Synthetic Vision, Memory and Learning", Comput. & Graphics, Vol. 19, No. 1, pp. 7–19.

Renault O., Magnenat Thalmann N. and Thalmann D. (1990) "A Vision-based Approach to Behavioural Animation", Journal of Visualization and Computer Animation, Vol. 1, No. 1, pp. 18–21.

Reynolds C. (1987) "Flocks, Herds, and Schools: A Distributed Behavioral Model", Proc. SIGGRAPH '87, Computer Graphics, Vol. 21, No. 4, pp. 25–34.

Reynolds C.W. (1993) "An Evolved, Vision-Based Behavioral Model of Coordinated Group Motion", in: Meyer J.A. et al. (eds), From Animals to Animats, Proc. 2nd International Conf. on Simulation of Adaptive Behavior, MIT Press, Cambridge, USA, pp. 384–392.

Reynolds C.W. (1994) "An Evolved, Vision-Based Model of Obstacle Avoidance Behavior", in: C.G. Langton (ed.), Artificial Life III, SFI Studies in the Sciences of Complexity, Proc. Vol. XVII, Addison-Wesley, Reading, MA.

Ridsdale G. (1990) "Connectionist Modelling of Skill Dynamics", Journal of Visualization and Computer Animation, Vol. 1, No. 2, 1990, pp. 66–72.

Rijpkema H. and Girard M. (1991) "Computer Animation of Knowledge-based Human Grasping", Proc. SIGGRAPH '91, pp. 339–348.

Roth-Tabak Y. (1989) "Building an Environment Model Using Depth Information", Computer, pp. 85–90.

Sims K. (1994) "Evolving Virtual Creatures", Proc. SIGGRAPH '94, pp. 15–22.

Slater M. and Usoh M. (1994) "Body Centred Interaction in Immersive Virtual Environments", in: Magnenat Thalmann N. and Thalmann, D. (eds), Artificial Life and Virtual Reality, John Wiley, Chichester, pp. 1–10.

Sowa J.F. (1964) "Conceptual Structures", Addison-Wesley, Reading, MA.

Tsuji S. and Li S. (1993) "Memorizing and Representing Route Scenes", in: Meyer J.A. et al. (eds), From Animals to Animats, Proc. 2nd International Conf. on Simulation of Adaptive Behavior, MIT Press, Cambridge, USA, pp. 225–232.

Tu X. and Terzopoulos D. (1994a) "Artificial Fishes: Physics, Locomotion, Perception, Behavior", Proc. SIGGRAPH '94, Computer Graphics, pp. 42–48.

Tu X. and Terzopoulos D. (1994b) "Perceptual Modeling for the Behavioral Animation of Fishes", Proc. Pacific Graphics '94, World Scientific Publishers, Singapore, pp. 165–178.

Tyrell T. (1993) "The Use of Hierarchies for Action Selection", in: Meyer J.A. et al. (eds), From Animals to Animats 2, Proceedings of the Second International Conference on Simulation of Adaptive Behavior, pp. 138–147.

van de Panne M. and Fiume E. (1993) "Sensor–Actuator Network", Computer Graphics, Annual Conference Series, pp. 335–342.

Wilhelms J. (1990) "A 'Notion' for Interactive Behavioral Animation Control", IEEE Computer Graphics and Applications, Vol. 10, No. 3 , pp. 14–22.

Index

292